AF568146

SOCIAL MATURITY
AND
TEACHING COMPETENCY

SOCIAL MATURITY AND TEACHING COMPETENCY

By

Dr. S.K. Panneer Selvam

Assistant Professor

Deptt. of Education

Bharathidasan University

Tiruchirappalli

Tamil Nadu

DISCOVERY PUBLISHING HOUSE PVT. LTD.

NEW DELHI-110 002

Published by:
Tilak Wasan
DISCOVERY PUBLISHING HOUSE PVT. LTD.
4831/24, Ansari Road, Prahlad Street
Darya Ganj, New Delhi-110002 (India)
Phone: +91-11-23279245, 43764432
Fax: +91-11-23253475
E-mail: parul.wasan@gmail.com
info@discoverypublishinggroup.com
web: www.discoverypublishinggroup.com

***First Edition:* 2011**
ISBN: 978-81-8356-722-0

Social Maturity and Teaching Competency

Printed at:
Shree Balaji Art Press
Delhi

Preface

Well thought out educational policies (both academic and technical), schemes and projects and proper and prompt implementation of them with a missionary zeal decide the growth of the knowledge of a state or nation, development of a country is the function of human knowledge and skills imparted in institutions. The end value of any stream of education is all mind development of human resources which in turn is the development of a nation. Across the world a number of persons connected with education are doing researches on current problems to find out solutions. To widen the dimensions of education multilevel researches with an eye on future prospects and visions is inevitable. So with an idea to discriminate the knowledge acquired by M.Phil (Education) students, these educations are brought out. This edition is mainly a sum total of research works and the findings M.Phil (Education) students. The originality of this edition owes to the originality of the contributed presentations and research papers submitted by the M.Phil (Education) students. As an editor I acknowledged all the contributors.

Author

Content

CHAPTER 1

Social Maturity and Teaching Competency

—S. MOHANA

PROBLEMS AND ITS PERSPECTIVES

Introduction

Emergence of the Problem

Every difference of environment means a difference in one's habit and one's way of living in so far as these differences create a different environment, a dynamic equilibrium of life is maintained through a processing of constant selections and constant adaptations. The society is not the world but is directly related to every one's life and maturity. The more complex the adaptation with society becomes, the more complex the social maturity of intelligence, maturity according to the need.

Society is significant medium where certain quality of life and certain types of activity and occupation are provided with the aim of securing child's development based on the social needs. Since it is a stem of growth characteristics of teacher trainees should adapt to the society in which they live and to which they also expected to adjust and contribute, the social maturity receives importance at the present context. The conduct of many individual in the society tells about the trainees social maturity through which he can respond right according to the teaching situation.

At the present age of competitive world, every human being meets a lot of problems in his daily activities. The root of most of human psychological problems is more socially based than psychologically based. It is in social situation, a lack of competence as well as social maturity. So every human need knowledge about teaching competence and social maturity for leading a very healthy life in this world.

The present study takes a position that teaching competency and social maturities are very important to the students who live and grow in the complex social environment. Hence there is a need to find out if there is any correlation between teaching competency and social maturity. Hence the problem emerged to study the two variables teaching competency and social maturity.

STATEMENT OF THE PROBLEM

The title of the problem is a follows: Social Maturity and Teaching Competency of Student Teachers in Tti and DIET in Chennai

OPERATIONAL DEFINITION

Social Maturity

Maturity assumes accountability, constantly assesses, judges and takes appropriate decisions. Maturity develops a balanced emotional outlook, helping the individual to accept himself, his talents and limitation and to accept others as they are. It analysis values and internalises them consistently. It helps towards progressive advancement in spiritual growth, impelling the individual to adapt himself to change and to life without emotional crisis.

Abraham Sperling (1967) defined social maturity in the following words, "An adolescent should get along with others. He ought to develop self-reliance in matter of taste and ought to develop tolerance of human differences".

Nazarath Maria E. Waples (1978) defines as, "Maturity is the blossoming of man's character into a unified totality. It discerns the process that contributes to the psychological and physical growth and well being of man".

Henry E. Garrett (1969) states "Social maturity is the degree of social participation as measured by child's activities, attitudes and play interests. It is related to physical growth and maturity and to mental ability. Every individual develops his own unique way of adjustment in the society. An individual, since his birth attempts to adjust to his environment".

EDUCATION AND THE SOCIETY

Education is the fulcrum upon which hangs the peaceful evolutionary transition of society. It plays a vital role in building a society. A modern society cannot achieve its aim of economic growth, technical development and cultural advancement without fully harnessing the talents of its citizens. For the advancement in education proper social maturity, values and adjustment pattern should be there. Social maturity is related to value that are found in the society. Teacher educators are very well associated with the cultivation of social maturity among the student teachers. Then only they will develop an integrated personality, proper cultivation of values to cope with the environment amicably.

Society does not come out of an oak or a rock; it is the product of human mind reflecting the multi-dimensional hues of human personalities. The society throbs, grows and progresses in tune with the development of the human potentialities. So the "man" and the "society" do not confront each others as antagonistic concepts. The human mind and its potentialities are extending through its cognitive, emotive and affective capacities. But all these capacities flower into realties in the context of the society and social interaction. So the human mind finds its ideal foil in the society, which is instrumental in the actualisation of the immeasurable human potentialities.

Man doesn't stand – alone; he is only and essentially a social animal. Otherwise he may be described as a "beast" or a "god" but not as a "man". Similarly society is just an abstraction unless it mirrors the human values, norms, ambitions and goal society is never an aggregate of individuals. Its, in the sense, no predictable string of unity. Tandra Patanic (1986) states, 'The society is rather a peculiar amalgamation of unity in diversity, which characterizes the society that again reflects the nature of human mind" (p.04). Mind can be judged from various dimensions. It is considered powerful as a cognitive tool reflecting sensitivity and emotionality. Separately none of these qualities of the mind can be called to constitute the proper essence of the mind. So man and the society and their relation have been viewed here as a prism throwing multi-coloured spectrum of light. Yet the arrangement of colour may change in the direction of the light. Society is a prism; it's multiple facets along with its unique ability of adapting to the change of circumstances.

EDUCATIONS AS AN AGENCY OF SOCIETY

The process of education is deep significance to the growth and welfare of society. If the people are to keep pace with the fast changing social order, with scientific discoveries and with the explosion of knowledge in all parts of the world, the hidden talents of youth must be brought to the surface and be exploited for the good of the society. There is a great demand for creative ideas and creative talents, and education is the best means for the development of such talents. The events of out time are moving continually, accelerating the rate and if the people are to keep pace with them, the people must make sure that the talents of the youth are thoroughly developed.

Alexander. A. Scheidrs (1965) defines "Education is the total experiences that can transform the life of the individual person". Education can contribute much and in many different ways to the social, moral and religious growth of the adolescent to healthy social perspectives to adequate vocational attitudes and goals, and to the future roles that the adolescent will expect to play. By means of active participation on the playing field and through extracurricular activities such as oratory, debating, newspaper reporting or yearbook editing the adolescent can pick up many ideas, skills and general know-how that may be of great help to him later in his social relations and vocational aspirations.

MATURITIES AS A DETERMINANT OF PERSONALITY

Henery. E. Garrett (1968) says, "Social maturity is the degree of social participation as measured by child's activities, attitudes and play interests. It is related to physical growth and maturity and to mental ability".

One of the components of social maturity is adjustment. Maturity is the determinant of personality. A man's personality is the total picture of his organised behavior, especially as it can be characterised by his fellow men in a consistent way.

An individual, since his birth attempts to interact with his environment. Behaviour of an individual can be defined as an adjustment to his environment. Every individual develops his own unique way of adjustment in the society. Socially matured individuals are better able to adjust to the various changes in the environment and react appropriately thus making the right type of adjustment.

STAGES OF SOCIAL MATURITY

An individual takes time in his social development. So, we may think of some stages of social maturity according to the physical, mental, emotional and language development of the individual. They are,

- Awareness of the presence of another person.
- Mixing with others
- Understanding of social relationships.

Understanding of all the above three things refers to human stages of social maturity.

SOCIAL MATURITY AND ITS CHARACTERISTICS

Social maturity is the final expected outcome of social development and socialisation; certain characteristics of social maturity are, (*a*) A social matured person has a sense of his proper place and roles as a member of the social group. He is willing and able to orient himself in the various activities and customs to the group.

(*b*) He is able to assume a reasonable amount of responsibility, to adjust him to the inevitable limitations and restrictions of the community life.

(*c*) He can be original and yet conform to the broad pattern of his social environment.

(*d*) He evaluates social problems not form a purely selfish point of view but has regard to the right opinion of others.

(*e*) He accepts responsibility for his actions, does not indulge in self-pitying.

(*f*) He has a realistic self-concept being conscious of his assets and limitations.

(*g*) He is relatively secure and so open to new experiences, which contribute, to his continuous development.

In short, co-operations, pleasing manner, consideration for others, positive and optimistic outlook on life and teaching competence are signs of socially matured individual.

CHARACTERISTICS OF SOCIALLY MATURED INDIVIDUAL

Social maturity is evidenced in the capacity of the individual to maintain friendships that meet the needs of others as well as his own. Vatssyan (1990) states "A matures individual form the social stand point is one who co-operates with all those with whom he comes into contact and contradicts them only when such a course of action becomes inevitable. He is never ill-mannered choosing instead to appear very well mannered, considerate and friendly to all and sundry" (p.119), consequently has a large circle of friends. An adult, who has attended that stage as required by the standpoint, evinces great interest in art, study, games etc.

He studies the works of greatest authors and takes interest in games and forms of recreation suitable to his station in life. His activities and conduct are scrupulously in conformity with his age and sex. He has the power of independent decision and judgement. He gives every evidence of being well balanced and adjusted with himself and his behaviour towards other individuals.

Elizabeth B. Hurlock (1959) says, "The socially mature individual has sense of his proper place and role as a member of a group. He is willing and able to orient himself in the various activities with others and customs of the group, to make the proportionate contribution to the work to be done, to take a suitable part in the social exchange to assume a reasonable amount of responsibility and to adjust himself to the inevitable limitations and restrictions of community life without waste of energy or loss or satisfaction". He can be original and yet conform to the broad pattern of the cultural environment.

Taneja R.P. (1989) says, "Social maturity refers to degree of growth in social and vocational abilities". The socially mature individual treats the members of his family as friends. In this role he shows the affection, loyalty, consideration and respect for all family members. As a citizen the socially mature person accepts his obligations and performs them faithfully". He makes good adjustments to all types of people without prejudice based on their religion, race or skin colour.

The matured accepts his friends as they are and does not criticize or try to change them as a socially immature person does. He is loyal to them and feels a sense of responsibility towards them when they need his help. Although society may add greatly to his happiness, the mature persons is self-sufficient enough that he can be happy when circumstances make it possible for him to be with his family, friends or acquaintances.

The mature individual can be found to posses the trait of good humour and pleasantness. The important point is that he keeps himself alive, with vigorous interests that make him interesting to be with. The mature individual posses a feeling of social concern and gets very involved in situations that call for obedience to social norms too. The person equipped with the human sensitivities that make for maturity will usually have powerful concern with social problems and ways of alleviating them. For all his social-mindedness, for all his scoring of human relationships, the maturing individuals are not dependent on always having company.

The mature person knows that he has to go on choosing alternatives, that each alternative costs him something, and there are things he will never be able to do and experience. He also knows that there are things he will never be able to do again, that he can never recapture his youth or relive his first encounters with certain experience. He knows that his integration is continually threatened by practical demands, by seductive temptations, by concessions and compromises, by conflicting values, and can only be preserved at the cost of some psychic stream. He knows that the only real reward in life comes with continued growth, and that there is no room in the material life he has for major regrets. This individual who has approached maturity can know that he has loved, has done his work, has made his mark on people.

IMPORTANCE OF SOCIAL MATURITY

Social maturity has been defined as an indication of willingness and ability to orient. Oneself in the various activities and customs of the group to make a proportionate contribution to the work to be done, to take a suitable part in the social exchange, to assume a reasonable amount of responsibility and to adjust oneself to the inevitable limitations and restrictions of community life without waste of energy or loss of satisfaction.

Nazarath Maria. E. Waples (1978) defines, "Maturity is the blossoming of man's character into a unified totality. It discerns the process that contributes to the psychological and physical growth and well being of man".

Maturity assumes accountability, constantly assesses, judges and takes appropriate decisions. Maturity develops a balanced emotional outlook, helping the individual to accept himself, his talents and limitations and to accept others as they are. It analyses values and internalises them consistently. It helps towards progressive advancement in spiritual growth, impelling the individual to adapt himself to change and to life without emotional crises. Abraham Sperling (1967) states social maturity in the following words "An adolescent should get along with and well with others. He ought to develop self-reliance in matters of taste and ought to develop tolerance of human differences". Maturity is a gradual process that comes with self-knowledge and with self-realisation shaping man into a responsible adult.

CHALLENGES AND PROBLEM OF TEACHER EDUCATION

Teacher education has to support the efforts for the solution of problem of education of the country. These problems may be divided into two categories. First one is problems of education as a whole with special reference to school education and the second is problems of teacher education itself. The latter includes general problems as well those caused by school education curricula and teacher effectiveness which put the responsibility of its implementation on teachers.

The education system now faces challenges from neo-colonialism which is not the same as its traditional counterpart. It is economic, ideological and cultural. If not checked, it will lead to further 'educational divide'. Teacher education has to understand its many dimensional consequences and take appropriate safeguards against it.

The country has to fulfill its constitutional commitment of article 45 providing universal elementary education to all and achieve the goal. To meet this obligation many programmes have been initiated. For achieving the target, the country needs well qualified and properly trained teachers. The system has to prepare them and also train under qualified teachers professionally.

Population explosion of school going children, rising aspirations of the people and their greater desire for more useful knowledge, complete with explosion of knowledge and techniques for imparting knowledge have emerged as new challenges to teacher education. The possibility of acquiring knowledge from sources other than the teacher, books and from outside educational institutions has increased tremendously. Then educational system has to respond in full measure to this development. Technological development impact knowledge within a short span of time and use of new transactional strategies including all the resources. Students should be encouraged to pursue independent learning and make use of the skills of 'learning to learn'.

In the emerging context the possibility of teachers and educators becoming outdated and professionally less effective has increased. Constant re-education and in-service programmes for teachers and their educators have become the need for this present century.

Teacher education institutions need to forge stronger links with the system of education and also with the community they serve. Community linked teacher education, research and extension programmes need to be undertaken. The experts from community, if available, may be invited by teacher education institutions and teachers and educators may be encouraged to participate in the activities of the community and vice-versa.

Education requires interdisciplinary approach. For its enrichment it needs cross fertilisation and active support from allied subjects, and teacher education is no exception to this. Sociology and social and cultural anthropology can help in developing need based pedagogies. Economics and management science can add value and meaning to the courses of educational finance, economics of education, educational planning, management, administration and supervision. There is a need to harness inputs from these areas to courses of education for teachers. By doing so, the theoretical and practical component of teacher education will certainly become more meaningful and contemporary. Alternative programmes with increased duration may be tried out for qualitative improvement of teacher education.

Children process information acquires knowledge and learns in a cultural context and their personalities and mental make-up are influenced by cultural factors. There are difference in the levels of aspiration and perception of children coming from a metropolis and of those from a tribal background. They may interpret the some event or concept differently according to their socio-cultural backgrounds. Cultural specificity therefore, needs to be utilised to improve children's learning. Since there is no uniform process of learning and forming concepts, acquisitions of values, morality and character and personality development, there is a need for teachers and educators to understand how cultural traditions and factors outside the school affect pedagogical practices. To ignore these factors can adversely affect educational and learning out comes. To evolve culture-specific pedagogy and empower the teacher to do so in their specific context becomes an important function of teacher education.

Culture-specific pedagogy is influenced by many tangible and intangible factors operating in society. Chief among these are the practices of child rearing in the family and the community, well-established methods of teaching and learning, indigenous educational practices and the ideas of thinkers and educationists of the society. India provides valuable opportunity for binding all these together for evolving culture-specific pedagogy not only because it has preserved a rich cultural heritage, a large variety of educational practices outside the school in different regions but also because it has its own thinking on matters pertaining to education. The thought and practices of Indian educationists can be useful for reconstructing a need-based indigenous national and culture specific pedagogies considerable research has been carried out in teacher education, and some of its findings relevant to Indian context can help in the development of quality teacher education programmes.

Mass copying and leakage of question papers and unruly behaviour of students during after examinations demand that teachers should evolve a more reliable and continuous evaluation system. Misconceptions about decentralisation of education with special reference to Panchayati Raj need to be removed from the minds of the teachers. Mismatch in the supply and demand of teachers in certain sectors and states demand need-based manpower planning. Teacher education has to convince the state about it. Special attention needs to be paid to inculcating professionalism, its values and skills and to improve teachers work culture.

TEACHING COMPETENCY

The teacher has a major role in the educational development Gandhiji remarked that "no country can make any progress without good teachers". The quality and standard of education depends on the quality and standard of teachers. Teacher is the torch bearer of the race and guardian of the feature of the mankind.

According to Humagun Kabir: "Teachers are literally the architects of a nations destiny" Mrs.Indira Gandhi stated, "The nation's well being depends upon the teacher's well being our teachers are the 'custodians' of future. No society can afford to neglect them".

"Competency" ordinarily is defined as "Adequate for the purpose; suitable, sufficient, or as capable". In a sense it refers to adequate preparation to begin a professional career, and has a direct linkage to verification requirements.

Cooker (1976) defined "competence is seen as the ability to cope with a certain class of problems encountered on the job. A teacher who can deal with problems in certain area is said to be competent in that area a fully competent teacher is one who can cope successfully with any "propositional problem". Competency in teaching stems forms the capacity to reach out differing children and to create a rich and multidimensional environment for them (Joyce and Well 1985).

To study the effectiveness "competency based teacher training (CBTT) strategy" for developing following basic teaching competencies among pre service teacher,

1. Cognitive - based teaching competency
2. Performance - based teaching competency
3. Affective - based teaching competency
4. Consequence - based teaching competency
5. Managerial - based teaching competency

CONCEPTS OF TEACHING COMPETENCY

A competent teacher has good command of subject matter and solid core of teaching skills. They have excellent instructional strategies supported by methods of goal setting, instructional planning and classroom management. They know how to motivate, communicate and work effectively with students. The teachers play an important role in molding and shaping the attitudes, habits, and manners and above all, the character and personality of the students. The teacher with competency does the planning, organisation, reading and controlling of teaching. He is free to perform various activities to provide a learning experience to the learners.

We expect scholars and leaders to be able to effectively communicate with others, and to be able to teach. Students can take coursework related to teaching and engage in a teaching mentorship with a faculty mentor. During the mentorship, students practice didactic, interactive and experimental teaching strategies in classroom setting. They also learn approaches to other forms of knowledge dissemination such as teaching and presentation. Teaching involves a conceptual understanding of how people learn and the ability to translate this understanding into constructing and delivering learning opportunities to diverse audiences.

According to Joki (1982), school boards can help improve the quality of teaching by writing strong, clear policies on administrative accountability (including provisions for instructional leadership); on teacher recruitment, supervision, and evaluation, on an instructional model keyed to specific objectives; and on in service training for administrators and teachers. Superintendents also might provide principals with clerical assistance to free more time for classroom observation, clinical supervision, demonstration teaching, and staff development (Joki 1982).

Teacher evaluation, in addition to its customary function of establishing basis for promotion, retention, in-service training of teachers can also be a valuable tool for improving instructional effectiveness. A good evaluation program should emerge from the cooperative efforts of teachers and their evaluators in identifying broad areas of responsibility and specific objectives (Joki 1982). Thus teachers will “own” an evaluation program, rather than have one arbitrarily imposed.

Besides monitoring teacher’s performance, a specific objective of teacher evaluation should be to set measurable job improvement targets (Sweeney and Manatt 1982). Once targets are set, the principal and teacher work out a specific plan of action within a given time frame, and then review the teacher’s progress in conference. Such clinical supervision promotes a school climate in which continuous improvement becomes an essential part of every teacher’s job.

In addition to setting and clarifying expectations, administrators can also employ incentives to induce teachers to excel in their profession. These include merit pay plans, career options (including career ladders), enhanced professional responsibilities (for example, master teacher plans), non monetary recognition such as annual awards, and improved working conditions.

The University of Waterloo's Competency portfolio Project emphasizes the need for student "to learn in ways that help deal with a range of contexts, many, if not all, unique" (Bowden and Marton, 1988) and be able to demonstrate that knowledge in a variety of learning contexts. This means that faculty members need to model desired competencies for students in their teaching. For history, it is important that students learn, not just about the "facts" but also about how historians really "do" history. In other words, we need to teach them about what it means to be a historian.

In my own practice, this has translated into a much more skilled-based approach to my teaching. This should not be taken to mean, however, that I see history courses as being just about "skill-building" I believe that by helping students to "see" their own competence in history they will be able to transfer their knowledge to other learning contexts. In order to foster this change in students 'behaviour I go beyond simply articulating my learning goals for them in terms of the competencies that they will develop in my courses to encouraging (and, in fact, requiring) them to reflect on how they can use their knowledge (both content and skills) in other learning contexts (in the work place in their community and in other academic courses). You can find examples of student reflections in the "methods that prompt thoughtful and responsible learning" link below.

The approach to teaching history, we believe, translates into a more powerful learning experience because it encourages students to view learning as a life-long experience, rather than just a course – based experience. Below we will see the professional and discipline-specific competencies that are part of teaching excellence in higher education. Links to example of how the model these competencies for our students are provided.

The University of Wateloo's Competency Portfolio Project emphasizes the need for students "to learn in ways that help them deal with a range of contexts, many if not all, unique"

(Bowden and Marton, 1998) and be able to demonstrate that knowledge in a variety of learning contexts. This means that faculty members need to model desired competencies for students in their teaching. For history, it is important that students learn, not just about the "facts" but also about how historians really "do" history. In other words, we need to teach them about what is means to be a historian.

DEFINITIONS

In the words of Murthy and Lulla, "Competence based teacher education is that type of professional education of class room teachers that takes the pre-determined competence of teaching behaviours as the base of teacher education programs".

The Education Commission (1964-66) observed, "Of all the different factors, which influence its quality of education and it's contribute to national development, the quality, competence and characters are undoubtedly the most significant".

COMPETENCIES TO BE DEVELOPED

Competence in the use of any methodology involves being able to choose intelligently with the knowledge, experience and skill to make chosen methods work effectively. This can only be acquired by experience, which requires confidence, risk taking and reflection on what happens, so the competencies that are to be developed among the teacher trainees are as follows.

1. Competence to understand the sight process of learning, including learning, learning by doing, learning to be, learning to do and learning to become.
2. Competence to devise dynamic methods in the day-to-day situations based on the needs and interests of children.
3. Competence to organise the class room in such a manner that different kinds of activities may be

organised in it so that children may receive required guidance from teacher.

4. Competence to become an example of qualities that he/she wants to develop among his/her students, realising that example is superior to mere instruction and preaching.
5. Competence in regard to language, delivery of speech and other method of communication.
6. Competence in regard to the contents of the subject that he / she are supposed to teach. The teacher should be able to answer questions that belong to the immediate reason or even to some remotely related subject matter, which may occur in subsequent reason.
7. Competence to engage children in a meaningful manner so that children my develop capacity to ask question and may be inspired to find out the answers by themselves.
8. Competence to innovate so as to create proper environment in the classroom to enable children to develop wider horizons of perceptions.
9. Competence to develop among students a scientific temper, which is often confined to cultivation of various attitudes, includes objective observation, experimentation and consideration of every point of view relevant to the enquiry in a logical manner.

The competencies mentioned above suggest that the school teacher in the developing countries may inspire a change in the impulses of the pupils growing personality so as to have a balanced blending of knowledge, power, love and skills that are required for his / her development as a good individual and useful member of the society. The teacher has to develop competence to innovative methods oriented and learner's need based. The teachers may be apprised what they are supposed to teach.

COMPETENCY AREAS

National Council for Teacher Education (NCTE) has identified ten competency areas in teacher preparation:

(*i*) Contextual competencies including development of education in society and teacher's role in it.

(*ii*) Conceptual competencies comprising various concepts of education and learning and psychological, sociological and physiological aspects of education.

(*iii*) Curricula and content competencies relating different stages of education like primary, upper-primary and secondary.

(*iv*) Transitional competencies as regards general subject-wise and stage-wise dimensions.

(*v*) Competencies in other educational activities such as planning and organising morning assembly, etc.

(*vi*) Competencies relating to teaching-learning materials.

(*vii*) Evaluation competencies including preparation, selection, use of tools, justice etc.

(*viii*) Management competencies including organisation of classroom, school and community activities.

(*ix*) Competencies related to working with parents understand the role; discuss the problems; active co-operation; organise parent teacher meetings; explore and utilise educational resources etc.

(*x*) Competencies related to working with the community and other agencies, understand the importance; contribute for improvement; realize the objectives; develop wholesome relationship; explore and exploit community educational resources activities etc.

A TO Z OF TEACHING COMPETENCIES

Teaching is an interactive process involving many aspects of teacher, student, learning process and learning situations. So in order to be a competent teacher one must have competent in the following dispositions.

'A' is for alertness.

'B' is for business like attitude to keep busy in worthwhile tasks.

'C' is for clarity and co-operative teaching learning.

'D' is for devotion and discovery.

'E' is for enthusiasm, expecting children to learn and evaluation.

'F' is for feedback for the guidance of the learner and evaluation.

'G' is for goal setting and achieving.

'H' is for hard work, honest work, humility and humor.

'I' is for involvement of children.

'J' is for judicious attitude and just action.

'K' is for knowledge of the students, subject-mater of oneself.

'L' is for linking learning with daily experiences and life.

'M' is for motivation.

'N' is for need-based learning.

'O' is for objectivity and providing out of classroom learning experiences.

'P' is for practice and praising children when needed.

'Q' is for quiz organsing for monitoring learning progress.

'R' is for relationships and review.

'S' is for stimulation.

'T' is for tolerance and the technology of teaching learning.

'U' is for unbiased attitude and unexpected encounters and situations.

'V' is for a variety of learning experience.

'W' is for warmth and wisdom.

'X' is for x-ray of the learning process.

'Y' is for yearning and eagerness.

'Z' is for zeal.

ESSENTIAL QUALITIES OF A COMPETENT TEACHER

In order to be a competent teacher, he must possess certain special qualities such as

1. Qualities relating to professional requirements.
2. Qualities relating to character and personality.
3. Qualities relating to human relationship.
4. Qualifications related to professional educational / training.

JOB FUNCTIONS AND COMPETENCY

Competence refers to a state of being well qualified to perform an activity, task or job function. When a person is competent to do something, he or she has achieved a state of competence that is recognisable and verifiable to a particular community of practitioners. A competency, then, refers to the way that a state of competence can be demonstrated to the relevant community. According to the International Board of Standards for Training Performance and Instruction (IBSTPI), a competency involves a related set of knowledge, skills and attitudes that enable a person to effectively perform the activities of a given occupation or function in such a way that meets or exceeds the standards expected in a particular profession of work setting (Richey et al., 2001).

The structure and assessment of competencies may differ form one community of practice to another and even within a community. To facilitate a common understanding of competencies in the / context / if mobile and distributed learning some specifications have been elaborated (IMS, 2001). Typically, as competency is divided into specific indicators describing the requisite knowledge, skills, attitudes and context of performance.

There are different ways to validate that a person has demonstrated the relevant competencies (Le Boterf, 1998, 2000, 2001). One of them is through a certification process (Levy-Leboyer, 1999). Teacher certification is a common practice, and the notion of teacher competencies is fairly well established. However, competencies are generally associated with highly formalised professional activities and not applied to ill-defined tasks (those involving variable and uncertain circumstances, procedures and outcomes). III-defined tasks certainly include many forms of teaching.

This narrow view of competence runs counter to common sense and professional practice, but brings into attention the mainstream approach to elaboration of teacher competencies where it is essential to clearly identify the conditions of teaching (Paquay et al., 1998). The delivery environment (classroom-based, internet-based, laboratory-based, hybrid environments and so on) is a particularly relevant condition to identify competencies for online teaching.

COMPETENCY AND CLASS ROOM TEACHING

Information technology can be integrated into both online and classroom setting, but the interaction between these technologies and new approaches to learning and instruction may very (Spector and Anderson, 2000). The range of activities available in online settings and the multiple conditions of time in which they take place are evidence that the technology demands placed on online teachers are some what more significant than those associated with classroom teachers.

Much of what has already been published with regard to online teaching has focused on technical skills and requirements of successfully moderating and facilitating online discussion and chat sessions (e.g. Collision et al., 2000; Kersley, 2000; Rosenburg 2001). This body of literature suggests that becoming an effective online moderate requires training and that there are competencies unique to online environments.

In online discussions, the moderator's competencies involve (1) allowing learners time for reflection, (2) keeping discussion alive and on a productive path, and (3) archiving and organising discussion to be used in subsequent lesions.

In online synchronous discussion (e.g., chat), the moderator must

(1) establish ground rules for discussion, (2) animate interactions with minimal instructor intervention, (3) sense how online text message may appear to distant learners, and (4) be aware of cultural differences.

At the school level animating discussions, displaying cultural sensitivity and so on, apply to all teachers. At the environment level, however, the ways in which a teacher demonstrates such competence is quite different, which suggests that there are competence is quite different, which suggests that there are competencies unique to online settings. According to Belisle and Linard (1996) the use of technology in teaching calls for additional competencies adapted to new roles and circumstances. Teaching competencies and online teaching competencies have generally been considered separately. Problems and challenges in teacher education.

SIGNIFICANCE OF THE STUDY

A new concept social maturity with its significance is more important for one's daily life. It may be defined as one's unitary ability to know, feel, judge, behave and cooperate with a person's thinking process for behaving in a proper way with the ultimate realisation of happiness in him and in others. In view of its wide significance from the individual as well as social angles, it becomes quite imperative that serious efforts should be made for its proper development right from early childhood among human beings.

A person's social maturity helps him much in all spheres of life. Social maturity also helps a person to understand and give direction to live a very healthy life. Social maturity is related to teaching competency. A competent teacher can execute their work very effectively. So teachers should have good teaching aptitude and teaching competency. The primary level of education is a significant stage to import various skills like listening, speaking and writing. Unless the teachers are very competent they may not perform their work properly. So it is significant to know the teaching competency of the teacher trainees at this level.

Teaching is an interactive process, involving four aspects teacher, students, learning process and learning situation. A competent teacher possesses all the necessary qualities to interact with the school and community. Teacher with social maturity will be able to teach students with all capabilities. So the present study has been conducted to verify how social maturity is correlated with the teaching competency of the B.Ed. teacher trainees. It is expected that every teacher trainee should have social maturity and it will influence their teaching competency. Hence this study has been conducted to verify these interesting aspects.

OBJECTIVES OF THE STUDY

The following objectives are set for the present study.

1. To find out the significant difference between male and female teacher trainees on their social maturity.
2. To find out the significant difference between male and female teacher trainees on their components of teaching competency.
3. To find out the significant difference between TTI and DIET teacher trainees on their social maturity.
4. To find out the significant difference between TTI and DIET teacher trainees on their components of teaching competency.
5. To find out the significant difference between teacher trainees belonging to nuclear and joint families on their social maturity.

6. To find out the significant difference between teacher trainees belonging to nuclear and joint families on their components of teaching competency.
7. To find out the significant difference between teacher trainees from rural and urban area on their social maturity.
8. To find out the significant difference between teacher trainees from rural and urban area on their components of teaching competency.
9. To find out the significant difference of teacher trainees on their social maturity based on their parental income.
10. To find out the significant difference of teacher trainees on their components of teaching competency based on their parental income.
11. To find out the significant difference on social maturity of teacher trainees based on their communities.
12. To find out the significant difference on components of teaching competency of teacher trainees based on their communities.
13. To find out the significant difference on social maturity of teacher trainees based on their fathers qualification.
14. To find out the significant difference on components of teaching competency of teacher trainees based on their fathers qualification.
15. To find out the significant difference on social maturity of teacher trainees based on their mothers qualification.
16. To find out the significant difference on components of teaching competency of teacher trainees based on their mothers qualification.
17. To find out the significant difference on social maturity of teacher trainees based on their age.

18. To find out the significant difference on components of teaching competency of teacher trainees based on their age.
19. To find out the significant relationship between social maturity and components of teaching competency.

LIMITATIONS

The present investigation has the following limitations.

1. The investigation is limited to TTI and DIET students.
2. The study is restricted to three institutions.
3. The sample is restricted to 400 students.
4. Standardised test materials alone were used in this investigation.
5. The investigation was restricted only teacher trainee student of the study.
6. Students were chosen from 3 institutions.

CONCLUSIONS

The problem of the present study has been discussed briefly in this chapter, bringing out the characteristics, importance and objectives of the study etc. A detailed discussion of the related literature follows in the next chapter.

REVIEW OF RELATED LITERATURE

Introduction

The research takes the advantage to the knowledge, which has accumulated in the past as a result of constant human endeavour. Research can never be undertaken in isolation of the work that has already been done on the problem, which is directly or indirectly related to study proposed by a researcher. One of the important steps in the planning of any research study is careful review of the research journals, books, dissertations, and other series of information on the problem to the investigated. A review of the related literature must precede any well-planned research study.

Review of the related literature allows the researcher to acquaint him with current knowledge in the field or area in which he is going to conduct his research. The important specific reason for reviewing the related literature is to know about the recommendation of previous researchers for further research, which they have listed in their studies. The present summary of research studies are related to problem "Social Maturity and Teaching Competency among TTI and DIET students".

IMPORTANCE OF REVIEW OF RELATED LITERATURE

Review of literature related to the problem is essential in order to determine three things.

- Whether studies already exists similar to what the purpose to undertake.
- Whether existing research provides guidance or sheds further light on the problem.
- Whether existing research provides a point of departure or a platform upon which the new research can build.

The investigations have added much to our knowledge. Thus the knowledge of related literature also enables investigator to define the frontiers of their field.

STUDIES RELATED TO SOCIAL MATURITY

Indian Studies

Ghosh. S (1975) has investigated social maturity of pre school Bengali children of Calcutta city belonging to different social-economic groups. Thirty five, nursery and kinder garden schools were randomly selected from the different regions of Calcutta and 40 pre-school children were selected from each school at random equally distributed in each area group. Data were also collected by using a standardised interview schedule on the mothers of these selected children.

The final sample included 1410 cases. The study revealed that sex had very insignificant role in imbibing social maturation. Economic status was insignificant as testimony of ability to enrich the social maturity level.

Rao. N. (1978) conducted a research work on social maturity of high school children in Bangalore city. A sample of 1020 students was chosen from 50 secondary schools in Bangalore. The self-constructed questionnaire was used in this study. The major findings were as follows; (I) Positive correlation between social maturity and intelligence (II) Positive relationship between social maturities and self-esteem (III) Girls generally scored higher then boys on social maturity (IV) There are class differences in social maturity among the children of lower grades (V) Private school children scored more on social maturity than Government Schools.

Puranik, S.D. (1985) has studied the relationship of social maturity of pupils with organisational climate and teachers' morale in the primary schools in Bangalore city. The sample consists of 70 schools 2634 students and 712 teachers. The study indicated the development of social maturity; autonomous climate, private management and unaided students and urban location of schools were most conductive factors. No effect of moral of teachers of both senses was noticed on the development of social maturity of male (or) female students (or) on the students of both sexes even under the influence of organizational climate, school organisation and localities.

Asthana, Anju (1989) conducted a study of social maturity among school going children in city of Lucknow. The objectives were (I) to study whether social maturity increases with grade level (II) to study association of intelligence, socio-economic status academic achievement, adult dependence and sex of the child with social maturity. It was found that the social maturity increased with inverse in grade level, the growth rate being highest in the first school years. Intelligence, academic achievement and adult dependence were significantly associated with the social maturity of children although adult dependence and a negative association and SES were not found to contribute to social maturity at any of the five grade levels.

Sarojamma, Y.H. (1990) has conducted a comparative study of reaching ability and social maturity of over normal and underachievers of standard VIII, the final sample comprised of 476 boys and 524 girls. The social maturity scale by Sathyanarayana and Swadha was used. It was found that, there was significant difference in the reading ability of,

1. Normal and under achievers,
2. Over and normal achievers,
3. Girls and boys,
4. Students having high and low social maturity
5. Students in private and government schools.

The interaction effect of the variables on reading ability, hypothesized was not significant.

Malin, A.J. (1990) conducted a study on the relationship of social maturity with classroom climate and academic achievement. The sample consisted of 1200 students of classes VIII and IX. The tools used were Edward's social maturity state and achievements tests. The research points out students studying in classes IX had high maturity as compared to students of class VIII. The mean maturity scores of students having low achievement for both classes. Classroom climate and achievement has a significant effort on maturity scores of students of both the class.

Agnihotri, C.S. (1991) has conducted a cross cultural comparative study between tribal and non tribal first generation and traditional learners in relation to their social maturity and educational adjustment. The sample consisted of 113 first generation tribal learners and 108 traditional tribal learners. Social maturity was independent of traditions of learning. The tribal and non-tribal differed in terms of their placements on attribute of social maturity. The traditions of learning were found to be contributing to social maturity. It was found that, the social maturity and educational adjustment were only social ingredients. Psychological characteristics also influenced the social maturity and educational adjustment of children and social maturity was independent of traditions of learning.

Bhusham, A. (1994) conducted a study on social maturity across sex and family vocations. The sample comprised of 200 student teachers from two colleges, equally divided between two sexes. Major variable used were sex values, and family vocations. The tools used for data collections were the form D of value survey. The study highlights, male and female uniformly assigned highest importance to social maturity. Both male and female from service and non-service class had politeness as a subdivision on their maturity.

Foreign Studies

Vora, J.I. (1980) in his research works on social maturity of B.Ed., students in Gujarat. The sample size was 855 student teachers from Gujarat University, South Gujarat University and M.S. University. Some of the major findings were (I) The male students were superior to the female students in their social maturity (II) Age had no relation with social maturity (III) The arts students were more socially mature than science students (IV) The higher socio-economic status had better social maturity.

Savoluk Thongngamkhom (1983) has investigated the social maturity as a function of some psycho socio – adjustment factors of B.Ed., college students of north central region of Thailand. The scale was standardised on a sample of 922 students – including boys and girls. The study states that boys and girls having dominant personality traits were more socially matured than those having submissive personality traits. The two groups of B.Ed., students having high suggestibility and low suggestibility trait did not differ on social maturity. The study revealed that the college students with high SES background were found more socially matured than those of coming from low SES strata. The students having dominant personality trait were more socially matured than those of having submissive personality trait. The students having high leadership personality trait were more socially matured than those of having low leadership personality trait.

Pattramon JumpamGern (1986) investigated the social maturity of teachers, college students of western region of Thailand and found that the teachers – college student coming from urban areas were found to be more matured than those coming from rural areas. Students having good family adjustment were more socially matured than those having poor family adjustment. It was found that the higher secondary students coming from urban areas were found to be more matured than those coming from rural areas. The male higher secondary students were found superior to the female students. The higher secondary students with high SES were more socially matured than those with low SES.

Bances Ann Leslie (1995) conducted a study on measuring the effect of participation in a peer facilitation project on sixth graders self esteem, social maturity and patterns of social choice. The population chosen for the study was rural mainstream sixth grade students. The sample was tested by sociometric pattern of choice. It was found that some significant difference in social maturity for gender and there was significant relationship between self-esteem and social maturity.

Mulia, R.D. (1991) A comparative study of the social maturity of higher secondary students in the contest of their streams, sex and IQs. The objectives were (I) To study the stream effect on social maturity. (II) To study the sex effect on social maturity. (III) To study the effect of levels of IQs on social maturity. (IV) To study the interaction effect among independent variables on social maturity. It was found that there was no significant relationship in social maturity among students of three streams and between the two sexes, while IQ had main significant effect on social maturity streams and sex and no interaction effect of streams and sex as well as sex and IQs was found significant on social maturity.

Flymin Xavier, J., (2003) attempted a study on social maturity and academic achievement among higher secondary school students. The sample of 300 was taken from government, government aided and private higher secondary schools in Trivandrum. The samples were tested by Rao's social maturity scale. Some of the major findings were ((I) Gender has no influence on social maturity (II) Type of schools had no influence on social maturity

(III) Social maturity and academic achievement are positively correlated.

Mani, M., (2004) did study on social maturity and adherence to school regulation of higher secondary students. Taken the sample of 300 higher secondary school students studying in 5 different schools in Chennai. Rao's social maturity scale was used for administration. Some of the major findings were (I) Gender has significant bearing on social maturity (II) There is significant relationship between social maturity and adherence to school regulations (III) There is significant relationship between social maturity and academic achievement.

Saravanan, K., (2005) attempted a research on social maturity on self-concept among higher secondary school students. The sample of 249 boys and girls who studied XI standard in various schools in Chennai was taken. Rao's social maturity scale was used for administration. Some of the major findings were (I) Social maturity is found to be moderate (II) Gender has no influence on social maturity (III) Type of school had no significant difference on social maturity.

STUDIES RELATED TO TEACHING COMPETENCY

Indian Studies on Teaching Competency

Chatter Jee, B.B. *et al.* (1965) studied about the predication of teaching competency as a function of sharing a common frame of reference. The major findings were: The range of the scaled teaching competency scores given by the staff judges increased in the post-presentation assessments as compared to the pre-presentation predication, while the post-presentation scaled scores of teaching competency given by the instructors themselves were found to have low range compared two scores distributions obtained from the staff judges.

Saraswathi, L.S. (1973) conducted a study about the jobs held by home scientists and the competencies needed on the jobs held as perceived by the employed home scientists and their employees in the District. The major findings were: The high competency perception proportion indicated that majority of the items included in the competency tests were perceived by the two sets of respondents (Teachers and research workers and those on miscellaneous job) as required as the job with an exception of those of the jobs of the assistant lecturers in colleges and teachers in secondary schools.

Nair, S.R. (1974) reported about and impact of certain sociological factors on teaching ability in the classroom of government training college in Tiruchur. The major finding of this work was that private school teachers in general were found to have better teaching ability than the government school teachers. Sex was not found to be affecting teaching ability. A positive relationship existed between age and teaching ability. Caste and religion were not found to be affecting teaching ability.

Sharma, S.K. (1981) analyzed the various relationship of teaching effectiveness in terms of competency. The study was carried out at three different stages. In the final study 220 classrooms teaching learning situations were observed. The major findings were: There were no significant relationship between the ages of Hindi teachers, their attitude, interest and intelligence and their teaching competency. Male and female Hindi teachers did not differ significantly in their teaching competency. There was significant negative correlation the self-perception of Hindi teachers teaching at higher secondary level and their teaching competency. There was a significant positive correlation between the teaching competency of teachers at higher secondary level and academic achievement of their pupil of grade XI in Hindi. The teaching competencies identified were: giving assignments, loud reading, asking questions, introducing lessons, pacing, managing the classroom, presenting verbal mode, clarification, using the black board, using appropriate reinforcement, achieving closure, probing question, creation interest and improving pupils reading behaviour.

Rajan, S. Sathyagiri (1985) conducted a study about the competency, personality, motivation, perception and profession of college teachers. The major findings were: Teacher competency was related to intelligence, emotional stability, conscientiousness, tender-mindedness, trusted nature, and placed nature, self-sufficiency, placed and relaxedness factors of Cattell's 16PF questionnaires. It was significantly related to creativity, dynamism, organised demeanours and warmth and acceptance, self-actualisation and professional perception of teachers. The more competent teachers significantly differed from the less competent teachers in all the above variables. Those variables that correlated significantly with teacher competence intercorrelated with one another significantly.

Das, B.C. (1993) conducted a study about the effectiveness of concept attainment model in terms of teaching competency of pre-service student teachers. It was found that concept attainment model effectively developed the teaching competency of pre-service students teachers.

Naseema, C. (1994) reported about a teaching competence of secondary schools physical science teachers in relation to satisfaction of teaching physical science. The major findings were: It was found that 30.92 percent of physical science teachers differed in perceived teaching competence which can be attributed to work (0.01) rewards (1.73), context of work (0.87), self (0.61), others (0.56), 26.89 percent of physical science teachers different in observed teaching competence which can be attributed to work (0.86), reward (0.002) context of work (1.5), self (2.32), others (1.91).

Kukreti, B.R. (1994) reported about a correlation study between job motivation and teaching competency. The major findings were: the competent teachers had joined the teaching profession because they regarded teaching as a prestigious job. They believed that the teaching profession provided them reasonable salary, security, opportunity of social service, to establish human relation and enhance their knowledge. Incompetent teachers entered the teaching profession because they thought that their profession would get fame, personal freedom, influencing opportunity and enough leisure with little burden of work.

Thigarajan, A. *et al.* (1995) conducted a study about the teaching competency and achievement. The major findings were: The teaching competency and achievement of boys had significant relationships. The relationship between teaching competency and achievement of boys and girls differed significantly.

Panda, S.C., (1996) conducted a study about the effect of competency-based instruction in achieving MLL competencies in grade IV Oriya medium schools. The major findings were: There was remarkable difference in the achievement of both the groups. The competency-based instruction yielded significantly better results than the traditional method of teaching.

Shamala, S.K. (1997) reported about enhancing teaching competency through integration of art education for effective language teaching at the primary stage. The major findings were: Prior the implementation of MLL based curriculum, it was highly essential to orient the primary school teachers to know how to develop local specific competencies based different activities. There was a positive impact of module to empower primary school teachers in developing competency based local specific curriculum. The main objective are: To determine the value of high school teachers place on these elements; classroom climate, questioning, set induction, stimulus variation, reinforcement and closure. In this study classroom climate, questioning, set induction, stimulus variation, reinforcement and closure are sported as a set of selected elements for improving instruction.

Thamilmani, P. (2000) conducted a study on teacher competency, teacher personality and teacher attitude on student achievement in science in high schools. The study included a sample of 100 teachers (58 male, 42 female teaching science and 300 students X studying under those teachers). The tools used were: Teacher Competency – Student Rating Scale, Teacher personality and teacher attitude of science teachers are related to the academic achievement of X standard students in science. They revealed male and female teachers differed significantly in their personality traits and attitude towards teaching.

Palaniyandi, R. (2001) investigated the competency needs of pre-service teacher trainees. The teacher educators and student teachers from six DIETs constituting 273 pre-service teacher trainees 106 teacher educators and 462 practicing teachers working in these districts were the samples for the study. To identify the competency needs of pre-service teacher trainees as perceived by the pre-service trainees. They revealed learning process related competencies emerged as a group having the highest number of competencies.

Manjula P. Rao (2002) studied Teacher Competencies and learners' achievement in Tribal areas of Karnataka. Twenty schools belonging to 3 taluks, 261 students of third standard and 31 teachers teaching the same students constituted the sample of this study. The researcher tool used in this study are: The achievement test developed based on the competencies specified for class III in Languae, Mathematics, EVS-I and EVS-II to assess teachers' competence in subject areas. To study the relationship between teachers' competency and students achievement: in language, Mathematics, EVS-I and II. They found that majority of the teachers do not have the knowledge competencies in EVS-I (66.5%) and EVS-II (89.9%).

Amaladoss Xavirer, S. and Amlraj, A. (2002), conducted a correlative study on teaching competency and its dimensions in post-graduate chemistry teachers. The study included data from 89 post-graduate chemistry teachers of higher secondary schools in Kanyakumari District in Tamil Nadu. A Teaching Competency Rating Scale was used to assess the teaching competency of chemistry teachers. They revealed that there exists significant relationship between the low-level of post-graduate chemistry teachers with regard to the teaching competency dimensions: content, organisation, knowledge, clarity, communication, rapport, audio-visual aids and personality.

Jayakanthan, S. (2003) conducted a study of general teaching competency of secondary school teachers in relation to their attitude in teaching. The study included samples of 3000 teacher from 14 schools. The General Teaching Competency Scale of Passi *et al*, and Teacher Attitude Scale of Ahulwalia were used to carry out the study found that Government and aided school teachers differed significantly in general teaching competency. Male and female teaches differed significantly in teaching competency.

Krishna Prasad, B. and Mthiah, P.N. (2003) carried out a study on teacher effectiveness and temperament variables of secondary school teacher. The study was carried out to a sample of 300 teachers of various secondary schools in Thirunelveli District in Tamil Nadu. MTA-test of personality for measuring the variables of Temperament, Checklist on Teacher Effectiveness developed and validated by the investigators, and a Personal Information Schedule were used. They found that there exist significant differences among high, average and low effective teachers in five variables (inferiority, self sufficiency, sociability, stability, objectivity) of temperament.

Laxmidhar Bhara (2004) made an attempt to find out the performance of B.Ed trainees of IASEs and CTEs. Six fifty student-teachers (259 male and 391 female) drew purposively from two CTEs and one IASE of Orissa in two consecutive sessions 1995-96 and 1996-97. The major findings were: that women student teachers excel their male counter parts in their aggregate (theory and practical performance).

Jeba, A., (2005) studied that the teaching competency and mental health of student teachers in DIETs. The size of the sample was 300 student-teachers in a DIET undergoing D.Ed. Elementary Teachers Training course. Tools used in this study are: Mental Health status scale constructed by M.Abraham and K.C.B. Praszanna. Teaching Competency Scale the study was conducted to find out gender and group (Arts, Science) difference in teaching competency and mental health status, the relationship between teaching competency and mental health status of student teachers in DIET. Major findings were that there is no significant difference between man and women student teacher.

Foreign Studies on Teaching Competency

Gregrersen and Traves (1968) used the projective technique for making a study of the child concept of the teachers. They made use of drawing of children, environment, which have special significance for them. Choeng and Devault at University of Wisconsin also made similar study in 1966.

Richard M. Galger and Tom. D. Freyo (1974) investigated two research questions (*a*) would rewarding items on a questionnaire for evaluating faculty teaching effectiveness substantially affect students ratings (*b*) would students ratings of professors teaching quality be totally consistent with their ratings of benefits derived from courses? Results shows that students' ratings were affected very little by a major rewarding of items and that a substantial degree of linear independence existed between students perception of the quality benefited from the instructional process.

Garrett and George, W. (1978) studied the teacher's perception of selected factors affecting the success of teaching process. A study sought to determine how various groups of teachers rated selected factors in teaching success. A review of literature of the topic indicated that both teachers and non-teacher was conducted to collect data from teachers of 64 elementary and secondary schools that were part of the test.

Lawrenz, Frances (1987) studied the gender effects for students' perception of the classroom psycho-social environment. This study compared to classroom environments as perceived by fourth grade, seventh grade and high school boys and girls in classes taught by males and females to determine if any perceptual differences existed. The analyses showed no difference for fourth grade students, one for seventh grade students, and three for high school students.

Brosious Janice A. and Smith R. Lyle (1990) studied the impact of Teachers Attractiveness and Gender on Students Perception of the Teacher's Ability. A group of seventh grade maths students (N=28) was chosen for the experiment, the students rated photograph of teachers in the area of organisation, classroom management, motivation, communication, sensitivity, imagination and competence. The results of this analysis revealed a significant main effect of student perceptions due to the attractiveness of the teacher in the area of organisation, classroom significant main effect on student's perceptions due to the gender of the teacher. The students rated the female photographs higher than male photographs in the area of organisation. Finally, there was a significant interaction between the attractiveness of the teacher and gender of teacher in the areas of organisation, sensitivity and imagination. Overall, females rated higher than males and teachers considered attractive were given higher ratings than teachers considered average and unattracrtive.

Ocepek, Linda Jeanne (1993) tested some "selected elements of effective teaching: A study of perception of high school teachers in Illinois, Indian and Ohio". This study utilised an export correlational design. A 42 item Value Rating Scale (VRS) was mailed to a stratified random sample of 384 public high school teachers in Illinois, Indian and Ohio. The teachers rated 42 indicator behaviours subsumed under the six elements of effective teaching.

Kim Keyng Suk (1999) studied "Teacher's perceptions of competencies needed for working inclusive early childhood education programs". A survey using five-point Likert scales included 7 teacher competency domains, each with a set of competency statements, and 12 teachers roles needed for working in inclusive pre-school program. 23 ECE teachers and 52 ECSE teachers in non-inclusive programs and 39 ECE teacher and 25 ECSE teachers inclusive program participated in this study. To determine the early childhood education (ECE) and Early Childhood. Special Education (ECSE) teacher's perceptions of importance teacher competencies, current levels of these competencies and appropriate teacher roles for working in inclusive early childhood programme. They found the ECSE teacher had significantly higher perceptions than the ECE teachers of their self-proficiency of competencies related to child development, curriculum and instruction, assessment procedures, working with other adults, and professionalism.

Kastair, Jamal (1999) carried out a study on "An evaluation of professional teaching competency of the instructors of the institute of Agriculture Sabah, Malaysia". A survey was carried out at the institute involving the instructors, the principal and the first and second year students as respondents. Each instructor and the principal completed a questionnaire containing 40 competency items of 7 categories, while each of the first and the second year students completed a questionnaire containing 33 competency items on 5 categories. The respondents were asked to assess the competence level of the instructors based on a five point Likert type scales. Evaluation by the professional teaching competency of the instructors of the Institute of Agriculture Sabah, Malaysia. They found that instructors' competence level was relatively high was respect to personal characteristics / attribute category, and lower with respect to planning and application of the principles of teaching-learning process.

CONCLUSION

The survey of related literature has helped the investigator to have clear perspective of the problem chosen for the above review of related literature that very few studies had been carried out using both variables "Social Maturity and Teaching Competency". Hence the investigator has chosen to study these two variables on TTI and DIET students. The reviews based on Indian and Foreign studies, had helped the researcher to frame appropriate hypotheses.

In the light of the literature studied, the third chapter has been designed.

RESEARCH DESIGN AND METHODS OF INVESTIGATION

Introduction

This chapter gives an overall picture of the design of the study, research tools used for the study, nature and selection of the sample and a brief description of the procedure adopted for the collection of data, in the light of the other research studies.

Thyer (1993) defined research design as "a blue print for how research study is to be completed operationalising variables so they can be measured, selecting a sample of interest to study collecting data to be used as a basis for testing hypothesis and analyzing the results".

Research is always directed towards solution to a problem. It is a producer from known to unknown. The ultimate goal of any research work is to find out the cause and effect relationship between the variables.

HYPOTHESIS OF THE STUDY

The following hypothesis are set for the present study.

1. There is a significant difference between male and female teacher trainees on their social maturity.
2. There is a significant difference between male and female trainees on their components of teaching competency.
3. There is a significant difference between TTI and DIET teacher trainees on their social maturity.
4. There is a significant difference between TTI and DIET teacher trainees on their components of teaching competency.
5. There is a significant difference between teacher trainees belonging to nuclear and joint families on their social maturity.
6. There is a significant difference between teacher trainees belonging to nuclear and joint families on their components of teaching competency.
7. There is a significant difference between teacher trainees from rural and urban area on their social maturity.

8. There is a significant difference between teacher trainees from rural and urban area on their components of teaching competency.
9. There is a significant difference of teacher trainees on their social maturity based on their parental income.
10. There is a significant difference of teacher trainees on their components of teaching competency based on their parental income.
11. There is a significant difference on social maturity of teacher trainees based on their communities.
12. There is a significant difference on components of teaching competency of teacher trainees based on their communities.
13. There is a significant difference on social maturity of teacher trainees based on their fathers qualification.
14. There is a significant difference on components of teaching competency of teacher trainees based on their father's qualification.
15. There is a significant difference on social maturity of teacher trainees based on their mothers qualification.
16. There is a significant difference on components of teaching competency of teacher trainees based on their mothers qualification.
17. There is a significant difference on social maturity of teacher trainees based on their age.
18. There is a significant difference on components of teaching competency of teacher trainees based on their age.
19. There is a significant relationship between social maturity and components of teaching competency.

DESCRIPTION OF THE TOOLS USED

To verify the framed hypotheses the following tools and techniques were used in the present investigation.

1. Social Maturity Scale.
2. Teaching Competency Scale.

DESCRIPTION OF THE TOOL

The maturity outcomes of school going population can best be estimated in the light of paucity of such essential increasing instruments. The social maturity scale was developed by "Dr.Nalini Rao", Department of Education, Bangalore University. The frame work for the integrated conceptual virtues of social maturity was adapted from the psychological structure.

It was formulated by Green Berger et al. The final form of the questionnaire consists of 90 items known as "Rao's Social Maturity Scale" Rsms).

ADMINISTRATION

The social maturity scales were administered to the respondents in groups in the regular classroom situation. The instruction provided on the first page of the scale booklet is self-explanatory. Reading of the instructions by the examiner to the group however ensures better conditions for responding to the items of the scale. The answers were recorded by the respondent on the scale protocol.

The item required to complete the scale items are between 45 minutes and one hour classification sought by the student regarding any item is to be handled by the examiner through encouraging the respondents. In this way the administration procedure is carried out.

SCORING PROCEDURE

The final form of the questionnaire consists of 90 items. Each item was accorded a four point response speed, the intervals of which are labelled.

- Strongly agree
- Agree

- Disagree
- Strongly disagree

Table 1.1. Scoring Key of the Questionnaire According to the Nature of Items

Nature of Item	Strongly Agree	Agree	Strongly Disagree	Disagree
Positive 17, 21, 24, 26, 36, 39, 41, 42, 50, 51, 52, 54, 56, 57, 59, 63, 74, 77, 89, 90	4	3	2	1
Negative 1, 2, 3, 4, 5, 6, 7, 8, 9, 10, 11, 12, 13, 14, 15, 16, 18, 19, 20, 22, 23, 25, 27, 28, 29, 30, 31, 32, 33, 34, 35, 37, 38, 40, 43, 44, 45, 46, 47, 48, 49, 53, 55, 58, 61, 62, 63, 64, 65, 66, 67, 68, 69, 70, 71, 72, 73, 75, 76, 78, 79, 80, 81, 82, 83, 84, 85, 86, 87, 88	1	2	3	4

The successive response intervals were subsequently scored as 4, 3, 2 and 1 with the high score represents mature response. There was no right or wrong answers. The answer was checked against the key and point is given for each item ticked as per the key. The total point obtained gives a measure of social maturity. By this way the scoring is carried out for social maturity.

PILOT STUDY

A pilot study was conducted on 50 students to establish the reliability and validity of the different tools used in the present study.

ESTABLISHING RELIABILITY AND VALIDITY

The reliability of a test may be defined as the degree of consistency with which the test measures what it does measure. A test score is called reliable to be stable and trustworthy.

The reliability of the tool was calculated using Spearman Brown's formula for split half method.

$$r_{11} = \frac{2r_{hh}}{1+r_{hh}}$$

r_{11} = Reliability coefficient of the whole test.

r_{hh} = Reliability coefficient of the half-test, found experimentally.

SOCIAL MATURITY SCALE

Reliability

In order to establish the reliability of the social maturity scale, the split half method was used. The reliability of social maturity scale was found to be 0.76. Hence social maturity is considered as a reliable tool.

Validity

The index of validity, which is the square root of reliability, was found to be 0.78. Hence social maturity scale selection for the study was considered to have high valid.

TEACHING COMPETENCY SCALE: B.K.PASSI AND M.S.LALITA

Teaching constitutes one of the major tasks of a teacher. Competency over this task of teaching is the essence of successful educational system. The development of teaching competency among teachers necessitates a clear understanding of the term as well as the method for its assessment. With more than half a century of research in this area, there has been no consensus regarding the meaning of the terms "teaching competency" and hence 'teaching competency' itself. As regards the term teaching although defined in different ways (Bhattacharaya, 1974) there has been a trend in perceiving the process analytically as constituting a host of activities (Brown, 1975; Gage, 1972). This analytical approach to perceive teaching has given a basis for innovations in teacher education, like microteaching (Alien and Ryan, 1969).

The term 'competency' has also been a debatable term. It refers to the criteria that determine teacher effectiveness. Although the reviews of research on teacher effectiveness (Ebel, 1969) point out the futility of efforts in identifying teacher effectiveness criteria, the recent upsurge in research provides a cautious optimism (Rosen-shine, 1971). It can now be started with fairly high confidence that pupil outcomes like pupil achievement, student liking may be taken as the criteria of teacher effectiveness (Flanders and Simon, 1969). But the term Teaching Competency's as defined by various authors includes more than mere teacher effects or pupil outcomes.

According to some authors it includes knowledge, attitude, skill and other teacher characteristics (Haskew, 1956, Wilson, 1973). Some others perceive teacher competence as teacher behaviours that produce intended effects (Medley and Mitzel, 1973; Biddle, 1964) arriving at a more comprehensive definition, Rama (1979) defines teacher competency as 'the ability of a teacher manifested through act of over teacher classroom behaviours which is a resultant of the interaction between the presage and the product variables of teaching within a social setting'. This lack of consensus of the term 'teaching competency' highlights the difficulty of its measurement. The measurement of teaching competency has to be valid; objective and reliable one has to delimit to such variables.

THE GENERAL TEACHING COMPETENCY SCALE

This scale is generally used for measuring teaching competency of a teacher individually by a reliable observer or a group of reliable observers making different observation of his class room behaviour for the entire teaching period.

As the teacher teaches, the observer sits at the back for observations. At the end of the teaching period, he gives his ratings in the GTC scale against all the items. To facilitate this process, he may either mark frequencies or write verbal descriptions against each item which would help him in giving ratings more objectively.

SCORING PROCEDURE

The sum of the ratings against all the items constitutes the score on General Teaching Competency (GTC Score) of the teacher being observed. The maximum possible score is 147 and minimum is 21.

MAIN STUDY

The validated scales were used to collect the necessary data for the main study. The study was carried out on sample of 400 TTI and DIET students.

The sample was stratified on the basis of type of management viz, Government and Private Institutions and type of location viz, rural and urban environment.

It was also stratified on the basis of type of institution viz, boys only, girls only and co-education, type of family community viz, age viz, income viz, qualification viz.

Table 1.2. The Table Shows the Background Variables of the Samples

Institution Name	Type of Institution	Institution Location	Type of Management	No. of Samples
Rajalakshmi Teacher Training Institute	Girls only	Rural	Private	100
Stella Matutina Teacher Training Institute	Girls only	Urban	Private	100
DIET – Chennai	Co-education	Urban	Government	200

STATISTICAL TECHNIQUES USED

Suitable descriptive and inferential statistical techniques were used in the interpretation of data to draw out a meaningful picture of results from the collected data. In the present study the following statistical measures were used.

1. Mean

$$X = A + \frac{\Sigma fd}{\Sigma f} \times 1$$

Where,

A = Assumed mean
F = Frequency
D = Deviation from the assumed mean
I = Class interval

2. Standard Deviation

$$SD = \sigma\sqrt{\frac{\Sigma fd}{N} - \left(\frac{\Sigma fd}{N}\right)^2}$$

Where,

F = Frequency
D = Deviation from arithmetic mean
I = Class internal
σ = Standard deviation

3. Quartile Deviation

$$Q_1 = L1 + \left(\frac{N/4 - CF1}{F1}\right) \times 1$$

$$Q_2 = L3 + \left(\frac{3N/4 - CF3}{F3}\right) \times 1$$

$$Q_3 = \frac{Q_3 - Q_1}{2}$$

QD = Quartile Deviation
Q_1 = First QD
Q_3 = Third QD
L_1, L_3 = Lower limit of medium class
N = Total Frequency
$CF_1 CF_2$ = Cumulative frequency
F_1, F_2 = Frequency of the medium class

4. Standard Error Deviation

Standard error of mean deviation

$$SEMD = \frac{\text{Standard error of mean deviation}}{\frac{\sigma_1^2}{N_1} + \frac{\sigma_2^2}{N_2}}$$

σ_1 = SD of group I variable

σ_2 = SD of group II variable

N_1, N_2 = Total number of sample for group I, II

5. Critical Ratio

To compare the significance of difference between mean, critical ratio was used. Critical ratio was calculated from the relation.

$$C.R. = \frac{M_1 - M_2}{\sqrt{\frac{\sigma 1^2}{N_1} + \frac{\sigma 2^2}{N_2}}}$$

Where,

M.M = Mean of group, I, II variable

σ_1, σ_2 = Standard Deviation

N_1, N_2 = Total number of class

6. Analysis of Variance

Correlation coefficient (*r*)

$$r = \frac{N\Sigma xy - \Sigma x \Sigma y}{\sqrt{(N\Sigma x - (\Sigma x)^2 - (N\Sigma x - (\Sigma y)^2}}$$

7. F-Ratio

$$\text{F-ratio} = \frac{\text{Variance between group}}{\text{Variance within} - \text{group}}$$

Correlation term

$$C = \frac{\Sigma x_1 + \Sigma x_2 + \Sigma x_3}{N}$$

$$Tss = X_2\text{-}C$$

$$Bss = \frac{(\Sigma x_1)}{N} + \frac{(\Sigma x_2)}{N} + \frac{(\Sigma x_3)}{N}$$

$$Wss = Tss - Bss$$

Where

$\Sigma x_1, \Sigma x_2, \Sigma x_3$ are scores in different groups.

C = Correlation term

Tss = Total sum of squares

Bss = Between sum of squares

Wss = Within sum of squares

CONCLUSION

This chapter indicates the details regarding the design of the study, hypothesis, pilot study and statistical techniques used. A detailed discussion of analysis of study and interpretation of the study follows in the next chapter.

ANALYSIS AND INTERPRETATION OF THE DATA

Introduction

Research consists of systematic observation and description of the characteristics of properties for the purpose of discovering relationship starts with the description of the measures of the variables and goes on the higher level of statistics analysis. To develop the research plan, processing and analysis of data is necessary. It covers all the technical matters related to research work. This chapter describes the analysis of data and testing of hypotheses that have been framed on the basis of objectives using appropriate statistical techniques.

The data collected was carefully edited, systematically classified tabulated, analyzed interpreted and rationally concluded.

TESTING OF HYPOTHESES

Hypothesis 1

There is a significant difference between male and female teacher trainees on their social maturity.

Interpretation

The calculated value of "t" 4.617 is greater than the table value, so there is significant difference occur at 0.01 level. Thus the Hypothesis is accepted.

Hypothesis 2

There is a significant difference between male and female teacher trainees on their components of teaching competency.

Table 1.3. The Table Showing the 'T' Value of Male and Female Teacher Trainees on their Social Maturity

Variable	Gender	No. of student	Mean	Std. Deviation	Std. Error Mean	't' Value	Level of Sig.
Social	Male	100	203.46	23.645	2.364	4.617	0.01
Maturity	Female	300	214.58	19.859	1.147		

Table 1.4. The Table Showing the 'T' value of Male and Female Teacher Trainees on their Components of Teaching Competency

Variable Teaching Competency	Gender	No. of student	Mean	Std. Deviation	Std. Error Mean	't' Value	Level of Sig.
Planning	Male	100	18.03	5.981	.598	1.737	NS
	Female	300	19.32	6.553	.378		
Presentation	Male	100	46.88	13.409	1.341	2.329	0.05
	Female	300	50.64	14.178	.819		
Closing	Male	100	10.32	4.075	.407	.256	NS
	Female	300	10.50	6.496	.375		
Evaluation	Male	100	9.92	3.784	.378	1.154	NS
	Female	300	9.48	3.160	.182		
Management	Male	100	9.66	3.742	.374	.017	NS
	Female	300	9.65	3.186	.184		

Interpretation

From the table it is observed that there is significant difference occur on the teaching component of presentation. So the empirical hypothesis partially accepted. All other components in teaching competency do not differ each other. As far as presentation is concerned the female teacher trainees perform well than their male counterparts.

Hypothesis: 3

There is a significant difference between TTI and DIET teacher trainees on their social maturity.

Table 1.5. The Table Showing the 'T' Value of TTI and DIET Teacher Trainees on their Social Maturity

Variable	Type of Institute	No. of student	Mean	Std. Deviation	Std. Error Mean	't' Value	Level of Sig.
Social	DIET	199	217.37	20.251	1.436	5.35	0.01
Maturity	Private	201	206.29	21.105	1.489		

Interpretation

The calculated value of "t" 5.35 is greater than the table value, so there is significant difference occur at 0.01 levels. Thus the Hypothesis is accepted.

Table 1.6. The Table Showing the 'T' Value of TTI and DIET Teacher Trainees on their Components of Teaching Competency

Variable Teaching Competency	Type of Intitue	No. of student	Mean	Std. Deviation	Std. Error Mean	't' Value	Level of Sig.
Planning	DIET	199	20.76	5.268	.373	5.66	0.01
	Private	201	17.25	6.992	.493		
Presentation	DIET	199	55.37	11.812	.837	8.73	0.01
	Private	201	44.09	13.899	.980		
Closing	DIET	199	11.68	7.393	.524	4.18	0.01
	Private	201	9.23	3.770	.266		
Evaluation	DIET	199	10.22	2.985	.212	3.82	0.01
	Private	201	8.97	3.533	.249		
Management	DIET	199	10.42	2.975	.211	4.70	0.01
	Private	201	8.90	3.491	.246		

Hypothesis: 4

There is a significant difference between TTI and DIET teacher trainees on their components of teaching competency.

Interpretation

The calculated value of 't' is greater than the all table value, so there is significant difference occur at 0.01 level. Thus the Hypothesis is accepted.

Hypothesis: 5

There is a significant difference between teacher trainees belonging to nuclear and joint families on their social maturity.

Table 1.7. The Table Showing the 'T' Value of Teacher Trainees Belonging to Nuclear and Joint Families on their Social Maturity

Variable	Category	No. of student	Mean	Std. Deviation	Std. Error Mean	't' Value	Level of Sig.
Social	Nuclear	211	215.53	22.749	1.566	3.74	0.01
Maturity	Joint	189	207.64	18.971	1.380		

Interpretation

The calculated value of 't' 3.74 is greater than the table value, so there is significant difference occur at 0.01 level. Thus the Hypothesis is accepted.

Hypothesis: 6

There is a significant difference between teacher trainees belonging to nuclear and joint families on their Components of Teaching Competency.

Interpretation

From the table it is observed that there is significant difference occur on the teaching component of presentation. So the empirical hypothesis partially accepted. All other components in Teaching competency do not differ each other.

Table 1.8. The Table Showing the 'T' Value of Teacher Trainees Belonging to Nuclear and Joint Families on their Components of Teaching Competency

Variable Teaching Competency	Category	No. of student	Mean	Std. Deviation	Std. Error Mean	't' Value	Level of Sig.
Planning	Nuclear	211	19.21	6.276	.432	.701	NS
	Joint	189	18.76	6.609	.481		
Presentation	Nuclear	211	51.10	13.721	.945	2.115	0.05
	Joint	189	48.14	14.320	1.042		
Closing	Nuclear	211	10.13	4.974	.342	1.131	NS
	Joint	189	10.81	6.927	.504		
Evaluation	Nuclear	211	9.49	3.027	.208	.600	NS
	Joint	189	9.69	3.638	.265		
Management	Nuclear	211	9.67	2.960	.204	.114	NS
	Joint	189	9.63	3.706	.270		

Hypothesis: 7

There is a significant difference between teacher trainees from rural and urban area on their social maturity.

Table 1.9. The Table Showing the 'T' Value of Teacher Trainees from Rural and Urban Area on their Social Maturity

Variable	Category	No. of student	Mean	Std. Deviation	Std. Error Mean	't' Value	Level of Sig.
Social Maturity	Rural	214	216.42	20.239	1.383	4.750	0.01
	Urban	186	206.49	21.499	1.576		

Interpretation

The calculated value of 't' 4.75 is greater than the table value, so there is significant difference occur at 0.01 level. Thus the Hypothesis is accepted.

Hypothesis: 8

There is a significant difference between teacher trainees from rural and urban area on their Components of Teaching Competency.

Table 1.10. The Table Showing the 'T' Value of Teacher Trainees from Rural and Urban Area on their Components of Teaching Competency

Variable Teaching Competency	Category	No. of student	Mean	Std. Deviation	Std. Error Mean	't' Value	Level of Sig.
Planning	Rural	214	20.36	5.382	.368	4.653	0.01
	Urban	186	17.43	7.160	.525		
Presentation	Rural	214	54.32	12.289	.840	7.519	0.01
	Urban	186	44.39	14.138	1.037		
Closing	Rural	214	11.41	7.221	.494	3.470	0.01
	Urban	186	9.35	3.847	.282		
Evaluation	Rural	214	10.01	3.006	.206	2.773	0.01
	Urban	186	9.10	3.608	.265		
Management	Rural	214	10.21	3.031	.207	3.601	0.01
	Urban	186	9.02	3.546	.260		

Interpretation

The calculated value of 't' is greater than the all table value, so there is significant difference occur at 0.01 level. Thus the Hypothesis is accepted.

Hypothesis: 9

There is a significant difference of teacher trainees on their Social Maturity based on their parental income.

Interpretation

The calculated value of 't' (.534) is less than the table value, so there is not significant difference at 0.01 level. Thus the Hypothesis is rejected.

Table 1.11. The Table Showing the 'T' Value of Teacher Trainees on their Social Maturity Based on their Parental Income

Variable	Category	No. of student	Mean	Std. Deviation	Std. Error Mean	't' Value	Level of Sig.
Social Maturity	Low income	330	211.54	21.474	1.182	.534	NS
	High income	70	213.04	21.094	2.521		

Table 1.12. The Table Showing the 'T' Value of Teacher Trainees on their Components of Teaching Competency Based on their Parental Income

Variable Teaching Competency	Category	No. of student	Mean	Std. Deviation	Std. Error Mean	't' Value	Level of Sig.
Planning	Low income	330	18.68	6.448	.355	2.165	0.05
	High income	70	20.50	6.176	.738		
Presentation	Low income	330	48.84	13.885	.764	2.675	0.01
	High income	70	53.76	14.318	1.711		
Closing	Low income	330	10.43	6.140	.338	.161	NS
	High income	70	10.56	5.191	.620		
Evaluation	Low income	330	9.51	3.267	.180	1.023	NS
	High income	70	9.98	3.601	.430		
Management	Low income	330	9.58	3.659	.437	1.034	NS
	High income	70	10.03	3.255	.179		

Hypothesis : 10

There is a significant difference of teacher trainees on their Components of Teaching Competency based on their parental income.

Interpretation

From the table it is observed that there is significant difference occur on the teaching components of planning and presentation. So the empirical hypothesis partially accepted. All other components is teaching competency do not differ each other. As far as presentation is concerned by the parental income.

Hypothesis: 11

There is a significant difference on social maturity of teacher trainees based on their community.

Table 1.13. Anova Showing the Difference in Social Maturity of Teacher Trainees to Different Communities

Variable	Souce of variation	Sum of Squares	Degree of Freedom	Mean Squares	F	Level of Sig.
Social Maturity	Between Groups	4753.860	2	2376.930	5.308	0.01
	Within Groups	177793.54	397	447.843		
	Total	182547.40	399	—		

Interpretation

From the above table the calculated value of 'F' (5.308) is greater than the table value is significant difference at 0.01 levels. Thus the Hypothesis is accepted.

Hypothesis: 12

There is no significant difference on components of teaching competency of teacher trainees based on their communities.

Table 1.14. Anova Showing the Difference in Teaching Competency of Teacher Trainees to Different Communities

Variable Teaching Competency	Souce of variation	Sum of Squares	Degree of Freedom	Mean Squares	F	Level of Sig.
Planning	Between Groups	209.560	2	104.780	2.553	NS
	Within Groups	16294.430	397	41.044		
	Total	16503.990	399	-		
Presentation	Between Groups	97.368	2	48.684	.245	NS
	Within Groups	78870.230	397	198.666		
	Total	78967.598	399	-		
Closing	Between Groups	142.240	2	71.120	1.999	NS
	Within Groups	14120.858	397	35.569		
	Total	14263.098	399	-		
Evaluation	Between Groups	19.731	2	9.865	.891	NS
	Within Groups	4397.207	397	11.076		
	Total	4416.937	399	-		
Management	Between Groups	14.658	2	7.329	.660	NS
	Within Groups	4407.732	397	11.103		
	Total	4422.390	399	-		

Interpretation

The calculated value of 'F' for all the components of teaching competency is not significant at any level and thereby the hypothesis is rejected.

Hypothesis: 13

There is no significant difference on social maturity of teacher trainees based on their father's qualification.

Table 1.15. Anova Showing the Difference in Social Maturity of Teacher Trainees Based on Fathers Qualification

Variable	Souce of variation	Sum of Squares	Degree of Freedom	Mean Squares	F	Level of Sig.
Social	Between Groups	1865.813	2	932.907		
Maturity	Within Groups	180681.58	397	455.117	2.050	N.S
	Total	182547.40	399	—		

Interpretation

The calculated value of 'F' (2.050) is less than the table value is not significant difference at 0.01 levels. Thus the Null Hypothesis is retained.

Hypothesis: 14

There is no significant difference on components of teaching competency of teacher trainees based on their father's qualification.

Interpretation

The calculated value of 'F' is less than the table value is not significant difference at 0.01 levels. Thus the null hypothesis is retained.

Hypothesis: 15

There is no significant difference on social maturity of teacher trainees based on their mother qualification.

Interpretation

The calculated value of 'F' (3.862) is greater than the table value is significant difference at 0.05 level. Thus the null hypothesis is not accepted.

Hypothesis: 16

There is no significant difference on components of teaching competency of teacher trainees based on their mother's qualification.

Table 1.16. Anova Showing the Difference on Components of Teaching Competency of Teacher Trainees Based on Fathers Qualification

Variable Teacing Compet-ency	Souce of variation	Sum of Squares	Degree of Freedom	Mean Squares	F	Level of Sig.
Planning	Between Groups	104.960	2	52.480	1.270	NS
	Within Groups	16399.030	397	41.307		
	Total	16503.990	399			
Presentation	Between Groups	1338.179	2	669.089	3.422	NS
	Within Groups	77629.419	397	195.540		
	Total	78967.597	399			
Closing	Between Groups	76.679	2	38.339	1.073	NS
	Within Groups	14186.419	397	35.734		
	Total	14263.098	399			
Evaluation	Between Groups	15.522	2	7.761	.700	NS
	Within Groups	4401.415	397	11.087		
	Total	4416.938	399			
Management	Between Groups	2.229	2	1.115	.100	NS
	Within Groups	4420.161	397	11.134		
	Total	4422.390	399			

Table 1.17. Anova Showing the Difference in Social Maturity of Teacher Trainees Based on Mother Qualification

Variable	Souce of variation	Sum of Squares	Degree of Freedom	Mean Squares	F	Level of Sig.
Social Maturity	Between Groups	3484.033	2	1742.016	3.862	0.05
	Within Groups	179063.36	397	451.041		
	Total	182547.40	399	-		

Table 1.18. Anova Showing the Difference on Components of Teaching Competency of Teacher Trainees Based on Mothers Qualification

Variable Teacing Compet-ency	Souce of variation	Sum of Squares	Degree of Freedom	Mean Squares	F	Level of Sig.
Planning	Between Groups	97.106	2	48.553	1.175	NS
	Within Groups	16406.854	397	41.327		
	Total	16503.990	399			
Presentation	Between Groups	344.359	2	172.179	.869	NS
	Within Groups	78623.239	397	198.043		
	Total	78967.598	399			
Closing	Between Groups	33.438	2	16.719	.466	NS
	Within Groups	14229.659	397	35.843		
	Total	14263.098	399			
Evaluation	Between Groups	.398	2	.199	0.18	NS
	Within Groups	4416.540	397	11.125		
	Total	4416.938	399			
Management	Between Groups	10.361	2	5.181	.466	NS
	Within Groups	4412.029	397	11.113		
	Total	4422.390	399			

Interpretation

The calculated value of 'F' for all the components of teaching competency is not significant difference at any level. Thus the null hypothesis is retained.

Hypothesis: 17

There is no significant difference on social maturity of teacher trainees based on their age.

Table 1.19. Anova Showing the Difference in Social Maturity of Teacher Trainees Based on Different Age

Variable	Souce of variation	Sum of Squares	Degree of Freedom	Mean Squares	F	Level of Sig.
Social Maturity	Between Groups	1832.424	2	916.212	2.013	NS
	Within Groups	180714.97	397	455.201		
	Total	182547.40	399	-		

Interpretation

The calculated value of 'F' (2.013) is less than the table value is not significant difference at 0.01 levels. Thus the null hypothesis is retained.

Hypothesis: 18

There is no significant difference on components of teaching competency of teacher trainees based on their age.

Interpretation

The calculated value of 'F' is less than the table value is not significant difference at 0.01 level. Thus the null hypothesis is not accepted.

Hypothesis: 19

There is significant relationship between social maturity and components of teaching competency.

Interpretation

The calculated correlation co-efficient is significant at 0.01 level. So the hypothesis is accepted.

Table 1.20. Anova Showing the Difference in Teaching Competency of Teacher Trainees Based on Different Age

Variable Teacing Compet-ency	Souce of variation	Sum of Squares	Degree of Freedom	Mean Squares	F	Level of Sig.
Planning	Between Groups	23.277	2	11.639	.280	NS
	Within Groups	16480.713	397	41.513		
	Total	16503.990	399			
Presentation	Between Groups	575.098	2	287.549	1.456	NS
	Within Groups	78392.500	397	197.462		
	Total	78967.598	399			
Closing	Between Groups	21.151	2	10.575	.295	NS
	Within Groups	14241.947	397	35.874		
	Total	14263.098	399			
Evaluation	Between Groups	42.534	2	21.267	1.930	NS
	Within Groups	4374.404	397	11.019		
	Total	4416.937	399			
Management	Between Groups	30.707	2	15.353	1.388	NS
	Within Groups	4391.683	397	11.062		
	Total	4422.390	399			

DISCUSSION OF THE RESULTS

The results of statistical analysis of the present investigation interpreted here in terms of the purpose of the study and with respects to other studies, which have been conducted in related areas of research.

It was found that there is no significant difference on social maturity of teacher trainees on their father's qualification and mother's qualification and teacher trainee's age. But significant difference was found based on their gender, type of institution type of family, area, parental income, and community.

Table 1.21. Correlation Matrix Between Social Maturity and Components of Teaching Competency

Variable	Social maturity	Pla	Pre	Clo	Eva	Manage
Social Maturity	*	-	-	-	-	-
Teaching competency Planning	041 .	-	-	-	-	-
Presentation	.156	.481	-	-	-	-
Closing	.091	.289	.200	-	-	-
Evaluation	.061	.356	.492	.330	-	-
Management	.041	.353	.447	.332	.717	*

To find out the relationship between social maturity and teaching competency of TTI and DIET students

CONCLUSION

This chapter summaries the analysis of data, testing of hypothesis description and discussion of the table. A brief report of the research study together with the major findings and conclusion along with their educational implications has been presented in the succeeding chapter.

SUMMARY OF FINDINGS AND CONCLUSION

Introduction

In this chapter, after presenting briefly the statement of the problem and the description of the procedure used in the investigation, the findings and the conclusions are presented. In the light of the findings of the present study, a few suggestions have been proposed at the end of the chapter for further research in this field.

STATEMENT OF THE PROBLEM

The Problem is Titled as "Social Maturity and Teaching Competency of Students Teachers in TTI and DIET in Chennai".

OBJECTIVES OF THE STUDY

1. To find out the significant difference between male and female teacher trainees on their social maturity.
2. To find out the significant difference between male and female teacher trainees on their components of teaching competency.
3. To find out the significant difference between TTI and DIET teacher trainees on their social maturity.
4. To find out the significant difference between TTI and DIET teacher trainees on their components of teaching competency.
5. To find out the significant difference between teacher trainees belonging to nuclear and joint families on their social maturity.
6. To find out the significant difference between teacher trainees belonging to nuclear and joint families on their components of teaching competency.
7. To find out the significant difference between teacher trainees from rural and urban area on their social maturity.
8. To find out the significant difference between teacher trainees from rural and urban area on their components of teaching competency.
9. To find out the significant difference of teacher trainees on their social maturity based on their parental income.
10. To find out the significant difference of teacher trainees on their components of teaching competency based on their parental income.

11. To find out the significant difference on social maturity of teacher trainees based on their communities.
12. To find out the significant difference on components of teaching competency of teacher trainees based on their communities.
13. To find out the significant difference on social maturity of teacher trainees based on their fathers qualification.
14. To find out the significant difference on components of teaching competency of teacher trainees based on their fathers qualification.
15. To find out the significant difference on social maturity of teacher trainees based on their mothers qualification.
16. To find out the significant difference on components of teaching competency of teacher trainees based on their mothers qualification.
17. To find out the significant difference on social maturity of teacher trainees based on their age.
18. To find out the significant difference on components of teaching competency of teacher trainees based on their age.
19. To find out the significant relationship between social maturity and components of teaching competency.

HYPOTHESIS OF THE STUDY

1. There is a significant difference between male and female teacher trainees on their social maturity.
2. There is a significant difference between male and female trainees on their components of teaching competency.
3. There is a significant difference between TTI and DIET teacher trainees on their social maturity.
4. There is a significant difference between TTI and DIET teacher trainees on their components of teaching competency.

5. There is a significant difference between teacher trainees belonging to nuclear and joint families on their social maturity.
6. There is a significant difference between teacher trainees belonging to nuclear and joint families on their components of teaching competency.
7. There is a significant difference between teacher trainees from rural and urban area on their social maturity.
8. There is a significant difference between teacher trainees from rural and urban area on their components of teaching competency.
9. There is a significant difference of teacher trainees on their social maturity based on their parental income.
10. There is a significant difference of teacher trainees on their components of teaching competency based on their parental income.
11. There is a significant difference on social maturity of teacher trainees based on their communities.
12. There is no significant difference on components of teaching competency of teacher trainees based on their communities.
13. There is no significant difference on social maturity of teacher trainees based on their fathers qualification.
14. There is no significant difference on components of teaching competency of teacher trainees based on their fathers qualification.
15. There is no significant difference on social maturity of teacher trainees based on their mothers qualification.
16. There is no significant difference on components of teaching competency of teacher trainees based on their mothers qualification.
17. There is no significant difference on social maturity of teacher trainees based on their age.

18. There is no significant difference on components of teaching competency of teacher trainees based on their age.
19. There is a significant relationship between social maturity and components of teaching competency.

SAMPLE

The population consists of students who are studying in TTI and DIET institutions.

The investigator randomly selected 400 students from 3 TTI and DIET institutions.

TOOLS USED IN THIS STUDY

The following tools were used.

1. Social maturity scale by Dr.Nalini Rao
2. Teaching competency scale by B.K.Passi and M.S.Lalita.

MAJOR FINDINGS OF THE STUDY

The major findings are presented below.

1. It was found that significant difference occurred on the social maturity and teaching competency of male and female teacher trainees.
2. It was found that significant difference occurred on the social maturity and teaching competency of TTI and DIET students.
3. It was found that significant difference occurred on the social maturity and teaching competency of teacher trainees from joint and nuclear family of the teacher trainees.
4. It was found that there is a significant difference between TTI and DIET teacher trainees with respect to their social maturity and teaching competency on the basis of their community.
5. It was found that there is a significant difference between TTI and DIET teacher trainees with respect

to their social maturity and teaching competency on the basis of their urban and rural area.

6. It was found that there is no significant difference between TTI and DIET teacher trainees with respect to their social maturity and teaching competency on the basis of parental qualification.
7. It was found that there is no significant difference between TTI and DIET teacher trainees with respect to their social maturity and teaching competency on the basis of parental income.
8. It was found that there is no significant difference between TTI and DIET teacher trainees with respect to their social maturity and teaching competency on the basis of their age.
9. It was found that significant relationship occurred between social maturity and components of teaching competency of TTI and DIET students.

EDUCATIONAL IMPLICATIONS

Social maturity and teaching competency is an aspect that makes an individual adjusted to the society at large. It is related to the development of the personality of a student. Students studying in TTI and DIET are forced to adhere to institution regulations as well as social activities. We find that if the students fall in line with the social relationship system and obeying its regulations they may possess a higher social maturity and teaching competency. Therefore for teacher trainees social maturity and teaching competency is essential for their daily life to adopt the classroom situation.

Hence, the study has a direct impact on the educational practice. The following are some of the major recommendations to be implemented for the social maturity and teaching competency of the students.

- Educators and Administrators should bring about awareness among students to give more importance to develop social maturity and teaching competency.

- In order to develop social maturity and teaching competency intensive training should be provided.

SUGGESTIONS FOR FURTHER RESEARCH

- This study was conducted to 400 TTI and DIET students only. To make the study more comprehensive further studies can be conducted on a larger sample.
- The present is confined only to the TTI and DIET students. This study may be conducted B.Ed. teacher trainees and nursery school teacher trainees.

CONCLUSION

This study is aimed to know the social maturity and teaching competency of TTI and DIET students. In this chapter the hypotheses and major findings were given also further analysis has been recommended.

REFERENCE

1. Abraham Sperling (1967). Definition of Social Maturity, Vikas Publications, New Delhi.
2. Adams, Linda (1989). Be your best, New York: Putnam.
3. Adhiesehiah, W.T.V. and Pavanasam,R. (1974). Sociology in Theory and Practice, Shanthi Publishers, New Delhi, p. 38.
4. Adi Seshiah W.T.A. and Mrs.Sulochana Sekar (1977). Educational and Social Research, Nekan Pathipagam, Coimbatore.
5. Agnihotri. L.S. (1991). Conducted a cross-cultural comparative study between tribal and non-tribal first generation and traditional learners in relation to their social maturity and educational adjustment, M. Phil Theses in Psychology.
6. Albert and James Gardon ward. "Teacher competency and testing: A natural affinity". Educational Measurement: Issues and Practice I (Summer 1982): 6-9, 26. 1982 ED 223-716.

7. Arthur, L. (1957). "Educational Goals". Ed. Res. Bull 36: 29-36.
8. Barr A.S. (1950). "Teaching Competencies". Encyc. Ed. Res. New York, Macmillam, p. 1446-1454.
9. Bauses Ann Leslie (1995). Measured the effect of participation in a peer facilitation project on sixth grades self esteem, social maturity and patterns of social choice. Ph.D. Kent State University.
10. Bhusan. A. (1994). Conducted a study done on the social maturity across sex and family vocations. Buch, M.B., The Educational Research, Volume II.
11. Bruce (1985). "Models of Teaching". New Delhi, Prentice Hall of India.
12. Cron Bach, L.J. and Gleser, G.C. (1954). Review of the study of behaviours, Psychometric 19, 329-333.
13. Cuber, J.F. (1995). Sociology, New York: Appleton Century.
14. Das, R.C. et al. (1976). A study of effectiveness of micro teaching of teachers dept of teachers education. NCERT, New Delhi (Abridged Report).
15. Das, B.C. (1993). "Effectiveness of concept attainment model in terms of teaching competency of pre-service student teachers perspectives in Education. Indian Educational Abstracts (Issue – 4) 9(1): 34-35.
16. Downe, N.M. and Health, R.W.C. (1970). Basic Statistical Methods, New York: Harper and Row.
17. Flippo, Rona F. and Carol R. Foster. "Teacher competency Teaching and Its Impact on Educators". Journal of Teacher Education, 35 (March – April 1984), 10-13.
18. Frank.E. (1951). "Situational Factors in Teacher Placement and Success". Ed. 20: 121-177.
19. George. J. Mouley, (1963). The Science of Educational Research, Eurosia Publishing House (P) Ltd., New Delhi.
20. Ghosh S. (1975). A study of the social maturity of Bengali children, Applied Psychology, Calcutta University.
21. Hentry I. Garrent (1968). General Psychology. Eurasia Publishing House Pvt. Ltd., New Delhi, p. 88.

22. John W. Best (1977). Research in Education, Third Edition, Prentice Hall India Pvt. Ltd., New Delhi.
23. John W. Best and James V. Khan (1989). Research in Education, Prentice Hall (P) Ltd., New Delhi.
24. Joki, Russell A. "Make Teacher Competency your policy". American School Board Journal 169, (November 1982): 32.
25. Kukreti (1994). Job motivation and teacher competency. A correlation and study. Experiments in education. Indian Educational Abstract Issue-2. 22(1):10-14.
26. Mc Millan and Schumacher (1964). Research in Education, A Conceptual Introduction, Little Brow Boston.
27. Mursell, J.L. (1954). "Successful Teaching". McGraw Hill Book Company.
28. Narayan Rao.S. (1990). Educational Psychology. Wiley Eastern Limited, New Delhi.
29. Newton, E.H. and Brathwarte, W.E. (1987). The importance of Teaching Competency". Perspectives in Education 3: 169-180.
30. Panda, S.C. (1996). Effect of competency based instruction in achieving MLL competencies in Grade IV, National Council of Educational Research. Educational Abstract Issue – 6.
31. Pattraman Jempengern (1986). Social maturity of higher secondary students in Thailand, Dissertation Abstract International.
32. Pearson, Allen T. "The competency concept", Educational Studies (Summer 1980): 145-152.
33. Poplia and Olds S.W. (1987). Psychology, Mc Graw Hill, New York.
34. Raj, B.C. (2001). Social Psychology, Prakashan Kendra, Lucknow, p. 29.
35. Report of the Education Commission, 1964-66: Ministry of Education, Govt. of India, 1966.
36. Robert Fisher (1990). Teaching Children to Think, Basil Blackswell Ltd., Oxford Endland.
37. Robert Kerber and P.J.Verdoorn (1962). Research Methods in Economics and Business, New York.

38. Ronald, T. (1984). Teacher Competence: The Logic, The Law and the Implications". Journal of Teacher Education, 35, p. 14-18.

39. Sadhya Giri Rajan (1985). Competency and personality. Motivation and profession perception of college teachers. Fourth serve of research in education 1983-1988. Volume – 11.

40. Schacter, Richard, T. (1983). Sociology, Mc Graw_Hill Inc. New York, p. 328.

41. Shamal, S.K. (1998). Enhancing teaching competency through integration of arts education for effective language teaching at the primary stage. National council of educational research and training. Indian Educational Abstract Issue – 5.

42. Sharma,S.K. (1981). "The various relationship between Teaching Competency and Intelligence". Indian Psychological Review, 36(5): 75-83.

43. Smith, B.O. (1985). "Teaching: Definitions". In Ency. of Educ. Res. Vol. 9, T-2, Peregamon Press, New York, pp. 5097-5101.

44. Sorajamma Y.H. (1990). A comparative study of reading ability and social maturity of over normal and underachievers of standard VII. Ph.D. Edu. Bangalore University.

45. Stagner and Karvoski (1973). Quoted by L.D.Crow and Acrow, Educational Psychology, Eurasia Publishing House, New Delhi.

46. Stevens, S.S. (1939). "Psychology and the science of science". Psychol. Bull. 36: 221-63.

47. Sweeney, Jim and Richard Manatt. "Teacher Competence: The Past, Present and Future of its Assessment". 1982 ED 223.716.

48. Tandra Patnaik (1986). The man and the society, Anu Books, Shivaji Road, Meerut.

49. Thamilmani. P. (1990). Teacher competency and teacher personality in relation to achievement of High School. Students in science V Survey of Educational Research 11:19-26.

50. Wilkinson and Bhandarkar (1987). Methodology and Techniques of Social Research, Himalaya Publishing House, Bombay.

ABSTRACTS

1. Buch, M.B. (1978). "Second Survey of Research in Education".
2. Buch, M.B. (1987. "Third Survey of Research in Education".
3. Buch, M.B. (1991). "Fourth Survey of Research in Education".
4. Dissertation Abstracts International – Humanities and Social Sciences, Vol. 54, No. 8, Feb. 1994.
5. Dissertation Abstracts International – Humanities and Social Sciences, Vol. 50, No. 5011, May 1995.
6. Dissertation Abstracts International – Humanities and Social Sciences, Vol. 36, No. 10, Nov. 1995.
7. Dissertation Abstracts International – Humanities and Social Sciences, Vol. 52, No. 20, Jan. 1995.
8. Dissertation Abstracts International – Humanities and Social Sciences, Vol. 55, No. 9, Mar. 1995.

TOOL - I

SOCIAL MATURITY SCALE

Please fill up the followings:

1. Name :
2. Age :
3. Type of Instruction :
4. Type of Family : Nuclear / Joint
5. Community : FC / BC / MBC / SC / ST
6. Educational Qualification : Father
Mother :
7. Parental Income : Father
Mother :

INSTRUCTIONS

We face and experience several situations in our daily life and in every one of these situations, we have a view of our own. Some such situations where each one may have a opinion, are given below in the form of statements. Read them carefully. Each statement has a range of four responses. They are: Strongly Agrees (SA), Agree (A), Disagree (D), Strongly Disagree (SD), Each response denotes a different position. Out of which, you should choose any one which suggests your stand in respect of the statement. Accordingly, encircle the columns given on the right hand side. Study the examples given below:

Statements	Strongly Agree (SA)	Agree (A)	Disag-ree(D)	Strongly Disa gree (SD)
1. A study should not spend too much time in dressing and grooming.	(□)	□	□	□
2. One should help one's friends with their home-work.	□	□	(□)	□
3. Good books and instruments borrowed by class-mates are rarely returned.	□	(□)	□	□

There is no right or wrong answer. Please respond in way you believe.

National Psychological Corporation

(4/230, KACHERI GHAT, AGRA – 282 004 (India)

Statements	Strongly Agree (SA)	Agree (A)	Disa-gree (D)	Strongly Disagree (SD)
1. It is hard to stick to anything that takes a long time to do.	⑥	⑥	⑥	⑥
2. I often forget to listen to what others are saying	⑥	⑥	⑥	⑥
3. I would never go out of my way to help another person if it means giving up some personal pleasure.	⑥	⑥	⑥	⑥
4. The future is so uncertain, one cannot really make any plan.	⑥	⑥	⑥	⑥
5. There is no way to tell whom you can trust.	⑥	⑥	⑥	⑥

Statements	Strongly Agree (SA)	Agree (A)	Disa-gree (D)	Strongly Disagree (SD)
6. I cannot be friendly with people who do things which I consider wrong.	⑥	⑥	⑥	⑥
7. I get extremely hurt when people criticise me.	⑥	⑥	⑥	⑥
8. I fight to the last with my group if they do not carry out what I tell them.	⑥	⑥	⑥	⑥
9. Women should not be elected to top Government positions.	⑥	⑥	⑥	⑥
10. I often forget work I am supposed to do.	⑥	⑥	⑥	⑥
11. I find it hard to speak my thought clearly.	⑥	⑥	⑥	⑥
12. I am willing to give a lot of money to medical research on cancer or such deadly disease only if I know they would find a cure in my life time.	⑥	⑥	⑥	⑥
13. I feel very uncomfortable if I disagree will what my friends think.	⑥	⑥	⑥	⑥
14. Most people, I feel, would rather lie than tell the truth if they could get away with it.	□	□	□	□
15. I do not make close friends with crippled / handicapped persons though I do not like to admit this.	⑥	⑥	⑥	⑥
16. It is natural for anybody to feel extremely uneasy to speak to people whom he / she does now know.	⑥	⑥	⑥	⑥
17. I settle fights and differences among my friends.	⑥	⑥	⑥	⑥

Statements	Strongly Agree (SA)	Agree (A)	Disa-gree (D)	Strongly Disagree (SD)
18. A man should not cook dinner for his wife and children unless the wife is sick.	⑥	⑥	⑥	⑥
19. I often get behind in my work.	⑥	⑥	⑥	⑥
20. In a discussion, it is hard to understand what people are trying to say.	⑥	⑥	⑥	⑥
21. I often think about doing things so that people in the future can have things better.	⑥	⑥	⑥	⑥
22. Someone often has to tell me what to do.	⑥	⑥	⑥	⑥
23. They are more bad people than good people in this world.	⑥	⑥	⑥	⑥
24. There is a lot of useful things for the rest of us to learn from having a group of people of other communities living in our neighbourhood.	⑥	⑥	⑥	⑥
25. One feels miserable when one has to disagree with his friends.	⑥	⑥	⑥	⑥
26. I get along well with teachers and classmates in our school.	⑥	⑥	⑥	⑥
27. Many more women should be trained for jobs usually held by men.	⑥	⑥	⑥	⑥
28. I often don't finish the work I start.	⑥	⑥	⑥	⑥
29. Even if know how to do something, I find it hard to teach someone else.	⑥	⑥	⑥	⑥

Statements	Strongly Agree (SA)	Agree (A)	Disagree (D)	Strongly Disagree (SD)
30. Members of one religion should never ask money for some religious cause from people who are not of the same religion.	⑥	⑥	⑥	⑥
31. Others seem more in control in their lives than I do.	⑥	⑥	⑥	⑥
32. It is hard to ask even the best friend for help.	⑥	⑥	⑥	⑥
33. One should not offer food to people who belong to other caste as it is embarrassing to refuse food offered.	⑥	⑥	⑥	⑥
34. I am comfortable only with people of my own sex.	⑥	⑥	⑥	⑥
35. It is obvious that one get upset when one has to change all his/ her plans to adjust to someone else's.	⑥	⑥	⑥	⑥
36. If we do not encourage women to work, we are seriously reducing what the country could accomplish.	⑥	⑥	⑥	⑥
37. I tend to go from one thing to another before finishing the earlier.	⑥	⑥	⑥	⑥
38. It is hard for me to find anything to talk about when I meet a new person.	⑥	⑥	⑥	⑥
39. I want to spend more time in work to help the society I live in.	⑥	⑥	⑥	⑥
40. I keep my ideas to myself in class unless I am sure I am right.	⑥	⑥	⑥	⑥

Statements	Strongly Agree (SA)	Agree (A)	Disa-gree (D)	Strongly Disagree (SD)
41. You can be sure people will be honest with you if you are honest with them.	⑥	⑥	⑥	⑥
42. I would not mind living next door to a family that is much poorer than mine.	⑥	⑥	⑥	⑥
43. It is a source of great disappointment to me when the opinion of others differs from mine.	⑥	⑥	⑥	⑥
44. There is no point helping, others inconveniencing oneself.	⑥	⑥	⑥	⑥
45. I really worry the way many girls become doctors, engineers and lawyers these days.	⑥	⑥	⑥	⑥
46. I get upset if I am not immediately successful in learning something new.	⑥	⑥	⑥	⑥
47. My friends find it hard to figure out from what I say.	⑥	⑥	⑥	⑥
48. Why work for something that others will enjoy when you won't be able to enjoy yourself.	⑥	⑥	⑥	⑥
49. In a group I prefer to let other people make the decision.	⑥	⑥	⑥	⑥
50. Even though it is hard to believe, the radio and news papers give us true facts about important events.	⑥	⑥	⑥	⑥
51. I do not mind playing with people who speak a language differ from mine.	⑥	⑥	⑥	⑥

Statements	Strongly Agree (SA)	Agree (A)	Disa-gree (D)	Strongly Disagree (SD)
52. One should be able to laugh at oneself and take jokes easily.	⑥	⑥	⑥	⑥
53. If you haven't been chosen as the leader, you should not suggest how things should be done.	⑥	⑥	⑥	⑥
54. More men should train themselves for jobs like nursery school teachers and telephone operators which are usually held by women	⑥	⑥	⑥	⑥
55. I often don't get my most important work done because I have spent too much time on other work.	⑥	⑥	⑥	⑥
56. In a discussion, people find it easy to understand what I am trying to say.	⑥	⑥	⑥	⑥
57. I would be willing to work for a good plan to make a better life for the poor, even if it cost me money.	⑥	⑥	⑥	⑥
58. I usually let others take the lead.	⑥	⑥	⑥	⑥
59. If you can trust a person in one way, you know you can trust him in all ways.	⑥	⑥	⑥	⑥
60. I find more interest to work for friends whose caste is the same as mine.	⑥	⑥	⑥	⑥
61. It is obvious that one gets angry when one looses an argument	⑥	⑥	⑥	⑥
62. In my class, I need not accept any responsibility in which I am not interested.	⑥	⑥	⑥	⑥

Statements	Strongly Agree (SA)	Agree (A)	Disagree (D)	Strongly Disagree (SD)
63. If everyone is to be really equal, some people will have fewer advantages than they have now.	⑥	⑥	⑥	⑥
64. I give up the work I am doing, when things go wrong.	⑥	⑥	⑥	⑥
65. I am not good at describing things in writing.	⑥	⑥	⑥	⑥
66. It is possible to rush to neighbours to help them in all their troubles and needs.	⑥	⑥	⑥	⑥
67. The outcome of my life is a matter of luck.	⑥	⑥	⑥	⑥
68. A person is better off if he does not trust anybody.	⑥	⑥	⑥	⑥
69. I do not care to tell my ideas about God, when I know others will disagree with me.	⑥	⑥	⑥	⑥
70. I cannot keep cool when I get upset even though I am in a classroom or in a formal group.	⑥	⑥	⑥	⑥
71. I prefer to work for my own self than for the group I belong to.	⑥	⑥	⑥	⑥
72. Giving higher education to women is a national waste.	⑥	⑥	⑥	⑥
73. Hard work is never fun.	⑥	⑥	⑥	⑥
74. I have a talent for influencing people by just talking to them.	⑥	⑥	⑥	⑥
75. A person should not be expected to do anything for his community unless he is paid for it.	⑥	⑥	⑥	⑥

Statements	Strongly Agree (SA)	Agree (A)	Disa-gree (D)	Strongly Disagree (SD)
76. When things have gone wrong for me, it is usually because of something I could not do anything about.	⑥	⑥	⑥	⑥
77. A person who is completely trusting will have better experience in life than someone who is not.	⑥	⑥	⑥	⑥
78. I prefer to break with a friend who disagrees with me often.	⑥	⑥	⑥	⑥
79. I will not do the work I do not like though I am expected to do.	⑥	⑥	⑥	⑥
80. I make my point clear when I argue.	⑥	⑥	⑥	⑥
81. I do not care to cut the use of water and electricity with a view to help the Government when there are so many others who are wasting it.	⑥	⑥	⑥	⑥
82. I do not know whether I like a new dress / clothes / saree until I find out what my friends think.	⑥	⑥	⑥	⑥
83. One can safely trust strangers as much as people they know.	⑥	⑥	⑥	⑥
84. It is very difficult for me to be nice to people I do not like.	⑥	⑥	⑥	⑥
85. It is more important for a job to pay well than for a job to be interesting.	⑥	⑥	⑥	⑥
86. I understand what that teacher wants me to do.	⑥	⑥	⑥	⑥
87. I clear the papers off my desk around the place even though I did not put them.	⑥	⑥	⑥	⑥

Statements	Strongly Agree (SA)	Agree (A)	Disa-gree (D)	Strongly Disagree (SD)
88. It is not really all that important to do the home-work regularly.	⑥	⑥	⑥	⑥
89. I would find hard to give a talk in front of others in my class.	⑥	⑥	⑥	⑥
90. I would not mind giving money to a benefit fund for a school or hospital building even though it is not built in my own place.	⑥	⑥	⑥	⑥

TOOL - II

TEACHING COMPETENCY SCALE

B.K.Passi and M.S.Lalita
Name of the Student Teacher...
Class to be taught...
Topic...
Date......................Time Duration..
Published by

National Psychological Corporation

4/230, Kacheri Ghat, Agra – 282004 (U.P).

	Not at all				Very much		
	1	2	3	4	5	6	7
PLANNING (Pre-instructional)							
1. Objectives of the lesson were appropriate: clearly stated relevant to the content, adequate and attainable.	⑥	⑥	⑥	⑥	⑥	⑥	⑥
2. Content selected was appropriate: relevant and adequate with respect to the objectives of the lesson, and accurate.	⑥	⑥	⑥	⑥	⑥	⑥	⑥
3. Content selected was properly organised: Logical continuity and psychological organisation.	⑥	⑥	⑥	⑥	⑥	⑥	⑥
4. Audio-visual material chosen was appropriate: suited to the pupils and content, adequate and necessary for attaining the objectives.	⑥	⑥	⑥	⑥	⑥	⑥	⑥

	Not at all				Very much		
	1	2	3	4	5	6	7
RESENTATION (Instructional)							
5. Lesson was introduced effectively and pupils were made ready emotionally and from knowledge point of view to receive the new lesson: continuity in statements or questions, relevance, use of previous knowledge and use of appropriate device/ technique.	⑥	⑥	⑥	⑥	⑥	⑥	⑥
6. Questions were appropriate: well structured, properly put, adequate in number and made pupils participate.	⑥	⑥	⑥	⑥	⑥	⑥	⑥
7. Critical awareness was brought about in pupils with the help of probing questions: prompting, seeking further information, refocusing, redirection and increasing critical awareness.	⑥	⑥	⑥	⑥	⑥	⑥	⑥
8. Concepts and principles were explained (underst-anding brought about) with the help of clear, interrelated and meaningful statements: statements to create set, to conclude, statements which had relevancy, continuity appropriate vocabulary explaining links, fluency and had no vague words and phrases.	⑥	⑥	⑥	⑥	⑥	⑥	⑥

	Not at all				Very much		
	1	2	3	4	5	6	7
9. The concepts and principles were illustrated with the help of appropriate examples through appropriate media (verbal and non verbal): simple, relevant to the content and interest level of pupils.	⑥	⑥	⑥	⑥	⑥	⑥	⑥
10. Pupil's attention was secured and maintained by varying stimuli like movements, gestures, changing speech pattern, focusing, changing interaction styles, pausing, and oral-visual switching: Pupil's postures, and listening observing and responding behaviour of pupils.	⑥	⑥	⑥	⑥	⑥	⑥	⑥
11. Deliberate silence and non verbal cues were used to increase pupil participation	⑥	⑥	⑥	⑥	⑥	⑥	⑥
12. Pupil's participation (responding and initiating) was encouraged using verbal and non verbal reinforces.	⑥	⑥	⑥	⑥	⑥	⑥	⑥
13. Speed of presentation of ideas was appropriate: matched with the rate of pupil's understanding and there was proper budgeting of time.	⑥	⑥	⑥	⑥	⑥	⑥	⑥
14. Pupils participated in the class room and responded to the teacher and initiated by giving their own ideas and reacting to other's ideas.	⑥	⑥	⑥	⑥	⑥	⑥	⑥
15. The blackboard work was good legible, neat, appropriateness of the content written and adequate.	⑥	⑥	⑥	⑥	⑥	⑥	⑥

	Not at all				Very much		
	1	2	3	4	5	6	7
CLOSING							
16. The closure was achieved appropriately: main points of the lesson were consolidated, present knowledge was linked with the part knowledge, opportunities were provided for applying present knowledge, and present was linked with future learning (assignment)	⑥	⑥	⑥	⑥	⑥	⑥	⑥
17. The assignment given to the pupils was appropriate: suited to individual differences, relevant to the content taught and adequate.	⑥	⑥	⑥	⑥	⑥	⑥	⑥
EVALUATION							
18. Pupil's progress towards the objectives of the lesson was checked and the procedures of evaluation were appropriate: relevant to the objectives, valid, reliable and objective.	⑥	⑥	⑥	⑥	⑥	⑥	⑥
19. Pupil's difficulties in understanding a concept of principle were diagnosed by step-by-step questioning and suitable remedial measures were undertaken.							
MANAGERIAl							
20. Both attending and non attending behaviours of the pupils were recognised: attending behaviour was rewarded, directions were given to eliminate non	⑥	⑥	⑥	⑥	⑥	⑥	⑥

	Not at all				Very much		
	1	2	3	4	5	6	7
attending behaviour, questions were asked to check pupils' attending behaviour, pupils' feelings and ideas were accepted, and non verbal cues were used to recognise pupil's attending and non attending behaviours.							
21. Classroom discipline was maintained in the class: pupils followed teacher's instructions that were not related to the content: Comments (if any) :	⑥	⑥	⑥	⑥	⑥	⑥	⑥

CHAPTER 2

Self Acceptance and Locus of Control

INTRODUCTION

Education is a life long process that begins at birth and continues throughout our life. Knowledge or information is nothing but the experiences based on the sense of perception. The bodily faculties that give an ability to gain experience in this universe are called senses, viz. the senses of sight, hearing, smell, taste and touch. It is during this educational life many of the adolescents face different problem. To lead a secure life every one needs to adjust with the present environment and have the ability to control effectively. In order to arrive at such a level of positive interaction the individual needs to possess a positive self acceptance of himself during their educational period requires their ability of accepting himself as he is in order to live effectively and dynamically with the environment.

Adolescence is a period when the students need proper motivation to reach the goals set in the academic field. Thus motivation is closely related to locus of control. The focus on the two types of locus of control would enable the adolescence to develop the right mode of thinking leads to positive self-acceptance.

Adolescence is generally regarded as a period of great stress and strain. It is so because of the nature of the physical and mental development during the period. Adolescence is normally a period between 13 and 19 or 20 years of age. Some psychologists are of the view that it starts from twelfth year and stretches upto 21 or 23 years of age. Mostly the students between the age 14 to 16 or 17 are called teenagers and the educational system categories them as High school students ranging from VIII, IX and X standard. Some adolescents talk amongst themselves about their need of earning money. One will say 'he have no love for school'. The other will reply 'he deeply loves school'. It indicates that their tastes, interests and aptitudes vary. The main problem of adolescents are overzealous, idealists and fame-hungry, impatient behaviour, adverse effect of elders policy of double standard. But posing the factors of their failure on others especially on fate is high among the High school students.

DEFINITION OF SELF ACCEPTANCE

According to **Wayne Dyer,** "Self Acceptance means liking the entire physical you, and eliminating those cultural impositions to be proper or to merely tolerate your body when it behaves other than in a cosmetic fashion".

According to **Jersild (1963),** the sum total of a person's view of what he wishes, he was or think he ought to be, as distinguished from what he is generally called, self, acceptance. The adolescent's self acceptance has many facts, It includes aspirations he is vigorously striving to attain, or hopes dimly some day to relays.

According to **Roger** (1951), self-acceptance comprises what the person would like to be or holds out as a goal for individual development and achievement.

Garrison et al, (1967) says the term self acceptance has been shown to be valuable in determining the relationship between how the child sees himself and what he thinks he should be like. The self acceptance begins when the child identifies with as parental figure. During middle childhood and early adolescence it moves through a stage of romance and glamour and culminates in the late adolescence as a composite of desirable characteristics which may be symbolised by an attractive, real and visible young adult or perhaps even an imaginary person.

Hilgar (1971) expressed that the self consists of all the ideas, perceptions and values that characterise 'I' and 'me' it includes the awareness of ' what I am and what can do'.

Garrison et al (1967) says that the person who accepts himself is guided by his own standard. He has insight and understanding in relation to his ability, worth and in relation to others. In order to be able to accept himself, a person must have a Self Concept which is realistic and which is not too different from his ideal of what he should be the Self Accepting person is familiar with his weakness. He recognises those that he cannot change, those he must accept and live with. Such a person approves himself with his deficiencies and self acceptance promotes self evaluations. Such a person can be critical about him and has sense of responsibility for his actions. He don't blame others or destiny for his condition. Nor does he strive to put up a show in order to win the approval of others.

Sheerer (1949) in his study on the acceptance in the following manner.

(*a*) To perceive one's self as a person of worth, worthy of respect rather than condemnation

(*b*) To perceive one's standards as being based upon his own experience rather than the attitudes or desires of others.

(*c*) To perceive one's own feelings, motives and personal experience without distraction of the sensory data. It is found that if an individual thinks well of himself, he is likely to think well of others and a person who is highly Self Accepting also accepts others ideas and guidance.

THE CONCEPT OF SELF-ACCEPTANCE

Self-Acceptance is love and happy with whom you are now. Some call it **self-esteem**, others **self-love**, but whatever you call it, you'll know when you are accepting yourself cause it feels great. It's an agreement with yourself to appreciate, validate, accept and support who you are this very moment, even those parts you'd like to eventually change.

Self Acceptance is one of the influencing factors of personality to determine the quality of one's behaviour. Self-Acceptance is the fullest description of oneself of which a person is capable of, at one time.

No one, not even the greatest in any field, in the wildest imagination possible is born with a Self Acceptance. Self Acceptance is something that is developed through countless learning experiences as the child interacts with others and with his environment, as he discovers himself, as he becomes aware of what he is capable of doing and what he cannot do.

PROCESS OF ACCEPTANCE

Acceptance exists at the care of your being. It is your default status. In order to reach this base level of acceptance, you need only remove the items lying on top. To do this you must first identify all the things you do not accept about yourself. Then one by one eliminate them by examining and questioning your beliefs around the issue.

- Know yourself and you beliefs.
- Take a good hard look at your honesty level.
- Know you are doing the best you can.
- Relax your value judgments.
- Examine guilt.
- Understand your motivations.
- Ask yourself questions about what you don't accept.

SELF ACCEPTANCE AND ADOLESCENTS

Adolescence is the period when one thinks about one's own identity physical, intellectual, emotional and moral aspects that influence the development of one's self.

It is more difficult for girls to formulate a clear and accepting view of their feminine identity than it is for boys, to accept their masculinity. In their upbringing there is more incentive for boys to prefer to be boys than for girls to prefer to be girls. Boys have more privileges they are less strictly supervised, they are not judged as severely as girls for misconduct, they move in to a man's world very smoothly.

The masculine gender looks forward to an occupation and financial independence as a necessity in life than the feminine gender. As girls reach and advance through adolescence, the major occupation many of them look forward to is marriage and motherhood. It has been found that with increasing age boys become more secure in their masculine role whereas the girls become less firmly identified with their feminine role. This paves the way for the masculine and feminine gender to develop a positive self-acceptance.

MOTIVATION BEHIND THE ACCEPTANCE

Acceptance is a concept that sounds positive and also provides opportunities for positive development within an individual, but generally acceptance of self becomes difficult as adolescence do not look at them with a positive approach. The necessity for motivation becomes a driving force behind the concept of self acceptance.

The high school level of the student population requires a positive self acceptance to improve their achievement motivation. Motivation directs the Self Acceptance of the students. The Locus of Control, level of aspiration and their strength of need freely influence it. Internal locus of control may not improve their Self Acceptance but on the other hand. External locus of control has a direct influence on their self acceptance. Self acceptance plays a key role on academic achievement.

LOCUS OF CONTROL

Originally developed within the framework of Rotter's (1954) Social learning theory, the Locus of Control construct refers to the degree to which an individual believes the occurrence of reinforcement is contingent on his or her own behaviour. The factors involved with reinforcement expectancy are labelled "external" and "Internal" control. In short, internal locus of control refers to the perception of positive or negative events as being a consequence of one's own actions and thereby under one's own personal control. In contrast, external locus of control believes that her behaviour is guided by fate, luck. A locus of control orientation is a belief about whether the outcome of our actions is contingent on what we do (internal control orientation) or on events outside our personal control (external control orientation) (Zimloardo, 1985).

Thus the locus of control is conceptualised as referring to an undimensional continum ranging from external to internal.

INTERNAL LOCUS OF CONTROL

Individual believes that his/her behaviour is guided by his/ her personal decisions and efforts.

EXTERNAL LOCUS OF CONTROL

Individual believes that his/her behaviour is guided by fate, luck, or other external circumstances.

The locus of control is a concept in psychology, originally developed by Julian Rotter in the 1950's.The Locus of Control represents how a person's decision-making ability is influenced, essentially those who make choices primarily on their own are considered to have internal locus of control. People with external locus of control are generally more apt to be stressed and suffered due to depression as they are more aware of work situations since those who make decisions based more on what others think are said to have external locus of control. Women tend to have more external locus of control than men. Having an internal locus of control can also be referred to as "Personal control" or "Self - determination".

HISTORY OF LOCUS OF CONTROL

The locus of control construct originated from social learning theory, though the groundwork for his theory was laid by Fritz Heider (1958). According to social learning theory, the potential for any given behaviour to occur is function of the individual's expectancy that the behaviour will be effective in securing a desired end or reinforcement.

Social learning theory attempts to explain the person's selection of specific responses from a larger repertoire in predicting behaviour in social settings. Although social learning theory evolved from associationistics and instrumental conditioning theories, it encompasses a wide range of behaviour determinants including personality, motivation and situational context. Within this frame work, Rotter developed the concept of Locus of control.

Heider's speculations were refined and formalised also by Weiner, Frieze, Reed, Rest and Rosenbaum (1971). Weiner described the elements in the kinds of explanations individuals use to account for their performance. The internal versus external dimension of behaviours is known as locus of control orientation.

Internals believe that the reinforcements they receive are primarily a result of their own behaviour, ability, effort or characteristics. Individuals at the external end of the locus of control continuum attribute the control of their reinforcements to force outside themselves, such as luck, chance, fate or powerful others.

Individuals may learn to attribute to themselves greater control over their own behaviour and view themselves as agents who can affect the world, rather than as passive objects being victimised by environmental commands. This fact is one of the focal issues of the Bandura's (1977) self-efficiency theory. Self-efficiency is one's perceived capacity to meet some challenge or perform a particular response.

According to Rose (1981), teachers with a generalised expectancy of internal control perceive classroom events as being a consequence of their own actions and under their personal control. Teachers with an expectancy of external control perceive little contingency between their actions in the class room and student behavioural outcomes. The degree of contingency expected by individuals between their behaviour and its effect has been conceptualised by Rotter as the personality dimension Internal - External (I-E) Locus of Control.

According to Brown Autry and Lange back (1985), the Locus of Control construct is an element of attribution theory. Attribution theory is associated with the investigation of the perception of causality, the judgment of why a particular incident occurred.

THE CONCEPT OF LOCUS OF CONTROL

The essence of the Locus of Control concept is that each of us located the controlling elements in our lives either inside or outside ourselves. The person who believes that he can decide for himself what he will do or be that he is the 'captain of the soul'. Locates his control internally and the person who believes that what happens to him is largely a matter or luck or who depends on the decisions of other is locating his control externally. The Locus of Control construct originated from Rotter's (1966) social learning theory. So the concept of Locus of control is rather a recent origin. Many of the Psychologists are interested in this idea and a number of studies are going on in this new field.

DEFINITIONS OF LOCUS OF CONTROL

According to Roddin Considerable attention has been devoted to this construct since the 1980s, because many mental and physical outcome variables have been identified that depend largely on the extent to which the individuals actually are and even more importantly - perceive themselves to be in control of their lives and of the resources needed to make meaningful decisions about their life circumstances (Rodin et al.,) It has been argued that as adults age they experience an increasing number of life events over which they have little or no control.

TYPES OF LOCUS OF CONTROL

A number of researches have been conducted to find out whether Locus of Control is a too broad term. They have suggested that it might be better to breakdown the concepts internal and external into component parts. Levenson (1973) for instance, maintains that externals may be of two different sorts, people who believe the world as disordered (that things happen by chance) and people who believe the world as ordered but luck decides the fate or result.

Researches have developed a test that distinguishes between the internals who take responsibility primarily for his success and the internals who blame himself for his failures. These two types have been shown to follow different developmental courses and to have differences in the classroom situation.

INTERNAL LOCUS OF CONTROL

If one person perceives that an event or achievement is contingent on his own behaviors or his own relatively permanent characteristics, he is termed to have internal control.

Here he assumes that he is the master of his fate and the captain of his soul. He thinks he can do what he wants to do and achieve results by his own efforts. Such people have internal locus of control.

CHARACTERISTICS OF INTERNAL LOCUS OF CONTROL

1. Internals are more likely to seek information
2. They are more sensitive and alert
3. Internals pay more attention to relevant cues, when there are uncertainties in the situation.
4. They show more incidental learning

5. They are more responsive to information requirements.
6. Internals pursue goals by paying careful attention to demands of the taste.
7. They set realistic goals and take responsibility for their actions.

EXTERNAL LOCUS OF CONTROL

When the subject is following some action of his own, but not being entirely perceives reinforcement contingent on his action, then it is typically perceived as the result of luck, fate, etc. When the events are interpreted or attributed in this way by an individual, this signifies the belief in external control.

If one believes that his ability and his skill would not make much difference because luck and other people will govern the outcome of his efforts. He is said to have external locus of control.

CHARACTERISTICS OF EXTERNAL LOCUS OF CONTROL

1. Externals are more suspicions to social influences and social demands.
2. They pursue goals by relying more on behaviour-oriented outcomes towards the social agent in the situation.
3. They are not ready to take the responsibility of their actions.

LOCUS OF CONTROL Vs EDUCATION

It has often been said that obtaining a good education is the key to being successful in the world. Many things may contribute to school achievement and one variable that is over looked is locus of control. In the context of education, locus of control refers to the types of attributions that makes for reaching success and/or failure in school tasks. If someone believes that his or her successes and failures are due to the factors within their own control such as effort or ability, then that person is said to have an internal locus of control. On the other hand if someone believes that his or her successes and failures are due to factors outside of their own control, such as fate, luck, then person is said to have an external locus of control.

MODIFICATION OF STUDENTS LOCUS OF CONTROL

Attribution training, which concentrates on strengthening the students' internal locus of control (Deshler, Schumacher & Lenz, 1984), may be helpful in increasing motivation. Attribution training has been shown to increase internal locus of control and improve task persistence (Shelton, Anastopoulos & Linden, 1985). Usually the implementation of attribution training utilizes some form of self instructional set of statements. Students are trained to say positive things to themselves, first out loud, then in a whisper, then silently to themselves. This type of training is easy to implement & requires no special materials. For some students, attribution training can have a considerable impact on their overall efforts at school. When students are struggling or not putting forth much effort, it would be wise to consider locus of control as a possible contributor to the problem. A teacher's effort to motivate a student may prove futile, the child has external locus of control. Teaching children from a young age that hard work can pay off would be beneficial. If they were taught to believe in their own ability to control their lives and the reinforcements in their lives, they would be more likely to succeed in school.

DEVELOPMENT OF LOCUS OF CONTROL

Generally, the development of locus of control stems from family, culture and past experiences leading to rewards. Most internals have been shown to come from families that focused on effort, education, and responsibility. On the other hand, most externals come from families of a low socioeconomic status where there is a lack of life control.

NEED AND SIGNIFICANCE OF THE STUDY

The study of self acceptance and locus of control among high school students is very important. This study may help us to diagnose the psychological problem faced by the students. Mostly the students lack in their personality. Self acceptance is one of the main variables of personality which is taken for this study. And every person especially the students need some type of motivation to reinforce their attitude. Hence locus of control is one of the main variables of motivation which is also considered for this study. Our present society shows positive signs of self-empowerment. Our adolescent population have also empowered themselves to meet the exclusive challenges in the Society.

Viewing the state of their self acceptance the adolescent needs to be encouraged in the educational field, to think for them, act rationally and reach the goals they have set. The adolescents of our present time need to face problems and demand which needs to be tackled effectively. The school and the family provide the support and Guidance for them. The individual himself should learn to acquire self-confidence and self-acceptance.

Adolescence is the most crucial and significant period of an individual's life. It represents the culmination of childhood and an initiation of the adult who is to be. In this stage, human personality develops new dimensions. It is the period to learn new things. It is the period of anxiety and worries. Adolescents are tightly ambitious. They developed so many desires and ambitions to be filled. Despite their best planning and efforts they may not get the desired success. At times they find themselves in a state of utter confusion and bewilderment. All the paths that take them to face repeated failures lead them to distances. The main significance of Self Acceptance is once you truly accept yourself, you will waste no energy or time on self deception or deceiving others and you will develop clarity as to just what needs improving.

As every one know, generally in an educational setting knowledge flows from the teacher to the student. This type of environment could cause students to withdrawn. It is suggested that students take more of an active control in the learning process. It is also important to take into consideration whether each student has an external or internal locus of control.

STATEMENT OF THE PROBLEM

Self Acceptance and Locus of control among High School students in Tiruvallur District.

DEFINITION OF THE TERMS

(*a*) Self acceptance

Self acceptance is one of the influencing factors of personality as it governs the individual's reaction towards people and situations and determines the quality of one's behaviour.

Self-Acceptance as measured through this inventory in an assessment of factors such as sense of personal worth and satisfaction with self.

(*b*) Locus of Control

Locus of control refers to an individual's generalised expectations concerning where control over subsequent event resides. In other words, who or what is responsible for what happens.

OPERATIONAL DEFINITIONS

(*a*) Self Acceptation

Self Acceptance scores are obtained by administering self acceptance inventory constructed and standardised by Kakkar, Patiala, 1984.

(*b*) Locus Control

1. Locus of control scores are obtained by administering Locus of control Scale constructed and standardised by Stephen Nowicki, Strickland in 1973.

OBJECTIVES OF THE STUDY

1. To study the level of self acceptance among High School students.

2. To Study the level of locus of control among High School students
3. To find out the significant difference between boys and girls of High School students in their self Acceptance.
4. To find out the significant difference between boys and girls of High School students in their locus of control.
5. To find out the significant difference between different ages among High School students in their self acceptance.
6. To find out the significant difference between different ages among High School students in their locus of control.
7. To find out the significant difference between the high School students studying in different management in their self acceptance.
8. To find out the significant difference between the high School students studying in different management in their locus of control.
9. To find out the significant difference between joint and nuclear family of High School students in their self Acceptance.
10. To find out the significant difference between joint and nuclear family of High School students in their locus of control.
11. To find out the significant difference between rural and urban area High School students in their self acceptance.
12. To find out the significant difference between rural and urban area High School students in their locus of control.
13. To find out the significant difference between English and Tamil Medium of High School students in their self acceptance.
14. To find out the significant difference between English and Tamil Medium of High School students in their locus of control.

15. To find out the Significant Relationship of Self Acceptance and Locus of Control among High School students.

LIMITATIONS OF THE STUDY

- The sample is restricted to 300 students
- The study is restricted to High School students
- The study is limited to 5 Schools of Tiruvallur District.

CONCLUSION

The first chapter highlights the overview of the problem and the statement of the problem, need and significance of the study, objectives and limitations of the study.

Reviews of related literature are dealt in the chapter that follows.

REVIEW OF RELATED LITERATURE

Introduction

The purpose of present investigation is to study the effect of Locus of control and Self Acceptance. A large number of studies have been carried out in the field of Locus of control. The research literature is reviewed under the following captions.

(*a*) Study related to Self Acceptance

(*b*) Study related to Locus of Control

STUDIES RELATED TO SELF ACCEPTANCE

Studies Abroad

Fuster's (1964) : A Study on the relationship between Self Acceptance and acceptance of others among College Students.

According to Fuster, Self Acceptance implies the formation of a realistic Self concept which includes one's strength and weakness. Self Acceptance flows from that inner craving of waiting to be that person which is truly one. A fine feeling of being in this world for a purpose which is fully within his reach and which is achieving gradually as the years roll by Self Acceptance should be developed in Children because it makes a person comfortable with himself.

Self Accepted Child adopts a realistic approach to life situation. Such a Child can develop a positive attitude towards life.

Baker (1977) : studied the influence of psychological education to enhance Self-understanding and Self Acceptance in College Students.

The result shows that there is no demonstrated effect of the course on the participants' Self Acceptance because these Students were the kind of people who improve without participating in this course. Baker's Study also emphasizes the need for psychological education to improve Self Acceptance in Adolescents.

Hurley (1990) : Studied the "Constructive thinking and elevated ratings of self in interpersonal groups".

First they conducted the constructive thinking inventory (CTI) for one hundred and three university students. Results shows that constructive thinking and rating one's self above peers, especially, for acceptance of Self consistently correlated positively, suggesting an underlying sense of independence, From this study it is clear that constructive thinking can be inculcated in Children by proper Self Acceptance programme.

Fraley-Stephen-E. (1992) : From Self-Blame to Self-Acceptance: Freeing Myself in a Prison Undergraduate Programme.

A prison inmate who is a graduate psychology student reflects on how the study of social and behavioural sciences contributed to his moral and ethical growth.

Starn (1993) : Studied learning disabilities of male adolescents.

Thirty Seven 9th and 10th grade males from two suburban Midwestern School systems were administered the California psychological inventory (CPI) Self Acceptance taken as one of the variable. The data do not provide evidence that adolescents with learning disabilities experience greater dependence and greater isolation and loneliness than their non-learning disabled peers. Correlation showed that there is a significant relation between Self Acceptance and their disabilities.

Statman-Daniel (1993) : Studied Self-Assessment, Self-Esteem, and Self-Acceptance.

Discusses students self-esteem is best improved through self-acceptance rather than by comparisons with others. Argues that some comparisons are essential to the concept of self and therefore are important to self-esteem. Concludes that some students may have low self-esteem because they accurately assess their abilities with others.

Randolph, Elizabeth (1993) : Developed Self-Awareness and Self-Acceptance in Emotionally Handicapped Students through the Bibliotherapeutic Process.

This practicum involved the development, implementation, and evaluation of a program which used a bibliotherapeutic approach to develop specific behaviours with three second graders and seven fifth graders, all in a resource program for students with emotional handicaps. It needs assessment survey of mainstream teachers identified needs in the following areas: responsibility, cooperation, conflict resolution, and truthfulness. Although projected goals were not met, individual students made gains in each area. Students experienced attitude changes, improved self-concepts, and more realistic awareness of objective areas. Items in the appendix include the student contract, target behavior survey, the data collection chart, and critical thinking questions.

Mills-Brett-D. (1993) : Studied the Rehabilitation Counselling for Athletes Prior to Retirement: A Preventative Approach Using Self-Acceptance to Enhance Performance before and after Retirement.

This study suggests that collegiate and professional athletes preparing to retire should be provided with pre retirement and postretirement rehabilitation counselling. The counselling should involve a preventative approach centered on self-acceptance, to enhance the athlete's performance before and after retirement. The development of self-acceptance in an athlete helps him or her to experience less competitive cognitive anxiety. Questions are presented that athletes can ask themselves to examine their level of self-acceptance and that coaches can ask themselves to determine their enhancement of athletes' self-acceptance. Counsellors are encouraged to provide empathy and support, break the problem into manageable parts and develop a plan to tackle those parts, and determine the athlete's internal and external strengths and resources.

Yuan-Frances (1994) : Studied that moving toward self-acceptance among Students with Learning Disabilities.

This study describes a course developed at Lesley College (Massachusetts) to help students with learning disabilities accept their disability and develop self-understanding and self-advocacy skills. It describes the course model and major tenets, highlights some course components, and summarises results of a study of the courses impact.

Chromic (1996) : Studied the level of acquisition of Self advocacy attribution within a group of High School students with learning disabilities after being exposed to an instructional unit developed to teach Self - advocacy skills.

The subjects were high school students (10th - 12th) with learning disabilities who were receiving services within transition resource classes. The conclusion was that seven week Self advocacy unit was not powerful enough to effect a change in the self advocacy attributes of the students as measured by the CPI qualitative data. Results indicated that most students were able to identify individual strengths and weakness, but were able to describe effectively the nature of their disability.

Frederick, Verdine J (1997) : Studied the relationship among acceptance of a learning disability grade level at diagnosis and achievement of students with learning disabilities.

The study sample consists of fifty high schools. Only students whose records indicated that they had been designated as learning disabled by a board of education, special education, team were considered for participation. The tools were given to each of the 50 learning disabled students in their schools. The findings demonstrate that lower the students' grade level when a diagnosis of a learning disability is determined, the greater the students' Self Acceptance of his or her learning disability.

Brill (1999) : Studied Self Acceptance and a heightened sense of emotional vulnerability.

The transition period from child to adult arrives the adolescents' intense need for emotional security in the form of acceptance by peers. Throughout life emotional needs and fear are interpreted differently. Helpless infants have a moral fear of living abandoned. At childhood, our emotional security requires contribute reassurance of our lovability and acceptability. In adolescence, this core emotional needs become Focused upon Self and social acceptance. The unbearable emotional distress leads the adolescence to a variety of destructive behaviour patterns, some may become self-destructive, some may express in anger and violence. Self Acceptance makes a person emotionally balanced. Self accepted person can be well adjusted with the peers and society.

Levon (2001) : Studied Self Acceptance as the ability to see and recognise all aspects of self without judgment, either positive or negative.

Self Acceptance is not about living or approving one's self. It is simply about being aware of all of the parts of the self. It is about being awake and fully conscious. He also says that increase of self acceptance increase the raw material at disposal. It is about adding and expanding. It is the contrasts, conflicts, inconsistencies and polarities in life that make it interesting and awesome.

Sim T.N. (2003) : Studied Father and mother linkage in relation to adolescent academic and athletic competence and self worth.

A total of 140 Singapore undergraduates reported on themselves and their parents. Results indicate that some adolescent attributes exist only when mother's characteristics are considered. The link between father's responsiveness and athletic competence existed only when mother's responsiveness was high and that link between father's acceptance of individualisation and athletics competence existed only when mother's acceptance of individualisation was moderate or high.

Studies In India

Arora (1981) : studied the problems of students in professional courses of medicine, law, engineering and education in relation to personality factors.

In this study Self Acceptance was taken as one of the variable. A student's problem checklist consisting of 10 areas were administered to a sample of 800 boys & girls preparing for the first professional degree in medicine, law, engineering and education. Result shows that high problem students in general, found to have lower personality adjustment, lower creative persons, and higher level of aspirations, and high Self Acceptance than low problem students.

Waheeda (1989) : Studied the behavioural training in improving personality characteristics of juvenile delinquents in relation to Self Acceptance.

The sample was drawn from Government Special Home for boys at Chengelpet and Government special home for girls at Kilpauk, Madras, run by Government of Tamil Nadu. The samples were chosen by administering kakkar's Self Acceptance inventory to a group of 50 male and female delinquents. The samples were given Jerner's personality inventory to assess the personality characteristics of the juvenile delinquents. His major findings were that the high self acceptance experimental low acceptance group, no significant difference was found in both the high Self Acceptance and low self acceptance group among males and females and the high self acceptance group showed improvement in a social index whereas the low self acceptance group had no improvement.

Sunanda. Y. (1991) : Conducted a study of reaction of frustration as related to life satisfaction and self acceptance among the aged.

The objective is to relate frustration reaction to the acceptance of age- linked changes. The 'Sample comprised under middle age (40-49 years) advanced middle age (50-59 years) young old (60-69 years) and old age (70+ years). The tools used included frustrations reaction of life satisfaction. Scale, Jamuna and Ramamoorthy is Assessment of self acceptance and a bio-data schedule. The collected data was subjected to statistical analysis. Mean, S.D, 't' test, correlation and analysis of variance was calculated. He found that self acceptance among the aged was positively related to life satisfaction.

Bharadwaj (1998) : Studied Parental rejection, acceptance and adolescent value conflict.

In a sample of 500 adolescents by employing a two group design. Tools used were parenting scale constructed and standardised by Bharadwaj et al. and value conflicts scale constructed and standardised by Bharadwaj.

STUDIES RELATED TO LOCUS OF CONTROL

Studies Abroad

Guss, Thomas (1990) : Studied Integrating Underemployment and Hardship: Using Locus of Control to Develop a Profile among Married Men. The role of marital issues and individual characteristics in hardship, and the emphasis in the literature of the traditional provider role, there is a need to explore the experience of underemployment among married men. Only husbands were selected for this project. A random sample of a non-metropolitan northwest community produced 137 couples with a variety of incomes.. Husbands in hardship were more oriented to chance, while non hardship providers were more internal. Results suggest that locus of control is a distinguishing characteristic among married men.

Thompson,-Josephine-T. (1991) : Established the Locus of Control among Ninth Graders: Using Peer Mentors To Reduce Student Disengagement, Absenteeism, and Failures.

An intervention program was implemented to reduce absences, stimulate responsibility for assignments, and increase participation in extracurricular activities among disengaged ninth-grade students (N=18). Mentors felt the greatest benefits were showing disengaged students that someone cares and that if attitudes towards school could be improved needless failures and dropouts could be prevented.

Martin,-Janice-E.; et. al. (1991) : studied the relationship among Internal-External Locus of Control and Rational-Irrational Beliefs.

The study investigated the relationship between Internal-External Locus of Control Scale and Irrational Beliefs Test (IBT) scores. The independent variable was locus of control; the dependent variables were IBT full-scale and subscale scores. Data were collected through administering these instruments to state human service agency employees (N=105). Statistical analyses indicated that there was a significant correlation between internal-external locus of control and IBT full-scale scores and that there were significant correlations between internal-external locus of control and 8 out of 10 IBT subscale scores. Internal locus of control subjects exhibited more rational beliefs. Likewise, external locus of control subjects maintained more irrational beliefs.

Hipps,-Elizabeth-Smith; Halpin,-Glennelle (1991) : Studied Job Stress, Stress related to performance-based accreditation, Locus of Control, Age, and Gender As Related to Job Satisfaction and Burnout in Teachers and Principals.

The purpose of the study described here was to: (1) determine the amount of variance in burnout and job satisfaction in public school teachers and principals which could be accounted for by stress related to the state's performance-based accreditation standards; (2) examine the relationship between stress related to state standards and the age and gender of the educators; and (3) develop measures of educator job stress common to both teachers and principals and stress related to the state performance-based accreditation standards. Surveys were sent to teachers (N=445) and principals (N=128). Responses were received from 219 teachers and 58 principals.

Whitney,-Patricia (1991) : Studied Children's Locus of Control and Intrinsically Motivated Reading.

Study investigated the relationship between locus of control and intrinsically motivated reading for children. To find the hypothesis that students with an internal locus of control would be more productive readers than those with an external locus of control, a matched sample was drawn. The t-test for matched samples and the Pearson product-moment both indicated non-significant differences between intrinsic motivation of internal and external subjects. The most revealing factor was that the students felt they were "too busy" for free-choice reading. To find the hypothesis that students with an internal locus of control would be more productive readers than those with an external locus of control, a matched sample was drawn. The t-test for matched samples and the Pearson product-moment both indicated non-significant differences between intrinsic motivation of internal and external subjects.

Evans,-Jan-Holmgren (1991) : Studied the Relationship between Internal Locus of Control and Rehabilitation Prognosis.

Studies involve the subject groups selected and the indexes of outcome, as well as the manipulation of treatment, structures cause limited general ability. Different studies contradict each other probably too frequently for strictly scientific purposes. The importance of internal locus of control on the rehabilitation process of any illness or disability tends to have numerous methodological problems. Questionnaires exist that measure a person's internal locus of control; however, that extra inner essence of a person defies scientific exploration and measurement.

Ayersman,-David-J. (1992) : studied the effect of a Summer Enrichment Program for At-Risk Youths on Locus of Control and the Relation to Motivational Orientation.

Examining locus of control, and showing an effective treatment program for transitioning from externality to internality, it may be possible to predict other behaviours and eliminate negative behaviours (drug use, low self-esteem, poor grades) associated with externality which will assist in keeping children in school. This study examined the relationship between locus of control and motivation. Statistical significance was also found by age and gender with younger females being the most external and older males being the most internal. A moderate negative correlation was found linking one of the five motivation subscales (independent judgment) with locus of control.

Thompson,-Bruce; et.al.(1992) : Studied the Nature of Children's Health Locus of Control Beliefs.

The study was to explore the structure of the health locus of control beliefs of children, using the Multidimensional Health Locus of Control Scales. People's beliefs about the origins of their health, sometimes referred to as health locus of control, have been shown to influence a variety of important behaviours. Two samples of 4th and 6th-grade students were utilised to allow for cross-validation of results. The first group had 780 subjects; the second group had 524 subjects. Confirmatory methods were employed in this study.

Martin,-Janice-E.; et.al (1992) : Studied the effects of internal-external Locus of Control and Selected Demographic Variables on Rational-Irrational Beliefs.

This study evaluated whether or not locus of control mediates rational-irrational beliefs. Results support the view that internally oriented individuals maintain more rational beliefs than do externally oriented people. Nine tables present study data. Data were generated investigating the impact of an internal-external orientation and selected demographic variables (age, race, gender, education, and occupation) on rational-irrational beliefs. Independent variables were locus of control and demographic characteristics, and the dependent variable was beliefs. Data were collected by administering the Internal-External Locus of Control Scale and the Irrational Beliefs Test to 105 state human service agency employees (81 internals and 24 externals). A one-way analysis of variance uncovered significant differences in internal and external females. In addition, there were significant differences in beliefs between internal and external subjects at different educational levels.

Sisco,-Sharon-S. (1992) : Using Goal Setting To Enhance Self Esteem and Create an Internal Locus of Control in the At Risk Elementary Student.

Study examined the effects of a program designed to enhance the self-esteem of at-risk students by developing an internal locus of control in the students. The Piers-Harris Children's Self-Concept Scale was administered as a pretest and post test, providing the data from which the discrepancy gap for showing improvement in self-esteem was formulated. The program consisted of six major components: (1) a specified vocabulary and format; (2) goal identification and description by students; (3) student evaluation and selection of alternative actions to accomplish goals; (4) student journal writing showing reflective evaluation and identification of successful and unsuccessful behaviours; (5) a scale to evaluate student goals; and (6) peer encouragement through class meetings. Results indicated that students' self-esteem improved and fewer severe behaviour referrals were necessary. However, attendance was not significantly affected. Related materials are appended.

Freedman,-Susan-A. (1992) : Studied Sex, Gender and Locus of Control in College Students.

Study was undertaken to examine the relationship between locus of control and gender role. Locus of control has most frequently been measured using Internal versus External measures. A non significant trend for the interaction of sex by locus of control was found. Findings further indicated that Internal locus of control may be over-represented in some college populations.

Enger,-John-M.; et.al (1993) : Studied Internal/ External Locus of Control and Parental Verbal Interaction of At-Risk Adolescent Black Males.

The academic and discipline problems of young black male students in a small southern town, the Positive Impact Program (PIP) was developed for at-risk black males. Two possible at-risk factors, locus of control and the quality of parental verbal interaction, were studied for participants in the PIP. Locus of control and communications with parents were compared to those of previously normed groups. The Verbal Interaction Questionnaire (developed by P. C. Blake in 1991) scores were comparable to those for rural predominantly white male and female high school students. In general, students more internally controlled reported having more positive parental verbal communication, while those more externally controlled had more negative parental verbal communication. Eighteen of the 42 boys were in the PIP, but no significant differences were found for these students on either measure, or no locus of control scores were available from the period before PIP participation.

Bernhard,-Judith-K.; Siegel,-Linda-S. (1994) : Increasing Internal Locus of Control for a Disadvantaged Group: A Computer Intervention.

Discussion of locus of control (LOC), gender, and mathematics and technical subjects focuses on a study of preschool girls and boys Highlights include treatment of experimental and control groups; gender differences; parent questionnaires; and pretests and post-tests.

Reeh,-H.-Elise; Reilly,-Karen-J. (1995) : A Quasi Meta Analysis of the Health Locus of Control Construct.

The study about the Internal HEALTH LOCUS OF CONTROL (HLOC) is related to health-promoting behaviour, positive health status, health knowledge, information-seeking, and treatment success. The results of this analysis indicate that HLOC research is primarily conducted in the United States by a fairly even distribution of male and female researchers, who are often members of psychology faculties. Studies are mostly published in psychology journals, with some research appearing in medical journals. These studies have included a wide variety of participants, including hospital patients, employees, school children, and university students. HLOC research is generally of an applied nature, and is most often correlation in design.

Fournier,-Genevieve; St-Onge,-Susan (1995) : Studied about the Shaping Vocational Locus of Control through Beliefs.

Presents a survey of rudimentary results, and proposes a typology of vocational beliefs. Presents a synthesis of the theoretical foundations implemented in an investigation of the principal vocational beliefs of individuals having difficulty with their career choice. Suggests principles of intervention to help young adults facing difficulty in career decisions

Hawkes,-Brent-B (1995) : Studied Locus of Control in Early Childhood Education

This study discusses research on locus of control, particularly as it relates to early childhood education. Some measures of children's sense of locus of control are discussed, including the Optimism-Pessimism Test Instrument and the Stanford Preschool Internal-External Scale. Factors which inhibit the assessment of children's sense of locus of control are detailed, including: (1) lack of development of children's vocabulary and communication skills; (2) children's tendency to select the last possible answer offered in a structured interview situation; (3) children's tendency to respond "yes" to yes or no questions; and (4) the prevalence of a research bias which assumes that elementary school children do not have well-developed self-awareness. The review concludes by noting that locus of control appears to be an important element of children's experiences and potential success in school.

Tyler,-Doris-Kennedy; Vasu,-Ellen-Storey (1995) : Studied Locus of Control, Self-Esteem, Achievement Motivation, and Problem-Solving Ability: LogoWriter and Simulations in the Fifth-Grade Classroom.

The effects of using LOGO, or problem-solving- oriented simulation software on locus of control, self-esteem, and achievement motivation for fifth-grade students. The importance of these variables in predicting LOGO mastery and far-transfer problem-solving ability was also examined.

Santa-Rita,-Emilio (1995) : Studied the Effect of Computer-Assisted Student Development Programs on Entering Freshman Locus of Control Orientation.

To determine the effect of SUCCESS programs on students' perceived locus of control and empowerment study was conducted at New York's Bronx Community College of two entering freshmen classes in fall 1995 (n=35). The experimental class received six SUCCESS assignments over 14 weeks related to basic college survival information and calculations of grade point averages and financial aid data. The Nowicki-Strickland Internal-External Control Scale was administered to both groups at the beginning and again at the end of their first semester to determine differences in student sense of power versus helplessness, persistence with parents in achieving goals, and perception of luck as a determinant in obtaining goals. Comparison of pre- and post-test scores for both groups indicated that students who completed the SUCCESS assignments did not shift significantly with respect to overall perceived control of reinforcement and there were no significant differences between the experimental and control groups' sense of persistence with parents. The SUCCESS students did however perceive luck as having a considerably lesser effect on the attainment of desired outcomes than the control group

Cook,-Ann; Troike, Roger (1995) : Studied Adolescent Parenting: Contrasts in Self-Esteem and Locus of Control.

Of the 17,051 women who become pregnant every day in America, 2,795 or 16% of them are adolescents. The self-esteem and locus of control of 85 pregnant and parenting teens enrolled in the Ohio Graduation, Reality, Dual Role Skills (GRADS) Program were measured and compared to the scores of 85 non-parenting peers. Self-esteem was measured using Rosenburg's Self-Esteem Scale. Locus of control was measured by Rotter's Internal-External Locus of Control Scale. No significant differences in the mean scores were discovered. This supported the assumption that involvement in the GRADS Program allowed pregnant and parenting teens to retain a level of self-esteem and locus of control equivalent to their non-parenting peers. The results of this study substantiate the worth of in-school support groups for high risk adolescents.

Studies In India

Pani, Mina (1991) : Studied the effect of culture and locus of control.

The performance among 40 tribal and 40 non-tribal Indian students in grade 3. Both tribal and non-tribal students were divided into internal Vs external locus of control groups. Reading task included both oral comprehension and several metalinguistic tasks. The poorest performance was evidenced by tribal students and students with external locus of control.

Saeeduzzafar and Sharma, Rama (1991) : studied the effect of religion (Hinduism and Islam) on locus of control and dependence proneness among externally oriented and internally oriented individuals.

The results showed that Muslim students were more dependent prone than Hindu Students. Externally oriented students were more depended than internally oriented students. However, the interactional effect of religion and locus of control was insignificant.

CONCLUSION

The survey of the related literature has helped much to have a proper perspective of the problem chosen for the study. The review of related literature has enabled the investigator to formulate relevant literature also resulted in providing insight into the selection and use of effective methods of study, analysis and interpretation.

DESIGN OF THE STUDY

Introduction

This chapter describes in detail, the design of the study, nature and selection of sample, a brief description of the tools of investigation and the criteria for their investigation. It also gives a description of the procedure adopted for the collection of data, for its scoring and classification, finally the proposed statistical treatment of the data for testing the hypothesis that were formulated are explained.

HYPOTHESIS

The following hypothesis have been set for the present study

1. The level of Self Acceptance among High School Student is Average.
2. The internal Locus of Control is predominant among High School Student.
3. There is a significant difference between boys and girls of High School students in their self acceptance.
4. There is a significant difference between boys and girls of High School students in their locus of control.
5. There is a significant difference between different ages among High School students in their self acceptance.
6. There is a significant difference between different ages among High School students in their locus of control.
7. There is a significant difference between the high School students studying in different management in their self acceptance.

8. There is a significant difference between the high School students studying in different management in their locus of control.
9. There is a significant difference between joint and nuclear family of High School students in their self Acceptance.
10. There is a significant difference between joint and nuclear family of High School students in their locus of control.
11. There is no significant difference between rural and urban area High School students in their self acceptance.
12. There is no significant difference between rural and urban area High School students in their locus of control.
13. There is a significant difference between English and Tamil Medium of High School students in their self acceptance.
14. There is a significant difference between English and Tamil Medium of High School students in their locus of control.
15. There is a significant relationship of self acceptance and locus of control among High School students.

TOOLS AND MATERIALS USED

To test the hypothesis, two inventories were used for the present investigation viz., Self Acceptance inventory and Locus of control inventory.

THE SELF ACCEPTANCE INVENTORY

The Self Acceptance inventory constructed and standardised by Dr.Kakkar (Patiala, 1984) was used in this study. It consists of 34 statements with positive and negative statements. The nature of items of Self Acceptance Inventory has been presented below.

ADMINISTRATION

The following instructions were given to the students before administrating the inventory. The purpose of this questionnaire is to detect the type of Self Acceptance students have about themselves. There are 34 items in the questionnaire. The subjects were asked to read each statement carefully and respond by putting a tick on "True" column. If it is not applicable, put tick (x) on "False" column.

Table 2.1. Showing the nature of the items of self acceptance inventory

S.No	Nature of item	Item number
1.	True	3,6,9,11,13,15,16,19,22,23,24, 25,28,30,33,34
2.	False	1,2,4,5,7,8,10,12,14,17,18,20,21,26,27

SCORING

For one correct answer, one score is provided according to key. Scoring through a template is also possible where circles which show through the template are counted and the total entered in the proper cell of the last page is treated as raw score.

LOCUS OF CONTROL INVENTORY

The Locus of Control Inventory constructed and standardised by Stephen Nowicki and Strickland in 1973 was used in this study. It consists of 40 statements. The nature of items of Locus of Control has been presented below.

Table 2.2. Showing the nature of the items of locus of control inventory

S.No.	Nature of item	Item number
1.	Yes	1,3,5,7,8,10,11,12,14,16,17,18,19,21, 23,24,27,29,31,33,35,36,37,39
2.	No	2,4,6,9,13,15,20,22,25,26,28, 30,32,34,38,40

ADMINISTRATION

The following instructions were given to the students before administrating the inventory. The purpose of this questionnaire is to detect the type of Locus of Control students have about themselves. There are 40 items in the questionnaire. The subjects were asked to read each statement carefully and respond by putting a tick on "Yes" or "No" in all the responses.

SCORING

For one correct answer, one score is provided according to the key. The total number of agreements between the answers and the ones on the key is a raw score.

PILOT STUDY

A pilot study was conducted to assess the reliability of the tools. Pilot study also helped in understanding the difficulties faced by the subject in answering the questionnaires. The pilot study was conducted on 50 students to assess the reliability and validity.

RELIABILITY OF THE TOOLS

The reliability coefficient of the self acceptance inventory has been computed by using the odd even method. The reliability coefficient was computed by spearman brown formula. Obtaining a value of 0.747 indicating, that the tool was highly reliable.

The reliability coefficient of the Locus of Control has been computed by using the odd even method. The reliability coefficient was computed by Spearman Brown formula obtaining a value of 0.866 indicating, that the tool was highly reliable.

VALIDITY OF THE TOOLS

The validity of the score was calculated by taking the square root of reliability. In the case of Self Acceptance inventory it is found to be 0.864, also suggesting that tool is valid. In the case of Locus of Control inventory it is found to be 0.93 indicating that the tool is valid.

SAMPLE

A stratified random sampling technique was adopted for the selection of sample. The school selected for this study is divided into different strata, namely Government, Aided and Private schools. 300 students were taken for the study.100 students were drawn from Government schools, 100 from Aided schools and 100 from Private schools.

Table 2.3. Showing the Composition of the Sample Selected for the Study of Gender, Type of School, Medium of Instruction and Locality of School.

S.No	Name of the School	Gender		Type of School			Medium		Locality of School	
		Boys	Girls	Govt	Aided	Private	English	Tamil	Urban	Rural
1.	Govt. welfare boys Hr. Sec school, Sevvapet.	47		47				47		47
2.	Govt. welfare girls Hr. Sec school , Sevvapet		53	53				53		53
3.	Siddhartha Matriculation school, Sevvapet	34	16			50	50			50
4.	Gnana vidyalaya matric school, Tiruvallur	12	38			50	50		50	
5.	Goudie Hr. Sec school, Tiruvallur	77	23		100		50	50	50	50
Total		170	130	100	100	100	150	150	100	200

MAIN STUDY

Permission was sought from the respective heads of the institution and explanation was given regarding the purpose and nature of the study. After having fixed the day and time for the distribution of questionnaire, the investigator administered the questionnaire to the sample of students selected standard VIII, IX and X.

The students were gathered in a classroom and the purpose of the investigation was explained to them. The nature of the questions and the method of answering were explained. Total confidentiality of views was assured in a bid to stimulate the students to answer freely. They were made to feel one with the purpose of the investigation. More instructions were given on the first page of the questionnaire.

STATISTICAL TECHNIQUES

Suitable descriptive and inferential statistical techniques were used in the interpretation of the data to draw more meaningful pictures of results from the collected data. In the present study the following statistical techniques were used.

- Mean
- Standard Deviation.
- Critical Ratio.
- Analysis of Variance.
- Correlaton Coefficient.
- Quartile Deviation.

CONCLUSION

This chapter outlines the design of the present study, the procedure followed and the nature of the sample. It describes the hypothesis to be tested, the tools used and method of administration and scoring.

ANALYSIS AND INTERPRETATION OF THE DATA

Introduction

Analysis of data means studying the tabulated material in order to determine the facts or meanings. The data, after collection has to be processed and analysed in accordance with the outline laid down for the purpose at the time of developing the research plan. This is essential for a scientific study and for ensuring that we have all relevant data for making contemplated comparisons and analysis. After analyzing the data the researcher has to accomplish the task of drawing inferences followed by report writing.

ANALYSIS AND INTERPRETATION OF THE DATA

The data collected was subjected to statistical calculations and the hypothesis formulated have been verified.

1. Descriptive statistics to understand the nature of Self Acceptance and Locus of control.
2. 't' test to find out the significant difference of Self Acceptance with respect to location, medium of instruction, gender. And same for the other variable Locus of control.
3. ANOVA to find out the significance of difference for self acceptance and Locus of control with respect to age, type of school.
4. Correlation to find out the relationship between Self Acceptance and Locus of control.

HYPOTHESIS – I

The level of Self Acceptance among High School Student is Average.

Table 2.4. Shows the frequency and percentage for the variable self acceptance

Category	Range	Frequency	Percentage
Low self acceptance	Below 14	57	19%
Moderate self acceptance	From 14- 18	191	63.36%
High self acceptance	Above 18	52	17.3%

From the above table, it is clear that more number of students lie in the category of moderate self acceptance (63.36%). So the level of self acceptance among high school students is moderate in nature. Hence the above hypothesis is accepted.

The score is graphically represented in figure 2.1

HYPOTHESIS –II

The internal locus of Locus of Control is predominant among High School Student.

Table 2.5. Showing the frequency and percentage for the variable locus of control

Category	Range	Frequency	Percentage
Average locus of control	Below 22	27	9%
High locus of control	Above 22	273	91%

From the above table, it is clear that more number of students lie in the category of high locus of control. So the level of locus of control among high school students is external in nature. Hence the above hypothesis is rejected.

The score is graphically represented in figure 2.2.

HYPOTHESIS–III

There is a significant difference between boys and girls of High School students in their self Acceptance

Table 2.6. Significance of difference in the self acceptance mean scores of high school students based on their gender

Variable	Gender	N	Mean	SD	C.R	L.S
Self	Male	170	17.10	2.72	1.221	N.S
Acceptance	Female	130	16.68	3.12		

From the above table, C.R value (1.22) which is lesser than the table value (1.96). Hence there is no significant difference between the male and female students of high school on their self acceptance. Therefore the above hypothesis is rejected.

The score is graphically represented in figure 2.3

HYPOTHESIS–IV

There is a significant difference between boys and girls of High School students in their locus of control

Table 2.7. Significance of difference in the self acceptance mean scores of high school students based on their gender

Variable	Gender	N	Mean	SD	C.R	L.S
Locus of	Male	170	21.30	3.01	3,487	0.01
control	Female	130	20.05	3.13		

From the above table, C.R value (3.487) is greater than the table value (2.58). Hence there is a significant difference between the male and female students of high school on their self acceptance. Therefore the above hypothesis is accepted.

The mean scores are graphically represented in figure 2.4.

HYPOTHESIS–V

There is a significant difference between different ages among High School students in their self acceptance...

From the above table it is clear that self acceptance of high school students of different ages has significant difference. So it is considered for further analysis.

Table 2.8. Showing the significant difference of self acceptance with respect to their different ages among high school students

Variable		Sum of Squares	DF	Mean Squares	F value	L.S
Self Acceptance	Between groups	54.845	2	27.423	3.305	0.05
	Within groups	2466.071	297	8.303		
	Total	2520.917	299			

Table 2.9. Showing the significance difference of ages of high school students for self acceptance

VARIABLE	AGE	N	MEAN	SD	SEM	C.R value	L.S
Self acceptance	14 yrs	115	16.86	2.91	0.37	0.832	N.S
	15 yrs	117	16.54	2.95			
Self acceptance	15 yrs	117	16.54	2.95	0.426	2.629	0.01
	16 yrs	68	17.66	2.71			
Self acceptance	14 yrs	115	16.86	2.91	0.426	1.877	N.S
	16 yrs	68	17.66	2.71			

From the above table, the C.R value is found to be significant difference in the Self Acceptance of high school students with respect to 15 and 16 years of age. So in this group only the hypothesis is accepted. In other groups table value shows no significance. So the hypothesis is partially accepted.

These scores are graphically shown in figure 2.5.

HYPOTHESIS –VI

There is a significant difference between different ages among High School students in their locus of control.

The above table value reveals that the obtained 'f' value

is lesser than the table value indicating no significant difference of Locus of control with respect to ages. Hence the hypothesis is rejected.

Table 2.10. Showing the significant difference of locus of control with respect to their different ages among high school students

Variable		Sum of Squares	DF	Mean Squares	F value	L.S
Locus of control	Between groups	5.779	2	2.889	0.295	N.S
	Within groups	2904.941	297	9.781		
	Total	2910.917	299			

HYPOTHESIS–VII

There is a significant difference between the high School students studying in different management in their self acceptance.

Table 2.11. Showing the significant difference of self acceptance with respect to their type of management among high school students

Variable		Sum of Squares	DF	Mean Squares	F value	L.S
Self Acceptance	Between groups	30.427	2	15.213	1.814	N.S
	Within groups	2490.490	297	8.385		
	Total	2520.917	299			

The above table value reveals that the obtained 'f' value is lesser than the table value indicating that the type of schools has no significant difference of self acceptance. Hence the hypothesis is rejected.

HYPOTHESIS–VIII

There is a significant difference between the high School students studying in different management in their locus of control.

Table 2.12. Showing the significant difference of locus of control with respect to their type of management among high school students

Variable		Sum of Squares	DF	Mean Squares	F value	L.S
Locus of control	Between groups	66.140	2	33.070	3.453	0.05
	Within groups	2844.580	297	9.578		
	Total	2910.720	299			

From the above table value it is clear that type of schools has significant difference in Locus of control of high school students. So it is considered for further analysis.

Table 2.13. Showing the significance difference between different types of management with respect to locus of control among high school students

Variable	Type of School	N	Mean	SD	SEM value	C.R.	L.S.
Locus of control	Private	100	20.77	3.83	0.478	1.17	N.S
	Aided	100	21.33	2.87			
Locus of control	Aided	100	21.33	2.87	0.374	3.06	0.01
	Govt	100	20.18	2.41			
Locus of control	Private	100	20.77	3.83	0.451	1.30	N.S
	Govt	100	20.18	2.41			

From the above table, the C.R value is found to be significant indicating that there is significant difference in the Locus of control of high school students with respect to their Aided and Government schools. So in these groups only the hypothesis is accepted. In other groups table value shows no significance. So the hypothesis is partially accepted. The scores are graphically shown in figure 2.6.

HYPOTHESIS–IX

There is a significant difference between joint and nuclear family of High School students in their self Acceptance.

Table 2.14. Significance of difference between self acceptances means scores of high school students based on their type of family

Variable	Type of Family	N	Mean	SD	C.R.	L.S
Self Acceptance	Joint	139	16.83	2.23	0.47	N.S
	Nuclear	161	16.99	2.97		

From the above table, C.R value (0.47) is lesser than the table value (1.96). Hence there is no significant difference between the type of family of high school on their self acceptance. Therefore the above hypothesis is rejected.

The mean scores are graphically shown in figure 2.7.

HYPOTHESIS –X

There is a significant difference between joint and nuclear family of High School students in their locus of control.

Table 2.15. Significance of difference between locus of control mean scores of high school students based on their type of family

Variable	Type of Family	N	Mean	SD	C.R.	L.S
Locus of control	Joint	139	21.02	3.23	1.35	N.S
	Nuclear	161	20.53	3.02		

From the above table, C.R value (1.35) is lesser than the table value (1.96). Hence there is no significance difference between the types of family of high school on their locus of control. Therefore the above hypothesis is rejected.

The mean scores are graphically shown in figure 2.8.

HYPOTHESIS –XI

There is no significant difference between rural and urban area high School students in their self acceptance..

Table 2.16. Significance of difference between self acceptances means scores of high school students based on their location

Variable	Location	N	Mean	SD	C.R.	L.S
Self Acceptance	Rural	200	16.68	2.42	1.78	N.S
	Urban	100	17.40	3.66		

From the above table, C.R value (1.78) is lesser than the table value (1.96). Hence there is no significant difference between the self acceptance of high school students on the basis of location. Therefore the above hypothesis is accepted.

The above mean scores are shown graphically in figure 2.9

HYPOTHESIS –XII

There is no significant difference between rural and urban area High School students in their locus of control.

Table 2.17. Significance of difference between locus of control mean scores of high school students based on their location

Variable	Location	N	Mean	SD	C.R.	L.S
Locus of control	Rural	200	20.78	2.98	0.15	N.S
	Urban	100	20.72	3.40		

From the above table, C.R value (0.15) is lesser than the table value (1.96). Hence there is no significance difference between the locus of control of high school students on the basis of their location. Therefore the above hypothesis is accepted.

The mean scores are graphically represented in figure 2.10

HYPOTHESIS–XIII

There is a significant difference between English and Tamil Medium of High School students in their self acceptance.

Table 2.18. Significance of difference between self acceptance mean scores of high school students based on their medium of instruction

Variable	Medium	N	Mean	SD	C.R.	L.S
Self Acceptance	Tamil	150	16.48	2.26	2.62	0.01
	English	150	17.35	3.38		

From the above table, C.R value (2.62) is greater than the table value (2.58) at 0.01 level. Hence there is a significant difference between the English and Tamil medium high school students on their Self acceptance mean scores, English medium scores (17.35) being higher than Tamil medium scores (16.48). Therefore the above hypothesis is accepted.

The scores are graphically represented in figure 2.11

HYPOTHESIS –XIV

There is a significant difference between English and Tamil Medium of High School students in their locus of control.

Table 2.19. Significance of difference between locus of control mean scores of high school students based on their medium of instruction

Variable	Medium	N	Mean	SD	C.R.	L.S
Locus of control	Tamil	150	20.40	2.65	2.008	0.05
	English	150	21.12	3.50		

From the above table, C.R value (2.008) is greater than the table value (1.96) at 0.05 level. Hence there is a significance difference between the English and Tamil medium high school students on their Locus of control mean scores. Therefore the above hypothesis is accepted.

The scores are graphically shown in figure 2.12.

HYPOTHESIS-XV

There is a significant relationship of self acceptance and locus of control among High School students.

Table 2.20. Shows the correlation between self acceptance and locus of control among high school students

Variable	N	Correlation Coefficient	L.S
Self acceptance Locus of control	300	–0.0241	N.S

The above table shows that there is no significant relationship between self acceptance and locus of control. Hence the above hypothesis is rejected.

CONCLUSION

The above analysis clearly shows that there is no significant relationship between the self acceptance and locus of control. The analysis and interpretation of data represent the application of deductive and inductive logic to the research process. The data are often classified by division into subgroups and then analyzed and synthesized in such a way that hypothesis may be verified or rejected. The final result may be a new principle of generalisation. Like interpretation of results, the formulation of conclusion and generalisations also demands keen observations, wide look and power of logical thinking.A brief report of the present research study together with major findings and conclusions has been presented in the succeeding chapter.

SUMMARY, FINDINGS AND CONCLUSION

In this chapter we have tried to assimilate, what we have done so far in the previous chapter by reinstating the statement of the problem, tools used for investigation, about the samples and finally presenting the major findings of the study. In the light of the major findings some useful recommendations for improvements and suggestions for research are proposed.

STATEMENT OF THE PROBLEM

Self acceptance and locus of control among high school students in Tiruvallur district.

OBJECTIVES OF THE STUDY

1. To study the level of self acceptance among High School students.
2. To Study the level of locus of control among High School students
3. To find out the significant difference between boys and girls of High School students in their self Acceptance.
4. To find out the significant difference between boys and girls of High School students in their locus of control.
5. To find out the significant difference between different ages among High School students in their self acceptance.
6. To find out the significant difference between different ages among High School students in their locus of control.
7. To find out the significant difference between the high School students studying in different management in their self acceptance.
8. To find out the significant difference between the high School students studying in different management in their locus of control.
9. To find out the significant difference between joint and nuclear family of High School students in their self Acceptance.
10. To find out the significant difference between joint and nuclear family of High School students in their locus of control.

11. To find out the significant difference between rural and urban area High School students in their self acceptance.
12. To find out the significant difference between rural and urban area High School students in their locus of control.
13. To find out the significant difference between English and Tamil Medium of High School students in their self acceptance.
14. To find out the significant difference between English and Tamil Medium of High School students in their locus of control.
15. To find out the Significant Relationship of Self Acceptance and Locus of Control among High School students.

HYPOTHESIS OF THE STUDY

1. The level of Self Acceptance among High School Student is Average.
2. The internal Locus of Control is predominant among High School Student.
3. There is a significant difference between boys and girls of High School students in their self Acceptance.
4. There is a significant difference between boys and girls of High School students in their locus of control.
5. There is a significant difference between different ages among High School students in their self acceptance.
6. There is a significant difference between different ages among High School students in their locus of control.
7. There is a significant difference between the high School students studying in different management in their self acceptance.
8. There is a significant difference between the high School students studying in different management in their locus of control.

9. There is a significant difference between joint and nuclear family of High School students in their self Acceptance.
10. There is a significant difference between joint and nuclear family of High School students in their locus of control.
11. There is no significant difference between rural and urban area High School students in their self acceptance.
12. There is no significant difference between rural and urban area High School students in their locus of control.
13. There is a significant difference between English and Tamil Medium of High School students in their self acceptance.
14. There is a significant difference between English and Tamil Medium of High School students in their locus of control.
15. There is a significant relationship of self acceptance and locus of control among High School students.

SAMPLE

The present study is concerned with High School Students. Random Sampling technique is used among the Government, Aided and Private Schools in Tiruvallur district. The investigator selected randomly two Government School, Two Private School and one Aided School. The sample composes of 300 High School students.

TOOLS USED

The following tools and techniques were used:

1. Self acceptance inventory. (Dr.Kakkar ,Patiala, 1984).
2. Locus of control inventory. (Dr.Stephen Nowicki, Jr., and Dr.Strickland in 1973).

MAJOR FINDINGS

1. It is found that the levels of self acceptance among High School students are average in nature.
2. It is found that the level of locus of control is high (external) in nature.
3. It is found that boys and girls of High School students have no significant difference in their self acceptance.
4. It is found that boys and girls of High School students have significant difference in their locus of control.
5. It is found that the different ages of High School students has significant difference in their self acceptance.
6. It is found that the different ages of High School students has no significant difference in their Locus of control.
7. It is found that the type of school of High School students has no significant difference in their self acceptance.
8. It is found that type of schools of high school students has significant difference in their locus control.
9. It is found that type of family of High School students has no significant difference in their self acceptance.
10. It is found that type of family of High School students has no significant difference in their local of control.
11. It is found that the locality of High School students has no significant difference in their self acceptance.
12. It is found that locality makes no significant difference in their locus of control
13. It is found that the medium of instruction of High School students has significant difference in their self acceptance.
14. It is found that the medium of instruction of High School students has significant difference in their locus of control.

15. It is found that self acceptance and locus control of High School students correlation is not significant.

EDUCATIONAL IMPLICATIONS

In the educational scenario it is found that the High School parts of education in the schools are very significant milestone of a student. This is due to some psychological aspects like emotional, mental, physical changes of High School students. This change gives or paves the way for various problems. During the adolescent stage the students normally find it difficult to adjust with home, school, peer and social setting. They normally possess on unstable self-acceptance. Since the self acceptance is a personality variable the high school students must possess this in their behaviour.

This study in self acceptance and locus of control of High School students will throw more light on the impact of self acceptance and locus of control in relation to their education. If the self acceptance is high locus of control also would be better and thus it is found that the students also learn and perform better in their school subjects. Further the students are well adjusted to the school and also develop good habits.

SUGGESTION FOR FURTHER RESEARCH

Some suggestions with regard to possibilities of the record in the field of education are offered with a view to stimulate prospective research works in this area. These are as follows:

1. Self-acceptance in relation to personality and different kinds of adjustment behaviour such as personal adjustment, social adjustment etc., can be studied among High School students.
2. A study of self-acceptance and locus of control among the college students.
3. A study of self-acceptance and academic achievement could be conducted among higher secondary students.
4. A study of locus control and personality could be conducted among college students.
5. A study of self-acceptance and leadership behaviour of college students.

CONCLUSION

Self-acceptance plays a vital role in every human being. Self-acceptance requires consistency, stability, and tends to resist change. If self-acceptance changed readily, the individual would lack a consistent and dependable personality. Man is a social being thus self-acceptance helps him to understand the self and what other thinks about himself. When there is an available in self-acceptance it may tend to lead the locus of control. So they help man to live smoothly and at peace with one another. If the locus of control is not good then the person cannot live freely in the society especially in the present fast developing world. So it is extremely necessary to develop high self acceptance, which is turn, would positively complements locus of control.

REFERENCES

1. Arora R.K.,(1981), "*An investigation into the problems of study in professional courses of medicine law, engineering and education in relation to personality factors*", Third survey of Research in Education, National Council of Educational Research and Training, p. 105.
2. Ayersman,-David-J. (1992), "*Effect of a Summer Enrichment Program for At-Risk Youths on Locus of Control and the Relation to Motivational Orientation*".
3. Baker, Eugene M. (1977), "*Psychological Education to enhance Self Understanding and Self Acceptance in college students*", http://WWW.spd.org/sdp/diss.
4. Brill, Ronala R., "*Dealing with the hazards of adolescence*',http://www.emotionalhonesty.com/arthazadoles.html.
5. Bharadwaj .R (1998), "*Perceived parenting of rejection – Acceptance and adolescents value conflicts*", Indian psychological review, Vol L1 special issue p. 256
6. Bernhard,-Judith-K.; Siegel,-Linda-S. (1995) , "*Increasing Internal Locus of Control for a Disadvantaged Group: A Computer Intervention*".Journal: Computers-in-the-Schools; V. 11 N. 1, p. 59-77 1994

7. Chromic Daria, Theresa (1996), "*The American Dream and Self advocacy for students with learning disabilities*", Theory : Curriculum and Learner outcome, Dissertation Abstracts International DAI-A 57/08, p. 3455.
8. Chaube S.D, (1981), "*Adolescent Psychology*", M/S Vikas Publishing house, New Delhi.
9. Furnham, A. and Henry, J. (1980). Cross-cultural locus of control studies: experiment and critique. Psychological Reports, 47, 23-29.
10. Freud, S. (1900). *The interpretation of dreams. In the complete psychological works of Sigmund Freud.* London: The Hogarth Press, 1962.
11. Fraley,-Stephen-E. (1992) From, "*Self-Blame to Self-Acceptance: Freeing Myself in a Prison Undergraduate Program*". Journal-of-Correctional-Education; V. 43 N. 4, p. 178-81 Dec 1992.
12. Frederick, Veedine j (1997), "*The relationship among acceptance of a learning disability, grade level of diagnosis and achievements of students with learning disabilities*", Dissertation abstract international, DAI –A 58/05, p. 3083.
13. Garrison, Albert j, and Kingston (1976), Educational psychology, Bombay : Vakils, Feffer and Simons pvt. Ltd., p. 448
14. Hurley, John R. (1990), "*Constructive thinking and elevated of self in interpersonal groups*", Journal of Psychology Vol. CXXIIV, No. 5, pp. 563-575.
15. Jersild Arthur, (1963), "*The Psychology of Adolescence*", New York, T. Macmillan company, p. 63.
16. Kao, G. and Thompson, J. S. (2003). Racial and ethnic stratification in educational achievement and attainment. In K.S. Cook and J. Hagan (Eds.), Annual Review of Sociology (Vol.29, pp. 417-442). Palo Alto, CA: Annual Reviews.
17. Krampen, G. and Weiberg, H. (1981). Three aspects of locus of control in German, American, and Japanese university students. Journal of Social Psychology, 113, 133-134.
18. Lynch, Shirley; Hurford, David P.; and Cole, AmyKay. (2002) *Parental Enabling Attitudes and Locus of Control*

of At-Risk and Honors Students. Adolescence, 37(147) 527-549.

19. Levon, Dirk (2001), "*Self Acceptance, Ace up your sleeve*", http://www.masermuse.com/columistsreylogs/archives/00000056.
20. Rotter, J.B. (1954). Social learning and clinical psychology. Englewood Cliffs, NJ: Prentice Hall.
21. Rotter, J. B. (1966). Generalized expectancies for internal versus external control of reinforcement. Psychological Monographs: General and Applied, 80 (1, Whole No. 609).
22. Rogers, C. R. (1947). Some observations on the organization of personality. American Psychologist, 2, 358-368
23. Randolph,-Elizabeth (1993), "*Developing Self-Awareness and Self-Acceptance in Emotionally Handicapped Students through the Bibliotherapeutic Process*".
24. Reeh,-H.-Elise; Reilly,-Karen-J. (1995), "*A Quasi Meta Analysis of the Health Locus of Control Construct*".
25. Shelton, T. L., Anastopoulos, A. D., & Linden, J. D. (1985). An attribution training program with learning disabled children. Journal of Learning Disabilities, 18, 261-265
26. Sim T.N (2003), "The father – adolescent relationship in the context of the Mother – adolescent relationship, exploring moderating linkages in the late adolescent sample in Singapore", Journal of Adolescent Research,Vol XVIII, No. 4, pp. 383-403
27. Sisco, Sharon S. (1992), "Goal Setting To Enhance Self Esteem and Create an Internal Locus of Control in the At Risk Elementary Student".
28. Sheerer, Elizabeth (1949), "An analysis of the relationship between acceptance and respect for theself acceptance of and respect for others in ten counseling cases", Journal of counseling psychology, Volume XIII, pp. 169-175.
29. Sisco,-Sharon-S. (1992), "*Using Goal Setting To Enhance Self Esteem and Create an Internal Locus of Control in the At Risk Elementary Student*".
30. Sunanda Y (1991), *A study of reactions to frustration as related to life Satisfactions and self acceptance among the aged*, Ph.D Sri Venkateswara university IV survey, II p. 977.

31. Santa-Rita,-Emilio (1995), "*The Effect of Computer-Assisted Student Development Programs on Entering Freshman Locus of Control Orientation*". CS: Bronx Community Coll., NY. Dept. of Student Development.

32. Starn Richard Lic (1993), "*Californial Psychological inventory profiles of male adolescents with learning disabilities*", A comparison with norm group scores dissertation abstracts international DAI–A 54/04, p. 296.

33. Statman,-Daniel (1993), "*Self-Assessment, Self-Esteem, and Self-Acceptance*". Journal-of-Moral-Education; V. 22 N. 1, p. 55-62 1993.

34. Thompson,-Josephine-T. (1991), "*Establishing Locus of Control among Ninth Graders: Using Peer Mentors To Reduce Student Disengagement, Absenteeism and Failures*".

35. Thielker, V. *et al. The relationship between positive reinforcement and locus of control.* [Electronic version]. Retrieved December 5, 2004, from.

36. Tyler,-Doris-Kennedy; Vasu,-Ellen-Storey (1995), "*Locus of Control, Self-Esteem, Achievement Motivation, and Problem-Solving Ability: LogoWriter and Simulations in the Fifth-Grade Classroom*". Journal-of-Research-on-Computing-in-Education; V. 28 N. 1, p. 98-120.

37. Waheeda M (1998), "*Behavioral Training in improving personality characteristics of Juvenile delinquents in relation to Self Acceptance*", M.Phil Thesis in Psychology, Madras University, p. 63.

38. Whitney,-Patricia (1991), "*Children's Locus of Control and Intrinsically Motivated Reading*".

CHAPTER 3

Relationship between Social Intelligence and Life Satisfaction

THE PROBLEM AND ITS PERSPECTIVE

There is no duty we so much underrate as the duty of being happy. By being happy, we sow enormous benefits upon the world. —Robert Louis Stevenson

INTRODUCTION

People who are more satisfied by their lives tend to experience greater physical and psychological health than people who are less satisfied with their lives. From an economic point of view, it is important to know what causes people to be satisfied with their lives. From a psychological perspective, life satisfaction is an important theoretical concept to be understood.

What leads satisfaction with the life? According to the various hypothesis framed, people who have fewer life commitments and demand experiences greater life satisfaction. thus the person who relaxes on the beach is more satisfied with life than the hurried one but on the other hand, the busy, and involvement in the work creates a satisfied with life. (Bailey and Miller (1998)).

Factors that influence life satisfaction are the availability of social support, personal traits, self esteem, physical health, financial resources, a sense of connectedness, and locus of control. Several studies have explained the relationship between social support and life satisfaction. Most of the literature has indicated that there is positive relationships exist between social support and life satisfaction.

Life satisfaction has been related to job satisfaction, interpersonal relationship, socio economic status, education, family background and many other variables. All these relationships indicate that life satisfaction is a multidimensional concept. There are various resources found the relationship between life satisfaction and life involvement among the variety of population.

According to Cutrona and Altmair (1996) low education and socio economic levels and poor physical health with few social supports have low life satisfaction.

WHAT IS SOCIAL INTELLIGENCE?

Various individuals are using learned social skills to improve the quality of the life and relationships. Most of human psychological problems were associated with the society. The psychological problems like depression, fear, confusion, anger created by the lack of positive human emotions are critical to the happiness of the individual in the society. So social intelligence is created to bring the skills in to the world of human interaction and relations.

According to E.L. Thorndike (1920) the term intelligence refer the person's ability to understand and manage the people and also engage in adoptation in social interaction. It also refers the individuals fund of knowledge about the social word (Kihlstrom 1987).

Social intelligence is the ability to understand and manage men and women boys and girls and act wisely with human relations "similarly, moss and Hunt (1927) defined social intelligence as the "ability to get along with others" Vernon (1933) defined social intelligence as the person's "ability to get along with people in general ability to handle.

Social intelligence is highly combined with the personal and social competence and this is vital for healthy and productive life. Such intelligence is comprised of social competence, social awareness, and social skills. But these are very difficult measuring and various related researchers are proving that there is a direct relationship exist between these skills and the productivity of life (Emmerling 1999)

DEFINITIONS OF SOCIAL INTELLIGENCE

According to Howard Gardener (1983) Social Intelligence is the capacity to know oneself and to know others is on inalienable a part of the human condition as it is the capacity' to know objects of sounds and it deserves to be investigated not less than these other "less charged" forms.

Vernon (1933) : Provided the most wide-ranging definition of social intelligence as the person's "abilities to get along with people in general, social technique or ease in society, knowledge of social matters, susceptibility to stimuli from other members of a group, as well as insight into the temporary moods and underlying personality traits of strangers.

IMPORTANCE OF SOCIAL INTELLIGENCE

Social intelligence is at the heart of human happiness and emotional comfort. Symptoms of poor social intelligence skills that impact people and organisations include.

1. Half-heartedly listening to others, engaging in mostly surface conversations.
2. Low morale in the workplace.
3. Quickly judging others with no factual basis, often in a critical or demeaning manner.
4. Complaints of racism, sexism, and a hostile work environment.
5. Finding it hard to say "no" to others, even when they may be taking advantage of you.
6. High employee turnover and absenteeism.

NEEDS OF SOCIAL INTELLIGENCE

Anyone can benefit from social intelligence training and it has been especially successful with the following groups:

1. People in high stress jobs.
2. Single or divorced men and women who would like to find and build a healthy relationship.
3. Senior and mid-level managers
4. Couples experiencing problems in their relationship they would like to better understand and resolve.
5. Workers in a regular contact with the public.
6. Married partners who would like to achieve higher levels of intimacy with one another
7. Organisational trainers and instructors.

Social intelligence training is skills-based, not theoretical. The material is brought to life by skilled trainers who demonstrate problems and illustrate solutions that work in the everyday world.

FACTORS OF SOCIAL INTELLIGENCE

Patience, co-operative ness, confidence level, sensitivity, recognition of social environment, tactfulness, sense of humour, memory.

(*a*) Patient - calm endurance under stressful situations,

(*b*) Co-operativeness - ability to interact with others in a pleasant way to be able to view matters from all angles.

(*c*) Confidence level - firm trust in one self and one's chances,

(*d*) Sensitivity-to be acutely aware of and responsive,

(*e*) Recognition of social environment - ability to perceive the nature and atmosphere of the existing situation.

(*f*) Tactfulness - delicate perception of the right thing to say or do.

(*g*) Sense of humour - capacity to feel and cause amusement to be able to see the lighter side of life,

(*h*) Memory - ability to remember all relevant issues; names and faces of people.

LIFE-SATISFACTION AND STUDENTS

Life satisfaction has been related to job satisfaction, interpersonal relationships, socio economic status, education, family background, and many other variables. All these relationships indicate that life satisfaction is a multidimensional concept. Bailey and Miller (1998) explored the relationship between college student life satisfaction and life involvement.

What leads students to be satisfied with their lives? According to the scarcity hypothesis of life satisfaction, people who have fewer life commitments and demands should experience greater life satisfaction. Thus, the student who relaxes on the beach is more satisfied with life than the harried student involved in volunteer organisations, campus government, and the honor society. On the other hand, according to the expansion hypothesis, the busy, student with involvement in the work is more satisfied with life.

EMOTIONS AND LIFE-SATISFACTION

Depression, positive emotions and cheerfulness are the personality traits that most influence life satisfaction, which was reported Canadian psychology professor Ulrich Schemas of the University of Toronto, and colleagues.

The findings come from four studies and included data from surveys of 136 students at the University of Toronto, the University of Illinois at Urbana-Champaign, and the University of California, Riverside.

The students completed surveys about their personalities and life satisfaction. To get another perspective, the students asked their peers and family members to answer the same questions about the participants' life satisfaction.

Participants rated their life satisfaction and personalities by responding to statements such as, "I tend to be in a good mood", "I tend to be a cheerful and high-spirited person," "I tend to feel hopeless", and "I tend to feel discouraged."

It probably won't surprise many people that depression hinders life satisfaction, positive emotions and cheerfulness. But you might not have guessed just how powerful depression and cheerfulness are predicting life satisfaction. In other words, a sunny personality can predict your life satisfaction better than a full social calendar. And depression kills satisfaction more than other grim traits such as anxiety or anger. 'Wouldn't our intuitions predict that somebody who is disposed to experience more depression, anxiety, and anger has lower life satisfaction than somebody who is only disposed to experience more depression?" ask the researchers.

INDIVIDUAL DIFFERENCES AND LIFE SATISFACTION

The notion of individual differences in the inclination to engage in thoughtful activity was proposed early in the history of social psychology and was developed most distinctly through empirical studies on the need for cognition, initially defined by Cohen, Stotland and Wolfe (1955) as a need to understand and make reasonable the experimental world. More recently, Cacioppo and Petty (1982) described the need for cognition as individual differences in the tendency to engage in and enjoy effortful cognitive activity. Individuals high in the need for cognition are highly intrinsically motivated towards thinking, exhibiting a strong tendency to enjoy complex cognitive tasks. Individuals low in the need for cognition are described as "cognitive misers" (Taylor, 1981) who have to be motivated to expend energy on cognitive activities. Cacioppo and Petty (1982) developed a 34-item Need for Cognition Scale (NCS), which was reduced to an 18-item scale (Cacioppo, Petty, and Kao, 1984) in order to increase its administrative efficiency.

Campbell (1981) stated, "The literary image of the crotchety old person, dissatisfied with everything, is not a very realistic picture of older people" (p.203). This pleasant finding may be due to older people being healthier and staying involved in more life domains compared to past reduced to an 18-item scale (Cacioppo, Petty, and Kao, 1984) in order to increase its administrative efficiency.

The lack of significant decrease in life satisfaction across the life span suggests people's ability to adapt to their conditions. Declines in income and marriage occur across age cohorts in later adulthood, yet, life satisfaction is stable. Some researchers have suggested that these findings serve as evidence that people readjust their goals as they age (Campbell et al., 1976; Rapkin & Fischer, 1992). Continuing with this line of thinking, Ryff (1991) found that older adults, compared with younger people, demonstrate a closer fit between ideal and actual self-perceptions. Brandtstadter and Renner (1990) believe that overcoming adversities is performed either by changing life circumstances to personal preferences (assimilative coping) or by adjusting personal preferences and goals to given situational constraints (accommodative coping) Judging self well-being depends on life satisfaction, satisfaction with important life areas (for instance, work), experiencing many pleasant emotions and moods, and low levels of unpleasant emotional experiences. Once people achieve certain materialistic needs, they become more concerned with self-fulfillment.

RELATIONSHIP BETWEEN SOCIAL INTELLIGENCE AND LIFE SATISFACTION

Human society as we know it could not exist without minds and selves, since all its most characteristic features presuppose the possession of minds and selves by its individual members; but its individual members would not possess minds and selves if these had not arisen within or emerged out of the human social process in its lower stages of development-those stages at which it was merely a resultant of, and wholly dependent upon, the physiological differentiations and demands of the individual organisms implicated in it. There must have been such lower stages of the human social process, not only for physiological reasons, but also (if our social theory of the origin and nature of minds and selves is correct) for minds and selves. Consciousness and intelligence, could not otherwise have emerged; because, that is, some sort of an ongoing social process in which human beings were implicated.

NEED FOR THE STUDY

Socially intelligent people are more likely to succeed in everything they undertake in their life. Unlike what is claimed of I.Q. we can teach and improve in children and in any individual, some crucial social competencies, paying the way for increasing their social intelligence and thus making their life more healthy, enjoyable, successful and satisfied in the coming days. The concept of social intelligence is to be applauded, not because it is totally new, but because it captures the essence of what our children or all of us need to know for living a productive, happy and satisfied life.

Social intelligence as an important factor to get satisfaction in life. Sternberg identified three broad constellations of behaviour which his American interviewers perceived as being intelligent.

1. Practical problem - solving ability; 'keeps our open mind; 'responds thoughtfully to others ideas;
2. Verbal ability; speaks clearly and articulately'; 'is knowledgeable about a field'.
3. Social competence: 'admits mistakes; displays interest in the world at large; 'thinks before speaking and doing'.

Hence the investigator would like to see, if there is a relation between life satisfaction and social intelligence of higher secondary students. The knowledge of the relationship between these variables under the study would help teachers, parents and students to make the needed changes in the system of education.

SCOPE OF THE STUDY

A new concept, 'social intelligence' with its significance even more than one's general intelligence has emerged on the educational scene. It may be defined as one's unitary ability to know, feel and judge emotions in co-operation with a person's thinking process for behaving in a proper way, with the ultimate realisation of happiness in him and in others. In view of its wide significance from the individual as well as social angles, it becomes quite imperative that serious efforts should be made for its proper development, right from the early childhood among the human beings.

STATEMENT OF THE PROBLEM

Social intelligence and life satisfaction among higher secondary students was chosen as the topic for the present study. Government, Government aided and private schools were selected from tuticorin District to conduct the study. Data were collected from 300 students (150 boys and 150 girls). In order to test the hypothesis proposed, the investigator statistically analysed the collected data.

OBJECTIVES OF THE STUDY

- To relate life satisfaction with that of social intelligence.
- To find out the relationship between social intelligence with that of educational status of the parent in the case of total sample.
- To identify associations existing between educational status of the parents and life satisfaction of the total sample.
- To recognise the impact of type of family on social intelligence and life satisfaction of the total sample.
- To know the impact of Gender on type of school, social intelligence, life satisfaction and various factors of social intelligence.
- To interrelate various factors of social intelligence in the case govt., govt. aided and private school students.

DELIMITATIONS OF THE STUDY

Even though every attempt was made to make the study as precise as possible, certain following limitations have to consider in this study.

- Since the study has been conducted as part of the course, the investigator has to complete it with in the time limitation and also he decided to collect sample randomly in a particular area only, namely Tuticorin District.
- This study has been restricted only to the higher secondary students in government, government aided and private schools.
- Samples were collected partly from urban and partly from rural areas. This study was taken to 300 samples.
- The investigator has taken into consideration only for two variables namely social intelligence and life satisfaction to conduct the proper way of research.

Inspire of these limitations, the investigator believes that the findings of the present study will be useful to classroom teachers and educator for developing new trends and approaches in the teaching learning process.

CONCLUSION

The first chapter chiefly concerned with the conceptual frame work of the problem chosen for the study. The discussion on social intelligence and life satisfaction has been presented to highlight the connectional position with which this study has been planned and concluded.

REVIEW OF RELATED LITERATURE

The review of literature promotes a greater understanding of the problem and its crucial aspects. It also provides comparative data on the basis of which to evaluate and to interpret the significance of one's findings – Mouly (1964).

According to Good (1959) in order to be truly creative and original, one must read extensively and critically as a stimulus of thinking. Therefore careful study is carried out and is presented in this chapter under the following heads.

(*a*) Studies related to social intelligence.

(*b*) Studies related to life satisfaction.

STUDIES RELATED TO SOCIAL INTELLIGENCE

The study was under taken by **Buch M.B**. (1960) for assessing the social intelligence of individuals quantitatively and to study the effect of environmental factors as grades and occupational status on social intelligence. The subjects for the present study of social intelligence were selected on the basis of certain independent findings supported by the content analysis of the available tests of social intelligence. The sub tests included here were 1. judgement in social situations, 2. Memory for names and faces, 3. observation of human behaviour, 4. Recognition of the mental state of the speaker, 5. sense of humour, 6. social introduction.

Ray. T (1972) Aimed at developing a test in Bengali for the objective measurement of social intelligence. Final form of the test had eighty items distributed on six subjects corresponding to six different area of human behaviour namely, 1. Judgement of a social situation, 2. observation of human behaviour, 3. Recognition of mental status, 4. Memory for names and faces, 5. Appreciation of humour, 6. Adjustment.

On analyzing the various development trends in social behaviour. Social behaviour was studied in relation to physical, motor, personal language and intellectual development and participation in school activities by Devi C.L. (1975), frequency analysis was made for patterning social behaviour into three categories very high, average and low. Discriminating value between the two age groups was calculated for each aspects of social behaviour.

Singhai. S (1986) attempts to study the social interest and attitude of college students and to see how these attitudes will influence their future family organisation. It was found that the social interests and attitude of adolescent students were adequate, mature and stable. It was found that suitable environment influenced development of healthy social interest and attitude of students.

A study was done by **Gabrielsen, Eric** (1992) to examine the role of self monitoring in colleges. A self monitor is an individual who adopts a social orientation so that he / she can manage self presentation. Self monitors are likely to modify their academic choices fit social situations or others expectations. Data were collected using a four-part questionnaire that explored background, a self monitoring scale a personal freedom versus social conformity scale and a friendship scale. Results indicated that self monitoring played a role in selection of college major. However, data also indicated that the direct influence of close friends was not what most persuaded self monitors with regard to choice of major.

A comparative study was undertaken by **Boulon-Diaz, Frances** (1992) on school achievement of the following variables, intelligence, social class, early motor and language development, preschool experience, gender and composition of household. The subjects were 65 children of 9 to 11 years, in grades four to six, in Puerto Rican public schools. They were selected from the sample of 2,200 children used for children revised for the Puerto Rican population. The wise-R Puerto Rico was used to measure IQ.

Mathias, Jane. L (1992) conducted a study on social intelligence with 75 adolescents with mental retardation factor analysis measures of conceptual intelligence adaptive behaviour and social intelligence yielded a practice-interpersonal competence construct. The second study however failed to establish the criterion validity of this construct.

An investigation made by **Nettelbeck Tex** (1992) to define social intelligence, with a total of 125 adolescents with mental retardation, found high to very high inter rater reliability coefficients; moderate to very high internal reliabilities, and moderate to high test-retest reliabilities.

In an experimental study conducted by **michael, William. B**. (1993) on maximum likelihood, factor analysis determined how accurately each of several hypothesised combinations of first-order and higher order factors reflecting creativity in the social intelligent of 192 high school students described the co-variation in selected sub-matrixes from the total correlation matrix originally analysed.

Laosa, Luis. M (1995) studied that there is a resurgence of scientific and public interest and controversy centering on four interrelated themselves intelligence testing, racial, ethic and socio-economic differences in measured IQ, genetic and environment influences on abilities and the role of scientific research in social policy.

STUDIES RELATED TO LIFE SATISFACTION

A model of change in Organisational health to improve Quality of life

The paper attempts to develop an empirical model of relationship between organisational health and QOL. Organisational health has been conceptualised as a relatively but quasi-enduring state of physical, mental and social wellbeing of the organisation and not merely an absence of strike and lockout. A scale was developed to measure eleven attributes of organisational health. QOL refers to general wellbeing ness of employees. GHQ-12 was used to measure wellbeing ness of employees. Stratified random sampling was P followed to collect the data from the managers (n=82), supervisors (n=131) and rank and file workers (n=186) of two heavy engineering organisations in private and public sectors. Data were analysed in terms of multivariate statistics. It was found that each organisational health attribute was positively related with general health. Standardised partial regression analysis revealed that involvement, environmental awareness, creativity and physical health accounted for maximum variances of General health than the other attributes. [Dutta Roy, D. (1991)]

Awareness of external environment, environmental satisfaction and mental health [Chatterjee, A. & Dutta Roy, D (1991]

Samples (n = 400) of two heavy engineering organisations were interviewed with a structured questionnaire to study the relationship between two predictors-Awareness of external environment (EA), Environmental satisfaction (ES) and one predicted variable - mental health (MH). Results revealed more accountability of ES than EA to predict MH. However, EA alone failed to predict MH when ES was regressed from EA by standardised partial regression analysis. Possible explanations of the findings were discussed achievement motivation significant relationship existed between achievement motivation and teacher pupil relationship.

Organisational health and life satisfaction: A Path-analytic model

Organisational health and life satisfaction: A Path-analytic model Present study attempts to understand a causal relationship between perceived attributes of organisational health and life satisfaction as a whole. Eleven attributes of organisational health v/ere measured by organisational health scale developed by authors. Life satisfaction was measured by life satisfaction scale (Warr et al., 1979). Data were collected from 400 employees of two heavy engineering organisations in private and public sectors following stratified random sampling. Higher order partial correlation coefficient analysis suggests that each health attribute is casually related with life satisfaction. Path analytic model was proposed lastly to identify some of the strategic variables of organisational health to improve life satisfaction. (Dutta Roy, D. (1992)).

Work-Family conflict and Life satisfaction in female Graduate students: Testing mediating and moderating Hypothesis (Treistman, Dana Lynn, (2004)

Most of the research on work-family conflict has examined people working in the paid labour force while simultaneously juggling the roles of paid worker, partner, parent, and homemaker. There is limited research on female graduate students and their experiences of work-family conflict. The goals of the present study were to examine the relationship between work-family conflict (work-to-family conflict and family-to-work conflict) and global life satisfaction, the relationship between work-family conflict and domain-specific satisfactions (family satisfaction and work satisfaction), and the mediators and moderators of these relationships among a sample of female graduate students. Participants included 187 female graduate students. Both work-to-family conflict and family-to-work conflict were hypothesized to be negatively related to domain-specific and global life satisfactions variance to the prediction of achievement. The present experiments tell us that any relationship between motivation and achievement appears to depend on the person's knowledge about their current performance in the area of achievement being measured.

Life satisfaction for people with long-term mental illness

This study attempts to explore those factors and program elements leading to better overall life satisfaction for people with long-term mental illness. The research sample included 88 patients, coming from mental hospitals and a large residential home in Hong Kong. Quality of Life Interview, Perceived Social Support and Sense of Freedom were modified, developed and adopted for data collection purpose. Most of the studied sample suffered from schizophrenia and had been ill for more than twenty years. Results showed that three factors including: number of hospitalisation, perceived sense of freedom and social support could explain about one third of the variance in overall life satisfaction of research sample. Based on these findings, a quality of care model, which emphasis on preventing relapse & hospitalisation, enhancing sense of freedom and strengthening social support, has been proposed? This quality of care model is suitable for residential home care setting, which aims at promoting the quality of life for people with long-term mental illness.

The relationship between the need for cognition and life satisfaction

The relationship between the need for cognition and life satisfaction was explored among college students. The J8-item short Need for Cognition Scale (NCS; Cacioppo, Petty, & Kao, 1984] and the 5-item Satisfaction with Life Scale (SWLS; Diener, Emmons, Larsen, & Griffin, 1985) were administered to 157 undergraduate university students. Results of a correlation and stepwise multiple regression indicated that currently enrolled students high in the need for cognition expressed greater life satisfaction than students low in the need for cognition. This study supports the hypothesis that the need for cognition is a predictor of life satisfaction among college students.

Successful Aging, Life Satisfaction, and Generativity in Later Life (1995)

Explores meanings for older people attach to successful aging and life satisfaction and to differentiate these concepts, Content analysis of an open ended survey confirmed five features of successful aging: interactions with others, a sense of purpose, self-acceptance, personal growth, and autonomy. Findings suggest generativist contributes to successful aging and remains a vital developmental task in later life. [Fisher – Bradley.J]

Family Resources and Adolescent Family Life Satisfaction in Remarried Family Households (1995)

Examines how family resources and demographic variables relate to adolescent family life satisfaction in remarried family households. Self-report questionnaire data were collected from 95 high school students in remarried families. Showed that flexibility, regularity in household time and routines, and effectiveness in parent communication were significantly related to overall adolescent satisfaction in remarried family households. [Henry, -Carolyn-S.; Lovelace, -Sandra-G.]

Life Satisfaction of Single Middle-Aged Professional Women

Questionnaires were administered to single professional women (n = 152) in higher education institutions. Performance on life satisfaction was significantly explained by recourse to the variables of job satisfaction, internal locus of control, regrets regarding life circumstances, sexual satisfaction, and leisure-time activities. [Lewis, -Virginia-G. ; Borders, -L.-DiAnne.(1995)]

The Effect of Parental Supportive Behaviours on Life Satisfaction of Adolescent Offspring

Explored effects of parental support on adolescents' life satisfaction in sample of 640 adolescent's ages 12 to 16. Three facts of parental support were identified and their effects on child satisfaction were examined. Intrinsic support was strongest predictor of life satisfaction. No differences based on gender of child or parents were found. [Young, -Margaret-H.(1995)]

Validity and Reliability of a Five Dimensional Life Satisfaction Index

The validity of the Five Dimensional Life Satisfaction Index was evaluated with 48 adults with moderate mental retardation. Results showed reliability of alternate forms and internal consistency, convergent and discriminant validity, and construct validity. [Hawkins, Barbara-A.(1995)]

Conjoint Analysis of the Students' Life Satisfaction Scale and the Piers-Harris Self-Concept Scale

Study investigated the relationships between a children's life satisfaction measure, the Students' Life Satisfaction Scale (SLSS), and a self-concept measure, the Piers-Harris Self-Concept Scale (PHSCS). Analysis demonstrated a strong relationship between the SLSS and one PHSCS subscale, providing support for the construct validity of the SLSS. (RJM) –[Huebner, -E. –Scott (1994)]

The Influence of Separation Orientation on Life Satisfaction in the Elderly

Findings from 154 older adults indicated that separation orientation helped explain differential impact of environmental factors on life satisfaction. Overly dependent subjects were more adversely affected by poor self-rated health and inadequate formal activity than balanced or overly self-sufficient participants. Presence of confidence was associated with higher life satisfaction for overly dependent participants. (Park,-Douglas; Vandenberg,-Brian [1994]).

Family System Characteristics, Parental Behaviours, and Adolescent Family Life Satisfaction

Describes investigation examining adolescents' perceptions of overall family system characteristics, parental behaviours, and demographic factors in relation to adolescent family life satisfaction. Results indicate family bonding, family flexibility, parental support, and adolescent age are positively related to adolescent family life satisfaction, but parental punitiveness is negatively related. [Henry, -Carolyn-S(1994)].

CONCLUSION

The study of related literature has helped the investigator to have a clear perspective of the problem chosen for the present investigation. The review of the related literature has enabled the investigator to formulate the relevant hypothesis for the present study. Based on this review, a suitable methodology and well planed procedure for the present study is adopted and it is explained in the succeeding chapter.

DESIGN OF THE STUDY AND METHOD OF INVESTIGATION

Introduction

This chapter explains the methods and procedures that are used in shaping and framing of hypothesis regarding the social intelligence and life satisfaction of higher secondary school students. This chapter deals with the hypothesis of the present study, tools and techniques used to collect data, validity and reliability of the tools, administration of the tools, pilot study, main study. Statistical techniques used etc.

STATEMENT OF THE PROBLEM

Social intelligence and life satisfaction among higher secondary school students was chosen as the topic for the present study. Government, Government Aided and Private Schools were selected to conduct the study. Data were collected from 300 students (150 boys and 150 girls). In order to test the hypothesis proposed, the investigator statistically analysed the data.

SAMPLE

Total 300 students were taken for the study of which 150 were boys and 150 were girls. The sample was drawn from six schools chosen randomly from higher secondary schools. Out of 300 sample 100 students from Government school, 100 students from Government Aided School and 100 students from Private schools were included.

DISTRIBUTION OF THE TOTAL SAMPLE

Table

Type of School	Name of the School	Boys	Girls	Total
Government	Arulmigu Muthumallai Amman	25	25	50
	Govt. Hr. Sec. School	25	25	50
Government Aided	Margoschis Hr. Sec. school.	50	-	50
	St. Marks Hr. Sec. School.	-	50	50
	James Memorial Matriculation Hr. Sec. School	25	25	50
Private	Anitha Kumaran Matriculation Hr. Sec. School.	25	25	50
	Total	150	150	300

OBJECTIVES

- To relate life satisfaction with that of social intelligence.
- To find out the relationship between social intelligence with that of educational status of the parent in the case of total sample.
- To identify associations existing between educational status of the parents and life satisfaction of the total sample.
- To recognise the impact of type of family on social intelligence and life satisfaction of the total sample.

- To know the impact of Gender on type of school, social intelligence, life satisfaction and various factors of social intelligence.
- To interrelate various factors of social intelligence in the case government, government aided and private school students.

HYPOTHESIS

1. Life satisfaction scores of the students will modify social intelligence.
2. Social intelligence has no impact on education status of the students.
3. Social intelligence does not depend on the type of family.
4. Life satisfaction does not depend on education status.
5. Life satisfaction has no impact with the type of family.
6. Gender plays on important role on life satisfaction of students
7. Gender plays on important role on total score of social intelligence.
8. Gender plays very important role on various factors of social intelligence.
9. Various factors of social intelligence are related to each other in government schools.
10. Different factors of social intelligence are related to each other in the case of government aided school.
11. Various factors of social intelligence are interrelated among themselves in private school.

TOOLS AND TECHNIQUES

To verify the framed hypothesis, the following tools and techniques were used in the present investigation.

1. Social intelligence scale by Dr. N.K. Chadha
2. Life Satisfaction Scale by Dr. Promila Singh.

SOCIAL INTELLIGENCE SCALE

Description

This test consists of 54 items and 12 eminent persons constructed by Dr.N.K. Chadha. This tool deals with 6 factors of social intelligence. They are patience, confidence, cooperativeness, sensitivity, sense of humour and recognition of social environment.

Administration

The social intelligence tool is constructed with simple sentences. The following instructions were given to the subjects before administrating the test. "There are some statements regarding the way in which we behave, feel and act. We want your first response. Please try to make your best possible answer honestly and sincerely. Read and understand each question properly and then put your mark on any cell against every statement on the answer sheet by making the sign of cross (X) please do not omit any question. In part-I read the following statements carefully and among the three responses given for each of them, pick up the one which seems to you to the most likely way in which you would respond.

You have to choose only one response from a, b and c, and mark a cross (X) on the appropriate cell on the answer - sheet. In part-II select the word that most accurately describes the mental state of the person making the statement. Cross out (X) the correct answer on the answer - sheet. In part-III there are some statements regarding the way you behave and act. Each statement has a forced choice response of either 'yes' or 'No', try and decide whether 'Yes' or 'No' represents your usual way of behaviour and acting. If yes, cross out (X) the cell below 'Yes' and if no, then cross out (X) the cell below 'No'. In part-IV list of incomplete jokes are given. Against them, there are three choices with which to complete the joke. You are to select and cross out (X) the choice you consider to be the most humorous. In part-V list of eminent persons are given.

Scoring Procedure

In the case of the first four dimensions (patience, cooperativeness, confidence and sensitivity) scores of 1, 2 and 3 were given to three response alternatives. For e.g., in the confidence dimension a score of 3 would indicate a high degree of confidence, a score of 1, a lack of confidence and a score of 2, would reveal moderate confidence. In the other two dimensions (sense of Humour and Recognition of Social Environment) one of three alternatives given is the appropriate response. This response when given was allotted of scores of 1. In the case of the 'Tactfulness' dimension the responses were in the form of 'Yes' or 'No'. The appropriate response was awarded a score of '1'. The last dimension that of Memory was scored '1' or '0' depending on whether or not the subject's response was 'right' or 'wrong'.

LIFE SATISFACTION SCALE

Description

This test consists of 35 items constructed by Dr. Mrs. Promila Singh. She construct a life satisfaction scale based on the following dimensions

(*a*) Taking Pleasure in everybody activities (b) considering life meaningful,

(*c*) holding a positive self-image, (*d*) having a happy and optimistic outlook, (*e*) feeling success in achieving goals. The present scale was constructed by considering the above five dimensions of life satisfaction.

Administration

This questionnaire consists of simple statement, which expresses the different way in which students think, feel and behaviour in their life situation. They were asked to indicate their responses for each statement by putting a tick (V) against any one of the five boxes always, often, sometimes, seldom and never and which are respectively scored as 5 4, 3, 2 and 1.

Scoring Procedure

The scale consists of 35 items each item is to be rated on the five-point scale always, often, sometimes, seldom and never and which are respectively scored as 5, 4, 3, 2 and 1 . The items relate to the individuals all-round activities and thus give a global picture of ones life satisfaction level. The higher the score on the life satisfaction scale for the higher will be the level of life satisfaction.

Interpreting the Score of Life Satisfaction

Table

Satisfaction level	Range of scores
High	136-175
Average	81-135
Low	35-80

PILOT STUDY

A pilot study was carried out to know suitability of the time required to administer the test of social intelligence and life satisfaction and to establish the reliability and validity of the tools. So students were selected for the pilot study. The tools were given based on data reliability and validity of the social intelligence questionnaire and life satisfaction questionnaire were calculated for the present study.

ESTABLISHING RELIABILITY AND VALIDITY OF THE TOOLS USED IN THE STUDY

Reliability of Social Intelligence Scale

In order to establish the reliability of the social intelligence scale, the split half method was used. The reliability of social intelligence scale was found to be 0.817. Hence social intelligence scale is considered as a reliable tool.

Validity of Social Intelligence Scale

The index of validity which is the square root of reliability was found to be 0.9. Hence social intelligence scale selection for the study was considered to have high validity.

Reliability of Life Satisfaction Scale

The test-retest reliability computed after a lapse of 8 weeks turned out to be 0.91.

Validity of Life Satisfaction Scale

To determine validity of the life satisfaction scale co-efficient of correlation between the scale of Alam and singh (1971) was computed and the co-efficient of correlation was found to be 0.83. The scale also possesses face and content validity since experts judged each item.

STATISTICAL TECHNIQUES

Suitable descriptive and inferential statistical techniques were used in the interpretation of the data to draw out a more meaningful picture of results from the collected data.

Life Satisfaction and total social intelligence scores were classified as low, moderate and high.

In the present study the following statistical measures were used.

1. Arithmetic Mean ($\overline{x}$)

Mean is the simplest measures of central tendency, which is calculated by adding all the scores and dividing the sum by the number of scores.

$$\text{Mean } (\overline{x}) = A + \overline{\left(\frac{\Sigma fd}{\Sigma f}\right)} \times 1$$

Where,

A = Assumed Mean

d = Deviation from the assumed mean.

f = Frequency

i = Class interval.

2. Standard Deviation ($\bar{x}$)

The standard deviation is defined as the square root of mean of the squares of the items taken from the arithmetic mean of the distribution.

$$= i\sqrt{\frac{\Sigma fd^2}{N} - \left(\frac{\Sigma fd}{N}\right)^2}$$

Where,

i = Class Interval

f = Frequency.

N = Total No. of Frequencies

d = Deviation.

3. Karl Pearson's Correlation Coefficient:

$$= \sqrt{\frac{N\Sigma dx\,dy - \Sigma dx \Sigma dy}{\{[N\Sigma dx^2 - (\Sigma dx)^2]\{[N\Sigma dy^2) - (\Sigma dy^2)\}}}$$

Where dx = Deviation of continuous values of the variable X from the assumed mean A.

dy = Deviation of continuous values of the variable Y from the assumed mean B.

N4 = Number of Pairs

Σdx = Summation of deviations of continuous values of the variable X.

Σdy = Summation of Deviations of continuous values of the variable Y.

Σdx^2 = Summation of the square of deviations of continuous values of the variable X.

Σdy^2 = Summation of the square of deviations of continuous values of the variable Y.

$\Sigma dxdy$ = Summation of the product of deviations of continuous values of variables X and Y.

4. Chi-Square test (χ^2)

$$\square = \frac{\Sigma(f_0 - f_e)^2}{f_e}$$

Here $$f_e = \frac{\text{Row Total} \times \text{Column Total}}{\text{Total Frequency}}$$

Where f_0 = Observed Frequency

f_e = Expected Frequency

Degrees of freedom = (row-1) (column-1)

5. '*t*' Test

(*a*) If mean and standard deviation are given the 't' value is calculated from the following formula.

$$\text{'}t\text{' value} = \frac{\bar{X}_1 - \bar{X}_2}{\text{S} \cdot \text{E}_M}$$

Here $$\text{S.EM} = \sqrt{\frac{\square_1^{\;2}}{n^1} + \frac{\square_2^{\;2}}{n^2}}$$

(*b*) If Correlation coefficient is given, the '*t*' value is calculated by using the following formula.

$$\text{'t' value} = \square\sqrt{\frac{(n-2)}{1-\square^2}}$$

Where, *n* is the total number of samples and *y* is the correlation coefficient.

If the number of group is 2 then degrees of freedom is equal to $(n_{1-1}) + (n_{2-1})$.

Where n_1 and n_2 are the no. of sample of group 1 and 2.

CONCLUSION

This chapter outlines the design of the present study, the procedure followed and the nature of the sample. It describes the hypothesis to be tested, the tools to be used and the methods of administration and scoring. The method of investigation designed was found to be quite appropriate and effective for the study.

methods of administration and scoring. The method of investigation designed was found to be quite appropriate and effective for the study.

ANALYSIS AND INTERPRETATION OF DATA

Introduction

This chapter highlights the analysis of the data obtained regarding the variables of the present study social intelligence and life satisfaction among higher secondary school students using appropriate techniques and verifying hypothesis framed for the present study. The findings were interpreted and discussed in the light of findings of other research studies.

HYPOTHESIS-1

Life satisfaction scores of the students will modify social intelligence.

Table 3.1. To correlate social intelligence with that of life satisfaction of boys & girls of Private School

Variables	Gender	No	Mean	S.D	'r'	't'	L.S
Socal intelligence & life satisfaction	Boys	50	99.1	9.26	0.279	2.013	0.05
			126.28	18.32			
	Girls	50	106.46	7.6	0.3339	2.5	0.01
			138.7	12.177			

The tables 3.1 to 3.3 and from Fig. E it is understood that the calculated 'r' values were greater than that of table 'r' values in the case of boys & girls of Private School and boys of Government School. So hypothesis was accepted in these cases and proved life satisfaction scores of the students modified social intelligence scores. Where as in the case of boys and girls of Government Aided School and girls of

Government School, the calculated 'r' values were less than that of table 'r' values. Hence hypothesis was rejected in these cases.

Table 3.2. To correlate social intelligence with that of life satisfaction of boys & girls of Government Aided Schools

Variables	Gender	No	Mean	S.D	'r'	't'	L.S
Socal intelligence & life satisfaction	Boys	50	94.78	8.65	0.229	1.629	N.S
			131.7	14.66			
	Girls	50	103.5	8.39	0.094	0.65	N.S
			138.72	15.55			

Table 3.3. To correlate social intelligence with that of life satisfaction of boys & girls of Government Schools

Variables	Gender	No	Mean	S.D	'r'	't'	L.S
Socal intelligence & life satisfaction	Boys	50	101.62	7.07	0.321	2.14	0.05
			140.32	17.04			
	Girls	50	102.58	5.97	0.011	0.07	N.S
			136.78	13.36			

HYPOTHESIS-2

Social intelligence has no impact on Education status of the students.

Table 3.4. Chi square test between Education status and Social Intelligence of boys and girls of Private School

Variables	Gender	No	D.F.	χ^2	L.S
Socal Intelligence Vs Education Status	Boys	50	4	2.03	N.S
	Girls	50	4	5.05	N.S

The tables 3.4 to 3.6 shows that the calculate chi-square value were less than that of table chi-square values. Hence the hypothesis was accepted and proved that intelligence has no impact on education status of the students in the case of boys and girls from Government, Government aided & Private Schools.

Table 3.5. Chi square test between Education status and Social Intelligence of boys and girls of Government Aided School

Variables	Gender	No	D.F.	χ^2	L.S
Socal Intelligence Vs Education Status	Boys	50	4	8.4	N.S
	Girls	50	4	1.64	N.S

Table 3.6. Chi square test between Education status and Social Intelligence of boys and girls of Government School

Variables	Gender	No	D.F.	χ^2	L.S
Socal Intelligence Vs Education Status	Boys	50	4	4.29	N.S
	Girls	50	4	2.41	N.S

Table 3.7. To associate Social Intelligence with that of family status of boys and girls of Private School

Variables	Gender	No	D.F.	χ^2	L.S
Socal Intelligence Vs Family Status	Boys	50	2	1.87	N.S
	Girls	50	2	2.49	N.S

Table 3.8. To associate Social Intelligence with that of family status of boys and girls of Government Aided School

Variables	Gender	No	D.F.	χ^2	L.S
Socal Intelligence Vs Family Status	Boys	50	2	4.12	N.S
	Girls	50	2	0.56	N.S

HYPOTHESIS - 3

Social intelligence does not depend on the type of family of students.

Table 3.9. To associate Social Intelligence with that of family status of boys and girls of Government School

Variables	Gender	No	D.F.	χ^2	L.S
Socal Intelligence Vs Family Status	Boys	50	2	1.72	N.S
	Girls	50	2	0.75	N.S

The tables 3.7 to 3.9 show that the calculated chi-square values were less than that of table chi-square values. Hence the hypothesis was accepted and proved that intelligence did not depend upon the type of family of the students in the case of boys and girls from government, government aided and Private Schools.

HYPOTHESIS-4

"Life satisfaction does not depend on Education status".

Table 3.10. Chi square test between Education status and Life Satisfaction of boys and girls of Private School

Variables	Gender	No	D.F.	χ^2	L.S
Socal Intelligence Vs Education Status	Boys	50	4	1.02	N.S
	Girls	50	4	5.31	N.S

Table 3.11. Chi square test between Education status and Life Satisfaction of boys and girls of Government Aided School

Variables	Gender	No	D.F.	χ^2	L.S
Socal Intelligence Vs Education Status	Boys	50	4	13.2	0.05
	Girls	50	4	8.5	N.S

Table 3.12. Chi square test between Education status and Life Satisfaction of boys and girls of Government School

Variables	Gender	No	D.F.	χ^2	L.S
Socal Intelligence Vs Education Status	Boys	50	4	1.73	N.S
	Girls	50	4	4.93	N.S

The tables 3.10 to 3.12 shows that the calculate chi-square values were less than that of table chi-square values. Hence the hypothesis was accepted and proved that life satisfaction does not depend on education status of the students in the case of boys and girls from Private, Government School and girls from Government Aided School where as in the case of boys of Government Aided School. The calculated chi-square values were greater than the table chi-square values. Hence hypothesis was rejected in these cases.

HYPOTHESIS-5

Life satisfaction has no impact on the type of family.

Table 3.13. Chi square test between Life Satisfaction and family status boys and girls of Private School

Variables	Gender	No	D.F.	χ^2	L.S
Socal Intelligence Vs Family Status	Boys	50	2	0.71	N.S
	Girls	50	2	0.48	N.S

Table 3.14. Chi square test between Life Satisfaction and family status of boys and girls of Government Aided School

Variables	Gender	No	D.F.	χ^2	L.S
Socal Intelligence Vs Family Status	Boys	50	2	0.82	N.S
	Girls	50	2	3.27	N.S

Table 3.15. Chi square test between Life Satisfaction and of family status boys and girls of Government School

Variables	Gender	No	D.F.	χ^2	L.S
Life Satisfaction Vs Family	Boys	50	2	2.73	N.S
	Girls	50	2	0.94	N.S

The tables 3.13 to 3.15 show that the calculated chi-square values were less than that of table chi-square values. Hence the hypothesis was accepted and proved that life satisfaction had no impact on the type of family of the students in the case of boys and girls from government, government aided and Private Schools.

HYPOTHESIS 6

Gender plays an important role on life satisfaction of students.

Table 3.16. To differentiate life satisfaction of boys & girls of Private Schools

Variables	Gender	No	Mean	S.D	C.R	L.S
Life satisfaction	Boys	50	126.28	18.32	6.9	0.01
	Girls	50	138.7	12.177		

Table 3.17. To differentiate life satisfaction of boys & girls of Government Aided Schools

Variables	Gender	No	Mean	S.D	C.R	L.S
Life satisfaction	Boys	50	131.7	14.66	2.32	0.05
	Girls	50	138.72	15.55		

The table 3.16 to 3.18 shows that the calculated CR value is greater than the table CR values. Hence the hypothesis was accepted and proved that Gender played an important role on life satisfaction of student in the case of Private School and Government Aided School, where as in the case of

Government School the calculated CR value were less than that of table CR values. Hence the hypothesis was rejected in these cases.

Table 3.18. To differentiate life satisfaction of boys & girls of Government Schools

Variables	Gender	No	Mean	S.D	C.R	L.S
Life satisfaction	Boys	50	140.32	17.04	1.44	N.S
	Girls	50	136.78	13.36		

HYPOTHESIS-7

Gender plays an important role on total score of social intelligence.

Table 3.19. To differentiate the total score of social intelligence of boys & girls of Private School

Variables	Gender	No	Mean	S.D	C.R	L.S
Social intelligence	Boys	50	99.1	9.26	7.36	0.01
	Girls	50	106.46	7.6		

Table 3.20. To differentiate the total score of social intelligence of boys & girls of Government aided school

Variables	Gender	No	Mean	S.D	C.R	L.S
Social intelligence	Boys	50	94.78	8.65	5.11	0.01
	Girls	50	103.5	8.39		

Table 3.21. To differentiate the total score of social intelligence of boys & girls of Government School

Variables	Gender	No	Mean	S.D	C.R	L.S
Social intelligence	Boys	50	101.62	7.07	0.692	N.S
	Girls	50	102.58	5.97		

The tables 3.19 to 3.21 show that clearly that the calculated CR values were greater than that of the table CR values. Hence the hypothesis was accepted and proved that Gender played an important role on total score of social intelligence of student in the case of Private School and Government Aided School, where as in the case of Government School the calculated CR value were less than that of table CR values. Hence the hypothesis was rejected in these cases.

HYPOTHESIS-8

Gender plays an important role on various factors of social intelligence of the total sample.

Table 3.22. To differentiate patience between boys and girls of Private, Government aided and Government School

Variable	Type of School	Gender	No	Mean	S.D	C.R	L.S
Patience	Private	Boys	50	18.274	3.516	3.9	0.01
		Girls	50	20.5	2.10		
	Government Aided	Boys	50	17.74	2.7	13.7	0.01
		Girls	50	19.98	2.645		
	Government	Boys	50	19.18	2.1	0.769	N.S
		Girls	50	19.44	2.06		

Table 3.22 and Fig. F show that the calculated CR values were greater than that of table CR values. Hence the hypothesis was accepted and proved that Gender played very important role on patience factors of social intelligence in the case of boys and girls of Private School and Government Aided Schools. Where as in the case of Government School, the hypothesis was rejected and proved that Gender did not play important role on patience factors of social intelligence.

Table 3.23. To differentiate co-operatives between boys and girls of Private, Government aided and Government School

Variable	Type of School	Gender	No	Mean	S.D	C.R	L.S
Co-operativ-eness	Private	Boys	50	25.215	3.46	2.15	0.05
		Girls	50	26.58	2.81		
	Government Aided	Boys	50	24.54	2.8	1.607	N.S
		Girls	50	26.46	3.55		
	Government	Boys	50	26.96	2.42	0.264	N.S
		Girls	50	26.82	1.97		

The table 3.23 and Fig. G show that the calculated CR values were greater than that of table CR values. Hence the hypothesis was accepted and proved that gender played very important role on co-operativeness factors of social intelligence in the case of boys and girls of Private School. Where as in the case of boys and girls of Government Aided School and Government School, the hypothesis was rejected and proved that gender did not played important role on co-operativeness factors of social intelligence.

Table 3.24. To differentiate confidence between boys & girls of Private, Government aided and Government Schools

Variable	Type of School	Gender	No	Mean	S.D	C.R	L.S
Confidence	Priavate	Boys	50	18.901	2.5	3.15	0.01
		Girls	50	20.62	1.75		
	Government Aided	Boys	50	18.64	2.94	2.88	0.01
		Girls	50	20.08	2.2		
	Government	Boys	50	20.46	2.2	4.08	0.01
		Girls	50	22.22	1.95		

The table 3.24 and Fig. H show that the calculated CR values were greater than that of table CR values. Hence the hypothesis was accepted and proved that Gender played very important role on confidence factors of social intelligence in the case of boys and girls of Private School, Government Aided School and Government School.

Table 3.25. To differentiate sensitivity between boys & girls of private, Government aided and Government School

Variable	Type of School	Gender	No	Mean	S.D	C.R	L.S
Sensitivity	Private	Boys	50	20.529	2.6	1.03	NS
		Girls	50	21.26	2.04		
	Government Aided	Boys	50	19.48	2.22	0.99	NS
		Girls	50	20.66	2.84		
	Government	Boys	50	20.72	2.3	0.610	NS
		Girls	50	20.98	1.94		

The table 3.25 and Fig. I show that the calculated CR values were greater than that of table CR values. Hence the hypothesis was rejected and proved that Gender did not play important role on sensitivity factors of social intelligence in the case of Private School, Government Aided School and Government School.

The table 3.26 and Fig. J show that the calculated CR values were greater than that of table CR values. Hence the hypothesis was accepted and proved that Gender played very important role on recognition of social environment factors of social intelligence in the case of boys and girls of Government Aided School. Where as in the case of Private School and Government School, the hypothesis was rejected and proved that Gender did not play important role on recognition of social environment factors of social intelligence.

Table 3.26. To differentiate Recognition of Social Environment between boys & girls of Private, Government aided and Government School

Variable	Type of School	Gender	No	Mean	S.D	C.R	L.S
Recognition of social Environment	Private	Boys	50	0.84	0.7	1.33	NS
		Girls	50	0.62	0.7		
	Government Aided	Boys	50	1.06	0.7	27.5	0.01
		Girls	50	0.64	0.7		
	Government	Boys	50	0.94	0.8	0.133	NS
		Girls	50	0.92	0.7		

Table 3.27. To differentiate tactfulness between boys & girls of Private, Government aided and Government School

Variable	Type of School	Gender	No	Mean	S.D	C.R	L.S
Tactfulness	Private	Boys	50	3.627	0.87	3.16	0.01
		Girls	50	4.28	1.08		
	Government Aided	Boys	50	3.46	1.09	0.542	NS
		Girls	50	3.38	1.12		
	Government	Boys	50	3.88	1.13	2.39	0.05
		Girls	50	4.4	1.04		

The table 3.27 and fig. K show that the calculated CR values were greater than that of table CR values. Hence the hypothesis was accepted and proved that Gender played very important role on tactfulness in the case of boys and girls of Government School and Government aided School. Where as in the case of boys and girls of Government Aided School, the hypothesis was rejected and proved that Gender did not play important role on tactfulness factors of social intelligence.

Table 3.28. To differentiate sense of humour between boys and girls of private, Government aided and Government School

Variable	Type of School	Gender	No	Mean	S.D	C.R	L.S
Sense of Humour	Private	Boys	50	3.549	1.269	2.09	0.05
		Girls	50	3.68	1.7		
	Government Aided	Boys	50	3.24	1.17	0.36	NS
		Girls	50	3.16	1.03		
	Government	Boys	50	2.96	0.9	1.29	NS
		Girls	50	3.18	0.8		

The table 3.28 and Fig. L show that the calculated CR values were greater than that of table CR values. Hence the hypothesis was accepted and proved that Gender played very important role on sense of humour factors of social intelligence in the case of boys and girls of Private School. Where as in the case of Government Aided School and Government School, the hypothesis was rejected and proved that Gender did not play important role on sense of humour factors of social intelligence.

The table 3.29 and Fig. M show that the calculated CR values were greater than that of table CR values. Hence the hypothesis was accepted and proved that Gender played very important role on memory factors of social intelligence in the case of boys and girls of Government Aided School. Where as in the case of Private School and Government School, the hypothesis was rejected and proved that Gender did not play important role on memory factors of social intelligence.

Table 3.29. To differentiate memory between boys and girls of private, government aided and Government School

Variable	Type of School	Gender	No	Mean	S.D	C.R	L.S
Memory	Private	Boys	50	8.372	2.16	1.76	NS
		Girls	50	8.92	0.16		
	Government Aided	Boys	50	6.62	1.44	6.0	0.01
		Girls	50	8.54	1.71		
	Government	Boys	50	5.96	1.33	0.67	NS
		Girls	50	5.81	0.82		

HYPOTHESIS-9

Various factors of social intelligence are related to each other of Government School.

From the tables 3.30 to 3.43 shows the correlation values among different factors of social intelligence in the case of Government School, tables 3.30 and 3.31 when patience was correlated with confidence the calculated 'r' value were greater than that of table 'r' values. So hypothesis was accepted and proved that patience and confidence was, interrelated in the case of Government School boys and girls. When patience was related with co-operatives and sensitivity it was found to be significant in Government School Girls, where as other factor were correlated with patience it was found to be not significant in the case of boys and girls of Government School.

The tables 3.32 and 3.33 shows that co-operativeness was correlated with confidence and sensitivity, the calculated 'r' values were greater than that of table values. So hypothesis was accepted and proved that cooperativeness was related with confidence and sensitivity in the case of Government School boys & girls. When the cooperativeness was related with recognition of school environment and tactfulness it was found to be significant in Government School boys. Where as other factors were correlated with cooperativeness it was found not to be significant in the case of boys and girls of Government Schools.

Table 3.30. To correlate Patience with that of Co-operativeness, Confidence, Sensitivity, Recognition of Social Environment, Tactfulness, sense of Humour and Memory of Government School Boys

Variables	No	Mean	S.D	'r'	't'	L.S
Patience Vs	50	19.18	2.1	0.189	1.33	N.S
Cooperativeness	50	26.96	2.42			
Patience Vs	50	19.18	2.1	0.484	3.83	0.05
Confidence	50	20.46	2.2			
Patience Vs	50	19.18	2.1	0.252	1.80	N.S
Sensitivity	50	20.72	2.3			
Patience Vs	50	19.18	2.1	0.005	0.03	N.S
Recognition of Social Environment	50	0.94	0.8			
Patience Vs	50	19.18	2.1	0.025	0.17	N.S
Tactfulness	50	3.88	1.13			
Patience Vs	50	19.18	2.1	-0.14	0.97	N.S
Sense of Humour	50	2.96	0.9			
Patience Vs	50	19.18	2.1	0.141	0.98	N.S
Memory	50	5.96	1.33			

Table 3.31. To correlate Patience with that of Co-operativeness, Confidence, Sensitivity, Recognition of Social Environment, Tactfulness, sense of Humour and Memory of Government School Girls

Variables	No	Mean	S.D	'r'	't'	L.S
Patience Vs	50	19.44	2.06	0.375	2.80	0.01
Cooperativeness	50	26.82	1.97			
Patience Vs	50	19.44	2.06	0.289	2.09	0.05
Confidence	50	22.22	1.95			
Patience Vs	50	19.44	2.06	0.363	2.69	0.01
Sensitivity	50	20.98	1.94			
Patience Vs	50	19.44	2.06	0.228	1.62	N.S
Recognition of Social Environment	50	0.92	0.7			
Patience Vs	50	19.44	2.06	0.035	0.24	N.S
Tactfulness	50	4.4	1.04			
Patience Vs	50	19.44	2.06	0.21	1.48	N.S
Sense of Humour	50	3.18	0.9			
Patience Vs	50	19.44	2.06	0.076	0.52	N.S
Memory	50	5.81	0.82			

Table 3.32. To correlate Co-operativeness with that of Confidence, Sensitivity, Recognition of Social Environment, Tactfulness, Sense of humour and Memory of Government School Boys

Variables	No	Mean	S.D	'r'	't'	L.S
Cooperativeness Vs	50	26.96	2.42	0.32	2.33	0.05
Confidence	50	20.46	2.2			
Cooperativeness Vs	50	26.96	2.42	0.316	2.43	0.05
Sensitivity	50	20.72	2.3			
Cooperativeness Vs	50	26.96	2.42	-0.309	2.25	0.05
Recognition of Social Environment	50	0.94	0.8			
Cooperativeness Vs	50	26.96	2.42	0.183	1.29	0.05
Tactfulness	50	3.88	1.13			
Cooperativeness Vs	50	26.96	2.42	0.025	0.17	N.S
Sense of Humour	50	2.96	0.9			
Cooperativeness Vs	50	26.96	2.42	0.049	0.33	N.S
Memory	50	5.96	1.33			

Table 3.33. To correlate Co-operativeness with that of Confidence, Sensitivity, Recognition of Social Environment, Tactfulness, Sense of humour and Memory of Government School Girls

Variables	No	Mean	S.D	'r'	't'	L.S
Cooperativeness Vs	50	26.82	1.97	0.317	2.31	0.05
Confidence	50	22.22	1.95			
Cooperativeness Vs	50	26.82	1.97	0.286	2.06	0.05
Sensitivity	50	20.98	1.94			
Cooperativeness Vs	50	26.82	1.97	0.006	0.04	N.S
Recognition of Social Environment	50	0.92	0.7			
Cooperativeness Vs	50	26.82	1.97	0.133	0.92	N.S
Tactfulness	50	4.4	1.04			
Cooperativeness Vs	50	26.82	1.97	0.149	1.04	N.S
Sense of Humour	50	3.18	0.9			
Cooperativeness Vs	50	26.82	1.97	0.061	0.42	N.S
Memory	50	5.81	0.82			

Table 3.34. To correlate Confidence with that of Sensitivity, Recognition of Social Environment, Tactfulness, Sense of humour and Memory of Government School boys

Variables	No	Mean	S.D	'r'	't'	L.S
Confidence Vs	50	20.46	2.2	0.258	1.85	N.S
Sensitivity	50	20.72	2.3			
Confidence Vs	50	20.46	2.2	0.04	0.27	N.S
Recognition of Social Environment	50	0.94	0.8			
Confidence Vs	50	20.46	2.2	0.12	0.83	N.S
Tactfulness	50	3.88	1.13			
Confidence Vs	50	20.46	2.2	0.086	0.59	N.S
Sense of Humour	50	2.96	0.9			
Confidence Vs	50	20.46	2.2	0.234	1.66	N.S
Memory	50	5.96	1.33			

The tables 3.34 and 3.35 shows that when confidence was correlated with other factors, the calculated 'r' values were lesser than that of table 'r' values. So hypothesis was rejected and proved that confidence and various factors of social intelligence were not related in the case of Government School boys and girls.

Table 3.35. To correlate Confidence with that of Sensitivity, Recognition of Social Environment, Tactfulness, Sense of Humour and Memory of Government School Girls

Variables	No	Mean	S.D	'r'	't'	L.S
Confidence Vs	50	22.22	1.95	0.168	1.18	N.S
Sensitivity	50	20.98	1.94			
Confidence Vs	50	22.22	1.95	0.027	0.18	N.S
Recognition of Social Environment	50	0.92	0.7			
Confidence Vs	50	22.22	1.95	0.135	0.94	N.S
Tactfulness	50	4.4	1.04			
Confidence Vs	50	22.22	1.95	0.044	0.30	N.S
Sense of Humour	50	3.18	0.8			
Confidence Vs	50	22.22	1.95	0.046	0.31	N.S
Memory	50	5.81	0.82			

The tables 3.36 and 3.37 shows that when sensitivity was correlated with sense of humour, the calculated r values were greater than that of table 'r' values. So hypothesis was proved the sensitivity and sense of humour were interrelated in the case of Government School girls. When the sensitivity was related with other factors it was not found to be significant in the case of boys and girls of Government School.

Table 3.36. To correlate Sensitivity with that of Recognition of Social Environment, Tactfulness, Sense of humour and Memory of Government School boys

Variables	No	Mean	S.D	'r'	't'	L.S
Sensitivity Vs	50	20.72	2.3	0.012	0.08	N.S
Recognition of Social Environment	50	0.94	0.8			
Sensitivity Vs	50	20.72	2.3	0.178	1.25	N.S
Tactfulness	50	3.88	1.13			
Sensitivity Vs	50	20.72	2.3	0.119	0.83	N.S
Sense of Humour	50	2.96	0.9			
Sensitivity Vs	50	20.72	2.3	0.194	1.37	N.S
Memory	50	5.96	1.33			

Table 3.37. To correlate Sensitivity with that of Recognition of Social Environment, Tactfulness, Sense of humour and Memory of Government School Girls

Variables	No	Mean	S.D	'r'	't'	L.S
Sensitivity Vs	50	20.98	1.94	0.119	0.83	N.S
Recognition of Social Environment	50	0.92	0.7			
Sensitivity Vs	50	20.98	1.94	0.084	0.58	N.S
Tactfulness	50	4.4	1.04			
Sensitivity Vs	50	20.98	1.94	0.348	2.57	0.01
Sense of Humour	50	3.18	0.8			
Sensitivity Vs	50	20.98	1.94	0.113	0.78	N.S
Memory	50	5.81	0.82			

Table 3.38. To correlate Recognition of Social Environment with tactfulness, Sense of humour and Memory of Government School boys

Variables	No	Mean	S.D	'r'	't'	L.S
Recognition of Social Environment Vs	50	0.94	0.8	0.035	0.24	N.S
Tactfulness	50	3.88	1.13			
Recognition of Social Environment Vs	50	0.94	0.8	0.054	0.37	N.S
Sense of Humour	50	2.96	0.9			
Recognition of Social Environment Vs	50	0.94	0.8	0.002	0.01	N.S
Memory	50	5.96	1.33			

Table 3.39. To correlate Recognition of Social Environment with tactfulness, Sense of humour and Memory of Government School girls

Variables	No	Mean	S.D	'r'	't'	L.S
Recognition of Social Environment Vs	50	0.92	0.7	0.143	1.00	N.S
Tactfulness	50	4.4	1.04			
Recognition of Social Environment Vs	50	0.92	0.7	0.07	0.48	N.S
Sense of Humour	50	3.18	0.8			
Recognition of Social Environment Vs	50	0.92	0.7	0.01	0.06	N.S
Memory	50	5.81	0.82			

The tables 3.38 and 3.39 shows that when recognition of social environment was correlated with sense of humour, tactfulness and memory the calculated r values were less than that of table r values. It was found not to be significant. The hypothesis was rejected in these cases of boys and girls of Government School.

Table 3.40. To correlate Tactfulness with Sense of humour and Memory of Government School boys

Variables	No	Mean	S.D	'r'	't'	L.S
Tactfulness Vs	50	3.88	1.13	0.273	1.96	N.S
Sense of Humour	50	2.96	0.9			
Tactfulness Vs	50	3.88	1.13	0.257	1.84	N.S
Memory	50	5.96	1.33			

Table 3.41. To correlate Tactfulness with Sense of humour and Memory of Government School Girls

Variables	No	Mean	S.D	'r'	't'	L.S
Tactfulness Vs	50	4.4	1.04	0.0289	0.20	N.S
Sense of Humour	50	3.18	0.8			
Tactfulness Vs	50	4.4	1.04	0.108	0.75	N.S
Memory	50	5.81	0.82			

The tables 3.40 and 3.41 shows that when tactfulness was correlated with sense of humour and memory the calculated 'r' values were less than that of table 'r' values. So hypothesis was rejected in these cases of boys and girls of Government School.

Table 3.42. To correlate Sense of humour and Memory of Government School boys

Variables	No	Mean	S.D	'r'	't'	L.S
Sense of humour Vs	50	2.96	0.9	0.0144	0.09	N.S
Memory	50	5.96	1.33			

Table 3.43. To correlate Sense of Humour and Memory of Government School Girls

Variables	No	Mean	S.D	'r'	't'	L.S
Sense of humour Vs	50	3.18	0.8	0.317	2.31	0.05
Memory	50	5.81	0.82			

The tables 3.42 and 3.43 shows that when sense of humour was correlated with memory the calculated 'r' values were greater than that of table 'r' values. Hence the hypothesis was accepted and proved that sense of humour and memory were interrelated in the case of Government School girls. When the sense of humour were related with memory it was found not to be significant in the case of boys of Government School.

HYPOTHESIS-10

Different factors of Social Intelligence are related to each other in the case of Government Aided School.

From the tables 3.44 to 3.57 shows the correlation values among different factors of social intelligence in the case of Government Aided School. Tables 44 and 45 when patience was correlated with co-operativeness and sensitivity the calculated 'r' values greater than that of the table 'r' values . So hypothesis was accepted and proved that patience were interrelated with cooperativeness and sensitivity in the case of Government Aided School boys and girls. When the patience was related with confidence it was found to be significant in Government Aided School boys, where as other factors were correlated with patience it was not found to be significant in the case of Government Aided Schools boys and girls.

Table 3.44. To correlate Patience with that of Co-operativeness, Confidence, Sensitivity, Recognition of Social Environment, Tactfulness, sense of Humour and Memory of Government Aided School Boys

Variables	No	Mean	S.D	'r'	't'	L.S
Patience Vs	50	17.74	2.7	0.4019	3.04	0.01
Cooperativeness	50	24.54	2.8			
Patience Vs	50	17.74	2.7	0.298	2.16	0.05
Confidence	50	18.64	2.94			
Patience Vs	50	17.74	2.7	0.3607	2.67	0.01
Sensitivity	50	19.48	2.22			
Patience Vs	50	17.74	2.7	0.129	0.90	N.S
Recognition of Social Environment	50	1.06	0.7			
Patience Vs	50	17.74	2.7	0.283	2.04	0.01
Tactfulness	50	3.46	1.09			
Patience Vs	50	17.74	2.7	0.136	0.95	N.S
Sense of Humour	50	3.24	1.17			
Patience Vs	50	17.74	2.7	0.147	1.02	N.S
Memory	50	6.62	1.44			

The tables 3.46 and 3.47 shows that co-operativeness was correlated with confidence, the calculated 'r' values were greater than that of table 'r' values. So hypothesis was accepted and proved that co-operativeness and confidence were interrelated in the case of Government Aided School boys and girls. When the co-operativeness was related with sensitivity, it was found to be significant in Government Aided School boys. Where as, other factors were correlated with co-operativeness it was not found to be significant in the case of boys & girls of Government Aided School.

Table 3.45. To correlate Patience with that of Co-operativeness, Confidence, Sensitivity, Recognition of Social Environment, Tactfulness, sense of Humour and Memory of Government Aided School Girls

Variables	No	Mean	S.D	'r'	't'	L.S
Patience Vs	50	19.98	2.645	0.326	2.38	0.05
Cooperativeness	50	26.46	3.55			
Patience Vs	50	19.98	2.645	0.262	1.88	N.S
Confidence	50	20.08	2.2			
Patience Vs	50	19.98	2.645	0.63	5.62	0.01
Sensitivity	50	20.66	2.84			
Patience Vs	50	19.98	2.645	0.192	1.35	N.S
Recognition of Social Environment	50	0.64	0.7			
Patience Vs	50	19.98	2.645	0.011	0.07	N.S
Tactfulness	50	3.38	1.12			
Patience Vs	50	19.98	2.645	0.11	0.76	N.S
Sense of Humour	50	3.16	1.03			
Patience Vs	50	19.98	2.645	0.168	1.18	N.S
Memory	50	8.54	1.71			

The tables 3.48 and 3.49 shows that the confidence and correlated with sensitivity, the calculated 'r' values were greater than table 'r' values. So hypothesis was accepted and proved that confidence and sensitivity were interrelated in the case Government Aided School boys and girls. When the confidence was related with sense of humour it was found to be significant in Government Aided School girls, where as other factors correlate with confidence it was found not to be significant in the case of boys and girls of Government Aided School.

Table 3.46. To correlate Co-operativeness with that of Confidence, Sensitivity, Recognition of Social Environment, Tactfulness, Sense of humour and Memory of Government Aided School Boys

Variables	No	Mean	S.D	'r'	't'	L.S
Cooperativeness Vs	50	24.54	2.8	0.5828	4.96	0.01
Confidence	50	18.64	2.94			
Cooperativeness Vs	50	24.54	2.8	0.278	2.00	0.05
Sensitivity	50	19.48	2.22			
Cooperativeness Vs	50	24.54	2.8	0.17	1.19	N.S
Recognition of Social Environment	50	1.06	0.7			
Cooperativeness Vs	50	24.54	2.8	0.177	1.24	N.S
Tactfulness	50	3.46	1.09			
Cooperativeness Vs	50	24.54	2.8	0.214	1.51	N.S
Sense of Humour	50	3.24	1.17			
Cooperativeness Vs	50	24.54	2.8	0.264	1.89	N.S
Memory	50	6.62	1.44			

The tables 3.50 and 3.51 shows that when sensitivity was correlated with various factors of social intelligence, the calculated 'r values were less than that of table 'r' values. So hypothesis was rejected in the case of boys and girls of Government Aided School.

The tables 3.52 and 3.53 shows that when recognition of social environment and correlated with tactfulness and sense of humour the calculated 'r' values were greater than table 'r' values. So hypothesis was accepted and proved that recognition of social environment were interrelated with tactfulness and sense of humour in the case of Government Aided School girls. Where as other factors were correlated with recognition of social environment it was not found to be significant in the case of boys and girls of Government Aided School.

Table 3.47. To correlate Co-operativeness with that of Confidence, Sensitivity, Recognition of Social Environment, Tactfulness, Sense of humour and Memory of Government Aided School Girls

Variables	No	Mean	S.D	'r'	't'	L.S
Cooperativeness Vs	50	26.46	3.55	0.279	2.01	0.05
Confidence	50	20.08	2.2			
Cooperativeness Vs	50	26.46	3.55	0.246	1.75	N.S
Sensitivity	50	20.66	2.84			
Cooperativeness Vs	50	26.46	3.55	0.175	1.23	N.S
Recognition of Social Environment	50	3.38	0.7			
Cooperativeness Vs	50	26.46	3.55	0.0599	0.41	N.S
Tactfulness	50	3.38	1.12			
Cooperativeness Vs	50	26.46	3.55	0.086	0.59	N.S
Sense of Humour	50	3.16	1.03			
Cooperativeness Vs	50	26.46	3.55	0.061	0.35	N.S
Memory	50	8.54	1.71			

The tables 3.54 and 3.55 shows that when the tactfulness and correlated with sense of humour, the calculated 'r' values were greater than table 'r' values. So hypothesis was accepted and proved that tactfulness and sense of humour were interrelated in the case of Government Aided School boys. Where as other factors correlated with tactfulness it was found not to be significant in the case of boys and girls of Government Aided School.

The tables 3.56 and 3.57 shows that when the sense of humour correlated with memory, the calculated 'r' values were greater than table 'r' values. In the case of Government Aided School boys. Hence the hypothesis was accepted and proved that sense of humour and memory were interrelated. Where as in the case of Government Aided School girls, the calculated 'r' values were less than that of table 'r' values. So the hypothesis was rejected in this case.

Table 3.48. To correlate Confidence with that of Sensitivity, Recognition of Social Environment, Tactfulness, Sense of humour and Memory of Government School Aided school boys

Variables	No	Mean	S.D	'r'	't'	L.S
Confidence Vs	50	18.64	2.94	0.288	2.08	0.05
Sensitivity	50	19.48	2.22			
Confidence Vs	50	18.64	2.94	0.184	1.29	N.S
Recognition of Social Environment	50	1.06	0.7			
Confidence Vs	50	18.64	2.94	0.166	1.16	N.S
Tactfulness	50	3.46	1.09			
Confidence Vs	50	18.64	2.94	0.161	1.13	N.S
Sense of Humour	50	3.24	1.17			
Confidence Vs	50	18.64	2.94	0.066	0.45	N.S
Memory	50	6.62	1.44			

From the tables 3.58 to 3.71 shows the correlation values among different factors of social intelligence in the case of Private School. Tables 3.58 and 3.59 show that when patience was correlated with co-operativeness the calculated 'r' value was greater than table 'r' values. So hypothesis was accepted and proved that patience and co-operativeness were, interrelated in the case of boys and girls of Private School. When the patience was related with confidence, it was found to be significant in Private School boys, when the patience was related with sensitivity it was found to be significant in Private School Girls, were as other factor were correlated with patience it was found not to be significant in the case of Private School boys and girls.

Table 3.49. To correlate Confidence with that of Sensitivity, Recognition of Social Environment, Tactfulness, Sense of Humour and Memory of Government Aided School Girls

Variables	No	Mean	S.D	'r'	't'	L.S
Confidence Vs	50	20.08	2.2	0.337	2.47	0.05
Sensitivity	50	20.66	2.84			
Confidence Vs	50	20.08	2.2	0.196	1.38	N.S
Recognition of Social Environment	50	0.64	0.7			
Confidence Vs	50	20.08	2.2	0.053	0.36	N.S
Tactfulness	50	3.38	1.12			
Confidence Vs	50	20.08	2.2	0.271	2.02	0.05
Sense of Humour	50	3.16	1.03			
Confidence Vs	50	20.08	2.2	0.177	1.24	N.S
Memory	50	8.54	1.71			

Table 3.50. To correlate Sensitivity with that of Recognition of Social Environment, Tactfulness, Sense of humour and Memory of Government Aided School boys

Variables	No	Mean	S.D	'r'	't'	L.S
Sensitivity Vs	50	19.48	2.22	0.134	0.93	N.S
Recognition of Social Environment	50	1.06	0.7			
Sensitivity Vs	50	19.48	2.22	0.024	0.16	N.S
Tactfulness	50	3.46	1.09			
Sensitivity Vs	50	19.48	2.22	0.072	0.50	N.S
Sense of Humour	50	3.24	1.17			
Sensitivity Vs	50	19.48	2.22	0.172	1.20	N.S
Memory	50	6.62	1.44			

Table 3.51. To correlate Sensitivity with that of Recognition of Social Environment, Tactfulness, Sense of humour and Memory of Government Aided School Girls

Variables	No	Mean	S.D	'r'	't'	L.S
Sensitivity Vs	50	20.66	2.84	0.139	0.97	N.S
Recognition of Social Environment	50	0.64	0.7			
Sensitivity Vs	50	20.66	2.84	0.086	0.59	N.S
Tactfulness	50	3.38	1.12			
Sensitivity Vs	50	20.66	2.84	0.081	0.56	N.S
Sense of Humour	50	3.16	1.03			
Sensitivity Vs	50	20.66	2.84	0.176	1.23	N.S
Memory	50	8.54	1.71			

Table 3.52. To correlate Recognition of Social Environment with tactfulness, Sense of humour and Memory of Government Aided School Boys

Variables	No	Mean	S.D	'r'	't'	L.S
Recognition of Social Environment Vs	50	1.06	0.7	0.088	0.61	N.S
Tactfulness	50	3.46	1.09			
Recognition of Social Environment Vs	50	1.06	0.7	0.066	0.45	N.S
Sense of Humour	50	3.24	1.17			
Recognition of Social Environment Vs	50	1.06	0.7	0.142	0.99	N.S
Memory	50	6.62	1.44			

Table 3.53. To correlate Recognition of Social Environment with tactfulness, Sense of humour and Memory of Government Aided School girls

Variables	No	Mean	S.D	'r'	't'	L.S
Recognition of Social Environment Vs	50	0.64	0.7	0.370	2.75	0.01
Tactfulness	50	3.38	1.12			
Recognition of Social Environment Vs	50	0.64	0.7	0.377	2.81	0.01
Sense of Humour	50	3.16	1.03			
Recognition of Social Environment Vs	50	0.64	0.7	0.041	0.28	N.S
Memory	50	8.54	1.71			

Table 3.54. To correlate Tactfulness with Sense of humour and Memory of Government Aided School Boys

Variables	No	Mean	S.D	'r'	't'	L.S
Tactfulness Vs	50	3.46	1.09	0.279	2.01	0.05
Sense of Humour	50	3.24	1.17			
Tactfulness Vs	50	3.46	1.09	0.197	1.26	N.S
Memory	50	6.62	1.44			

Table 3.55. To correlate Tactfulness with Sense of humour and Memory of Government Aided School Girls

Variables	No	Mean	S.D	'r'	't'	L.S
Tactfulness Vs	50	3.38	1.12	0.139	0.97	N.S
Sense of Humour	50	3.16	1.03			
Tactfulness Vs	50	3.38	1.12	0.24	1.71	N.S
Memory	50	8.54	1.71			

Table 3.56. To correlate Sense of humour and Memory of Government Aided School Boys

Variables	No	Mean	S.D	'r'	't'	L.S
Sense of humour Vs	50	3.24	1.17	0.309	2.2	0.05
Memory	50	6.62	1.44			

Table 3.57. To correlate Sense of humour and Memory of Government Aided School Girls

Variables	No	Mean	S.D	'r'	't'	L.S
Sense of humour Vs	50	3.16	1.03	2.71	1.95	N.S
Memory	50	8.54	1710.82			

HYPOTHESIS-11

Various factors of social intelligence are interrelated among themselves of Private School.

The tables 3.60 and 3.61 shows that co-operative ness was correlated with confidence, the calculated 'r' values were greater than that of table 'r' values. So hypothesis was accepted and proved that co-operativeness and confidence were interrelated in the case of Private School boys and girls. When the co-operativeness was related with sense of humour it was found to be significant in Private School girls, when the co-operativeness was related with memory it was found to be significant in Private School boys. Where as, other factors were correlated with co-operativeness it was not found to be significant in the case of Private School boys and girls.

The tables 3.62 and 3.63 shows that when confidence was correlated with memory the calculated 'r' values were greater than that of table 'r' values. So hypothesis was accepted and proved that confidence and memory were interrelated in the case of Private School boys. Where as other factors were correlated with confidence it was found not to be significant in the case of Private School boys and girls.

Table 3.58. To correlate Patience with that of Co-operatives, Confidence, Sensitivity, Recognition of Social Environment, Tactfulness, sense of Humour and Memory of Private School Boys

Variables	No	Mean	S.D	'r'	't'	L.S
Patience Vs	50	18.274	3.516	0.474	3.72	0.01
Cooperativeness	50	25.215	3.46			
Patience Vs	50	18.274	3.516	0.474	3.72	0.01
Confidence	50	18.901	2.5			
Patience Vs	50	18.274	3.516	0.13	0.90	N.S
Sensitivity	50	20.529	2.6			
Patience Vs	50	18.274	3.516	0.079	0.54	N.S
Recognition of Social Environment	50	0.843	0.7			
Patience Vs	50	18.274	3.516	0.181	0.98	N.S
Tactfulness	50	3.627	0.87			
Patience Vs	50	18.274	3.516	0.121	0.84	N.S
Sense of Humour	50	3.549	1.269			
Patience Vs	50	18.274	3.516	0.15	1.05	N.S
Memory	50	8.372	2.16			

The tables 3.64 and 3.65 shows that when sensitivity was correlated with tactfulness and sense of humour, the calculated r values were greater than that of table 'r' values. So hypothesis was accepted and proved the sensitivity were interrelated with tactfulness and sense of humour in the case of Private School girls. Where as other factors were correlated with sensitivity, it was found not to be significant in the case of boys and girls of Private School.

Table 3.59. To correlate Patience with that of Co-operativeness, Confidence, Sensitivity, Recognition of Social Environment, Tactfulness, sense of Humour and Memory of Private School Girls

Variables	No	Mean	S.D	'r'	't'	L.S
Patience Vs	50	20.5	2.10	0.588	5.03	0.01
Cooperativeness	50	26.58	2.81			
Patience Vs	50	20.5	2.10	0.129	0.90	N.S
Confidence	50	20.62	1.75			
Patience Vs	50	20.5	2.10	0.488	3.87	0.01
Sensitivity	50	21.26	2.04			
Patience Vs	50	20.5	2.10	0.046	0.31	N.S
Recognition of Social Environment	50	0.62	0.7			
Patience Vs	50	20.5	2.10	0.133	0.24	N.S
Tactfulness	50	4.28	1.08			
Patience Vs	50	20.5	2.10	0.164	1.48	N.S
Sense of Humour	50	3.68	1.7			
Patience Vs	50	20.5	2.10	0.221	0.52	N.S
Memory	50	8.92	0.16			

The tables 3.66 and 3.67 shows that when recognition of social environment was correlated with sense of humour, tactfulness and memory the calculated 'r' values were less than that of table 'r' values. So hypothesis was rejected in these cases of boys and girls of Private School.

The tables 3.68 and 3.69 shows that when tactfulness was correlated with sense of humour and memory the calculated 'r' values were greater than that of table 'r' values. So hypothesis was accepted and proved that tactfulness were interrelated with sense of humour, and memory in the case of Private School boys. Where as other factor was correlated with tactfulness it was found not to be significant in the case of Private School girls.

Table 3.60. To correlate Co-operativeness with that of Confidence, Sensitivity, Recognition of Social Environment, Tactfulness, Sense of humour and Memory of Private School Boys

Variables	No	Mean	S.D	'r'	't'	L.S
Cooperativeness Vs	50	25.215	3.46	0.320	2.33	0.05
Confidence	50	18.901	2.5			
Cooperativeness Vs	50	25.215	3.46	0.011	0.07	N.S
Sensitivity	50	20.529	2.6			
Cooperativeness Vs	50	25.215	3.46	0.083	0.57	N.S
Recognition of Social Environment	50	0.843	0.7			
Cooperativeness Vs	50	25.215	3.46	0.142	0.99	N.S
Tactfulness	50	3.627	0.87			
Cooperativeness Vs	50	25.215	3.46	0.180	1.26	N.S
Sense of Humour	50	3.549	1.269			
Cooperativeness Vs	50	25.215	3.46	0.33	2.42	0.05
Memory	50	8.372	2.16			

The tables 3.70 and 3.71 shows that when sense of humour was correlated with memory the calculated 'r' values were greater than that of table 'r' values. Hence the hypothesis was accepted and proved that sense of humour and memory were interrelated in the case of Private School girls. When the sense of humour was related with memory it was found not to be significant in the case of boys of Private School.

Table 3.61. To correlate Co-operativeness with that of Confidence, Sensitivity, Recognition of Social Environment, Tactfulness, Sense of humour and Memory of Private School Girls

Variables	No	Mean	S.D	'r'	't'	L.S
Cooperativeness Vs	50	26.58	2.81	-0.325	2.38	0.05
Confidence	50	20.62	1.75			
Cooperativeness Vs	50	26.58	2.81	0.482	0.87	N.S
Sensitivity	50	21.26	2.04			
Cooperativeness Vs	50	26.58	2.81	0.1997	1.42	N.S
Recognition of Social Environment	50	0.62	0.7			
Cooperativeness Vs	50	26.58	2.81	0.0857	0.59	N.S
Tactfulness	50	4.28	1.08			
Cooperativeness Vs	50	26.58	2.81	0.4258	3.26	0.01
Sense of Humour	50	3.68	1.7			
Cooperativeness Vs	50	26.58	2.81	0.0109	0.07	N.S
Memory	50	8.92	0.16			

CONCLUSION

Statistical techniques used in this chapter analyzed the data comparing the social intelligence & life satisfaction of 300 students from government, government aided and Private Schools in the Tuticorin District based on the results obtained, hypothesis framed were either approved or disapproved. The succeeding chapter explains the brief summary about the present study.

Table 3.62. To correlate Confidence with that of Sensitivity, Recognition of Social Environment, Tactfulness, Sense of humour and Memory of Private School boys

Variables	No	Mean	S.D	'r'	't'	L.S
Confidence Vs	50	18.901	2.5	0.036	0.24	N.S
Sensitivity	50	20.529	2.6			
Confidence Vs	50	18.901	2.5	0.031	0.21	N.S
Recognition of Social Environment	50	0.843	0.7			
Confidence Vs	50	18.901	2.5	0.134	0.93	N.S
Tactfulness	50	3.627	0.87			
Confidence Vs	50	18.901	2.5	0.267	1.91	N.S
Sense of Humour	50	3.549	1.269			
Confidence Vs	50	18.901	2.5	0.366	2.72	0.01
Memory	50	8.372	2.16			

Table 3.63. To correlate Confidence with that of Sensitivity, Recognition of Social Environment, Tactfulness, Sense of Humour and Memory of Private School Girls

Variables	No	Mean	S.D	'r'	't'	L.S
Confidence Vs	50	20.62	1.75	0.081	0.56	N.S
Sensitivity	50	21.26	2.04			
Confidence Vs	50	20.62	1.75	0.003	0.02	N.S
Recognition of Social Environment	50	0.62	0.7			
Confidence Vs	50	20.62	1.75	0.124	0.86	N.S
Tactfulness	50	4.28	1.08			
Confidence Vs	50	20.62	1.75	0.0809	0.56	N.S
Sense of Humour	50	3.68	1.7			
Confidence Vs	50	20.62	1.75	0.1518	1.06	N.S
Memory	50	8.92	0.16			

Table 3.64. To correlate Sensitivity with that of Recognition of Social Environment, Tactfulness, Sense of humour and Memory of Private School boys

Variables	No	Mean	S.D	'r'	't'	L.S
Sensitivity Vs	50	20.529	2.6	0.060	0.41	N.S
Recognition of Social Environment	50	0.843	0.7			
Sensitivity Vs	50	20.529	2.6	0.0456	0.31	N.S
Tactfulness	50	3.627	0.87			
Sensitivity Vs	50	20.529	2.6	0.155	1.08	N.S
Sense of Humour	50	3.549	1.269			
Sensitivity Vs	50	20.529	2.6	0.222	1.57	N.S
Memory	50	8.372	2.16			

Table 3.65. To correlate Sensitivity with that of Recognition of Social Environment, Tactfulness, Sense of humour and Memory of Private School Girls

Variables	No	Mean	S.D	'r'	't'	L.S
Sensitivity Vs	50	21.26	2.04	0.007	0.04	N.S
Recognition of Social Environment	50	0.62	0.7			
Sensitivity Vs	50	21.26	2.04	0.368	2.74	0.01
Tactfulness	50	4.28	1.08			
Sensitivity Vs	50	21.26	2.04	0.35	2.58	0.01
Sense of Humour	50	3.68	1.7			
Sensitivity Vs	50	21.26	2.04	0.043	0.29	N.S
Memory	50	8.92	0.16			

Table 3.66. To correlate Recognition of Social Environment with tactfulness, Sense of humour and Memory of Private School boys

Variables	No	Mean	S.D	'r'	't'	L.S
Recognition of Social Environment Vs	50	0.843	0.7	0.194	1.37	N.S
Tactfulness	50	3.627	0.87			
Recognition of Social Environment Vs	50	0.843	0.7	0.0074	0.05	N.S
Sense of Humour	50	3.549	1.269			
Recognition of Social Environment Vs	50	0.843	0.7	0.159	1.11	N.S
Memory	50	8.372	2.16			

Table 3.67. To correlate Recognition of Social Environment with tactfulness, Sense of humour and Memory of Private School girls

Variables	No	Mean	S.D	'r'	't'	L.S
Recognition of Social Environment Vs	50	0.62	0.7	0.25	0.17	N.S
Tactfulness	50	4.28	1.08			
Recognition of Social Environment Vs	50	0.62	0.7	0.001	0.006	N.S
Sense of Humour	50	3.68	1.7			
Recognition of Social Environment Vs	50	0.62	0.7	0.079	0.54	N.S
Memory	50	8.92	0.16			

Table 3.68. To correlate Tactfulness with Sense of humour and Memory of Private School boys

Variables	No	Mean	S.D	'r'	't'	L.S
Tactfulness Vs	50	3.627	0.87	0.8	9.23	0.01
Sense of Humour	50	3.549	1.269			
Tactfulness Vs	50	3.627	0.87	0.318	2.32	0.05
Memory	50	8.372	2.16			

Table 3.69. To correlate Tactfulness with Sense of humour and Memory of Private School Girls

Variables	No	Mean	S.D	'r'	't'	L.S
Tactfulness Vs	50	4.28	1.08	0.268	1.92	N.S
Sense of Humour	50	3.68	1.7			
Tactfulness Vs	50	4.28	1.08	0.0188	0.13	N.S
Memory	50	8.92	0.16			

Table 3.70. To correlate Sense of humour with that of Memory of Private School boys

Variables	No	Mean	S.D	'r'	't'	L.S
Sense of humour Vs	50	3.549	1.269	0.141	0.98	N.S
Memory	50	8.372	2.16			

Table 3.71. To correlate Sense of humour with that of Memory of Private School Girls

Variables	No	Mean	S.D	'r'	't'	L.S
Sense of humour Vs	50	3.68	1.7	0.344	2.53	0.01
Memory	50	8.92	0.16			

SUMMARY, FINDINGS AND CONCLUSION

Introduction

The present study aims at bringing to highlight how we have proceeded the work sincerely in the subject of social intelligence and life satisfaction among XI standard students. This chapter furnishes a short description of all the preceding chapters, highlights the main findings of the study and point out some implications and recommendations for application of the findings.

SAMPLE

Total 300 students were taken for the study of which 100 from government school, 100 from government Aided school and 100 from Private Schools in each category it contains 50 boys and 50 girls. All the students chosen for the study were studying in XI standard in Tuticorin District.

STATEMENT OF THE PROBLEM

Social intelligence and life satisfaction among higher secondary school students was chosen as the topic for the present study. government school, government Aided school and Private Schools were selected to conduct the study. Data were collected from 300 students (150 boys and 150 girls). In order to test the hypothesis proposed, the investigator statistically analyzed the data.

OBJECTIVES

1. To relate life satisfaction with that of social intelligence.
2. To find out the relationship between social intelligence with that of educational status of the parent in the case of total sample.
3. To identify associations existing between educational status of the parents and life satisfaction of the total sample.
4. To recognise the impact of type of family on social intelligence and life satisfaction of the total sample.

5. To know the impact of Gender on type of school, social intelligence, life satisfaction and various factors of social intelligence.
6. To interrelate various factors of social intelligence in the case of Government School, Government Aided School and Private School students.

FINDINGS AND DISCUSSIONS

Hypothesis I

Life satisfaction scores of the students will modify social intelligence.

The hypothesis was accepted and proved that life satisfaction scores modified the level of social intelligence of boys and girls of Private School and the boys of Government School. Where as in the case of boys and girls of Government Aided School and girls of Government School it was not found to be significant hence the hypothesis was rejected in these cases.

Hypothesis II

Social intelligence has no impact on education status of the students.

The hypothesis was accepted and proved that intelligence had no impact on education status of the students in the case of boys and girls from Government School, Government Aided School and Private School.

Hypothesis III

Social intelligence does not depend on the type of family.

The hypothesis was accepted and proved that intelligence did not depend upon the type of family of the students in the case of boys and girls from Government School, Government Aided School and Private Schools.

Hypothesis IV

Life satisfaction does not depend on Education status.

The hypothesis was accepted and proved that life satisfaction did not depend on education status of the students in the case of boys and girls from Private School, Government School and girls from Government Aided School. Where as in the case of boys of Government Aided School, it was found to be significant. Hence hypothesis was rejected in this case.

Hypothesis V

Life satisfaction has no impact with the type of family.

The hypothesis was accepted and proved that life satisfaction had no impact with the type of family of the students in the case of boys and girls from Government School, Government Aided School and Private School.

Hypothesis VI

Gender plays an important role on life satisfaction of students.

The hypothesis was accepted and proved that gender played an important role on life satisfaction of student in the case of Private School and Government Aided School. Where as in the case of Government School. It was not found to be significant. Hence the hypothesis was rejected in this case.

Hypothesis VII

Gender plays an important role on total score of social intelligence.

The hypothesis was accepted and proved that gender played an important role on total score of social intelligence of student in the case of Private School and Government Aided School. Where as in the case of Government School, it was not found to be significant. Hence the hypothesis was rejected in this case.

Hypothesis VIII

Gender plays very important role on various factors of social intelligence of the total sample.

The hypothesis was accepted and proved that gender played very important role on patience factors or social intelligence in the case of boys and girls of Private School and Government Aided School. Where as in the case of

Government School, it was not found to be significant. Hence the hypothesis was rejected in this case.

The hypothesis was accepted and proved that gender played an important role on co-operativeness factors of social intelligence in the case of boys and girls of Private Schools. Where as in the case of boys and girls of Government Aided School and Government School, it was not found to be significant. Hence the hypothesis was rejected in these cases.

The hypothesis was accepted and proved that gender played very important role on confidence factors of social intelligence in the case of boys and girls of Private Schools, Government Aided School and Government School.

The hypothesis was rejected and proved that gender did not play important role on sensitivity factors of social intelligence in the case of Private Schools, Government Aided School and Government School.

The hypothesis was accepted and proved that gender played very important role on recognition of social environment factors of social intelligence in the case boys and girls of Government Aided School. Where as in the case of Private Schools and Government School, it was not found to be significant. Hence the hypothesis was rejected in these cases.

The hypothesis was accepted and proved that gender played very important role on tactfulness in the case boys and girls of Government School and Private School. Where as in the case of boys and girls of Government Aided School, it was not found to be significant. Hence the hypothesis was rejected in this case.

The hypothesis was accepted and proved that gender played very important role on sense of humour factors of social intelligence in the case of boys and girls of Private School. Where as in the case of Government Aided School and Government School, it was not found to be significant. Hence the hypothesis was rejected in these cases.

The hypothesis was accepted and proved that gender played very important role on memory factors of social intelligence in the case boys and girls of Government Aided School. Where as in the case of Private Schools and Government School, it was not found to be significant. Hence the hypothesis was rejected in these cases.

Hypothesis IX

Various factors of social intelligence are rejected to each other of Government School.

The hypothesis was accepted and proved that patience and confidence where, interrelated in the case boys and girls of Government School. When patience was related with co-operativeness and sensitivity it was found to be significant in Government School girls, where as other factor where correlated with patience it was not found to be significant in the case of boys and girls of Government School. Hence the hypothesis was rejected in this case.

The hypothesis was accepted and proved that co-operativeness was related with confidence and sensitivity in the case of boys and girls of Government School. When the co-operativeness was related with recognition of school environment and tactfulness it was found to be significant in boys of Government School. where as other factors were correlated with co-operativeness it was not found to be significant in the case of boys and girls of Government School. Hence the hypothesis was rejected in this case.

The hypothesis was rejected and proved that confidence and various factors of social intelligence were not related in the case of Government School boys and girls.

The hypothesis was accepted and proved that the sensitivity and sense of humour where inter related in the case of Government School girls. When the sensitivity were related with other factors it was found not to be significant in the case of boys and girls of Government School. Hence the hypothesis was rejected in this case.

The hypothesis was rejected when the recognition of social environment was correlated with sense of humour, tactfulness and memory. It was not found to be significant in the case of boys and girls of Government School.

The hypothesis was rejected when tactfulness was correlated with sense of humour and memory. It was not found to be significant in the case of boys and girls of Government School.

The hypothesis was accepted and proved that sense of humour and memory were interrelated in the case of Government School girls. When the sense of humour were related with memory it was not found to be significant in the case of Government School boys. Hence the hypothesis was rejected in this case.

Hypothesis X

Different factors of social intelligence are related to each other in the case of Government Aided School.

The hypothesis was accepted and proved that patience were interrelated with co-operativeness and sensitivity in the case of Government Aided School girls and boys. When the patience was related with confidence it was found to be significant in Government Aided School boys. Where as other factors were correlated with patience it was found not to be significant in the case of Government Aided School boys and girls. Hence hypothesis was rejected in these cases.

The hypothesis was accepted and proved that co-operativeness and confidence were interrelated in the case of Government Aided School boys and girls. When the co-operativeness was related with sensitivity it was found to be significant in Government Aided School boys. Where as other factors were correlated with co-operativeness it was not found to be significant in the case of boys and girls of Government Aided School. Hence the hypothesis was rejected in these cases.

The hypothesis was accepted and proved that confidence and sensitivity were interrelated in the case of Government Aided School boys and girls. When the confidence was related with sense of humour it was found to be significant in

Government Aided School girls, where as other factors were correlate with confidence it was not found to be significant in the case of boys and girls of Government Aided School. Hence the hypothesis was rejected in these cases.

The hypothesis was rejected and proved that sensitivity and various factors of social intelligence are not interrelated in the case of boys and girls of Government Aided School.

The hypothesis was accepted and proved that recognition of social environment were interrelated with tactfulness and sense of humour in the case of Government Aided School girls. Where as other factors were correlated with recognition of social environment it was not found to be significant in the case of boys and girls of Government Aided School. Hence the hypothesis was rejected in this case.

The hypothesis was accepted and proved that tactfulness and sense of humour were interrelated in the case of Government Aided School boys. Where as other factors correlated with tactfulness it was not found to be significant in the case of boys and girls of Government aided School. Hence the hypothesis was rejected in this case.

The hypothesis was accepted and proved that sense of humour and memory were interrelated. Where as in the case of Government Aided School girls. It was found not to be significant. Hence the hypothesis was rejected in this case.

Hypothesis XI

Various factors of social intelligence are interrelated among themselves of private school.

The hypothesis was accepted and proved that patience and co-operativeness were interrelated in the case of boys and girls of Private School. When the patience was related with confidence it was found to be significant in Private School boys. When the patience was related with sensitivity it was found to be significant in Private School girls, where as other factors were correlated with patience it was not found to be significant in the case of Private School boys and girls. Hence the hypothesis was rejected in these cases.

The hypothesis was proved that co-operativeness and confidence were interrelated in the case of Private School boys and girls. When the co-operativeness was related with sense of humour it was not found to be significant in Private School girls, when the co-operativeness was related with memory it was found to be significant in Private School boys. Where as other factors were correlated with co-operativeness it was not found to be significant in the case of Private School boys and girls. Hence the hypothesis was rejected in this case.

The hypothesis was accepted and proved that confidence and memory were interrelated in the case of Private School boys. Where as other factors were correlated with confidence it was not found to be significant in the case of Private School boys and girls. Hence the hypothesis was rejected in these cases.

The hypothesis was accepted and proved that sensitivity were interrelated with tactfulness and sense of humour in the case of Private School girls. where as other factors were correlated with sensitivity it was not found to be significant in the case of boys and girls of Private School. Hence the hypothesis was rejected in these cases.

The hypothesis was rejected when recognition of social environment was correlated with sense of humour, tactfulness and memory it was found not to be significant in the case of boys and girls of Private School.

The hypothesis was accepted and proved that tactfulness was interrelated with sense of humour, and memory in the case of Private School boys. Where as other factors was correlated with tactfulness it was not found not to be significant in the case of Private School girls. Hence the hypothesis was rejected in this case.

The hypothesis was accepted and proved that sense of humour and memory were interrelated in the case of Private School girls. When the sense of humour were related with memory it was not found to be significant in the case of boys of private school.

EDUCATIONAL IMPLICATIONS

The finding of the present investigation are important for the improvement in the quality of Education. The following are some of the major recommendation to implicate the Life satisfaction and social intelligence of the students.

1. Educators and administrators should bring about awareness among students to give more importance to develop Life satisfaction and social intelligence.
2. Parent's role is necessary to develop Life satisfaction of students through guiding, directing, stimulating and encouraging.
3. Lectures should provide inspiring leadership in developing Life satisfaction and social intelligence among students.
4. Emotional development programmes and seminor are to be arranged in the classrooms.
5. Early identification and environmental stimulation by teachers are very much essential. They should conduct Life satisfaction and social intelligence tests in the classrooms.

Emmons (1986) found that positive affect is related to the Degree to which one accomplishes their goals, negative affect is related to the individual's ambivalence about their goals and Conflict between their goals, and life satisfaction was highest for those who had goals that were very important to them. Cantor (1994) belaieves that an individual's goals are determined by one's life circumstances, expectations of the Culture, and the person's idiosyncratic needs. People can accomplish their goals in a variety of ways, but those with high Life satisfaction have developed effective strategies for meeting there needs within the constraints of cultural expectations and life circumstances. Intrinsic goals reflect inherent growth tendencies and satisfy inherent psychological needs whereas extrinsic goals are imposed on the individual by Society and are sought for the approval of others or some other end. Specially, the extrinsic goals of desire for material.

SUGGESTIONS FOR FURTHER RESEARCH

1. Social intelligence and academic achievement among the secondary school students.
2. Social intelligence in relation to creativity among higher secondary school students.
3. Life satisfaction and intellectual ability among the high school students.
4. Life satisfaction, intelligence and learning process among the higher secondary school students.
5. Life satisfaction and self confidence among the secondary school students.

REFERENCES

1. Bailey and Miller (1998), Predicting Life Satisfaction, Personality and Social Psychology Bulletin, in August Edition.
2. Binet, A. (1916), The Development of Intelligence in Children (translated by E.S. Kite). Vineland. N.J. : Training School.
3. Cacioppo, J. T., & Petty, R. E. (1982), The need for cognition. Journal of Personality and Social Psychology, 42, 116-131.
4. Campbell A., et. al (1976), The quality of American life New York: Rissell sage Foundation.
5. Cattell, R.B. (1940), Theory of Fluid and Crystalized intelligence: A critical experiment, Journal of Educational Psychology, 31, 161-179.
6. Chaplin, J.P (1965), Dictionary of psychology.
7. Chatterjee, A. and Dutta Roy. D (1991), Awareness of external environment, environmental sati Applied Psychology, 29, 2, 74-77.
8. Chauhan, S.S. (1996), Advanced Educational Psychology, Sixth Revised Edition, Delhi: Vikas Publishing House Pvt. Ltd.

9. Cheung, C. (2000), Studying as a source of life satisfaction among university students. College Student Journal, 34, 79-96.
10. Cohen, A. R., et.al., (1955), An experimental investigation of need for cognition. Journal of Abnormal and Social Psychology, 51, 291-294.
11. Diener, E., and R., Larsen, R., (1985), The Satisfaction with Life Scale. Journal of Personality Assessment 49, 71-75.
12. Dockrell, W.B. (1974), On Intelligence, London : Methuen.
13. Dr. Bhatnagar A.B. (2004), Educational Psychology, Meerut. Surya Publications.
14. Dr. Mangal S.K. (1983), Psychological Foundation of Education, Ludhiana: Rampracash Tandon.
15. Dr. R.S. Sharma (2004), Teaching of Social Science, by Surya Publicaitons.
16. Dutta Roy, D. & Mukhopadhyay, S. (1999), Organizational coping and organizational commitment across organizational hiearchies in heavy engineering organizations, Journal of Behavioural Sciences. 10, 2, 5-20.
17. Dutta Roy, D. (2000), Maximizing coefficient alpha of state anxiety inventory in repeated measurement design, Indian Journal of Psychometry and Education, 31, 2, 111-114.
18. Dutta Roy, D. and Mallik, R. (2000), Ranking General aptitudes for success in computer programming, Journal of the Indian Academy of applied Psychology, 26, 1-2, 135-139.
19. Dutta Roy, D.(1996), Personality model of fine artists,Creativity Research Journal, 9, 4, 391-394.
20. Dutta Roy, D. (1991), A comparative study of organizational awareness strategies in private and public sector, Decision, 18, 1, 41-44.
21. Dutta Roy, D. (2002), Computer programming job analysis, Management and Labour Studies. 27, 4, 255-262.

22. Dutta Roy, D.(1991), A model of change in Organizational health to improve Quality of life, Social Science International, Vol. 16, No. 4, pp. 189-191.
23. Esther N Goody (1995), "Social Intelligence and Interaction" Published by Cambridge University.
24. Fisher and Bradley. J (1995), Successful Aging, Life Satisfaction and Generativity in Later Life, International Journal of Aging and Human – Development, Vol. 1, No. 3, pp. 239-50. ERIC.
25. Guilford, J.P. (1967), The Nature of Human Intelligence, New York : McGraw Hill.
26. Guilford, J.P. Hopener, R. (1971), The Analysis of Intelligence, New York, McGraw Hill.
27. Harry Elmer Barnes (2004). History and Social Intelligence, Kessenger.
28. Hawkins and Barbara, A Validity and Reliability of a Five Dimensional Life Satisfaction Index, Mental Retardation, Vol. 33, No. 5, p. 295-303, Oct. 1995.
29. Henry – Caroln. S, and Lovelace Sandra. G. (1995), Family Resources and Adolescent Family Life Satisfaciton in Remarried Family Households, Journal of Family Issues; Vol. 16, No. 6, pp. 765-86, Nov. 1995.
30. Henry and Carolyn. S (1994), Family System Characteristics, Parental Behaviours and Adolescent Family Life Satisfaction, Family Relations, Vol. 43, No. 4, p. 447-55, Oct. 1994.
31. Hoffman, R.E. (1987). Computer simulations of neural information processing and the schizophrenia-mania dichotomy. Archives of General Psychiatry, 44:178-188.
32. Huebner and Scott. E. (1994), Life Satisfaction Scale and the Piers – Harris Self-Concept Scale, Psychology in the School, Vol. 33, No. 31, p. 273-77, Oct. 1994.
33. Humphreys, L.G. (1971), Theory of Intelligence, In R. Cancro (Ed), Intelligence : Genertic and Environmental Influences (31-55), New York; Grune and Stratton.
34. Hunt, T. (1928), The measurement of Social Intelligence, Journal of Applied Psychology, 12, 317-334.

35. Leone, C., & Dalton, C. (1988), Some effects of the need for cognition on course grades. Perceptual and Motor Skills, 67, 175-178.

36. Lewis, Virginia. G and Borders. L (1995), Life Satisfaction of Single Middle-Aged Professional Women, Journal of Counselling and Development, Vol. 74, No. 1, p. 100, Sep. 1995.

37. Mayer, J.D. and Salovey, P. (1993), The intelligence of Emotional Intelligence; 433-422.

38. Mc Clelland, B.C. (1973), Testing for competence rather than Intelligence, American Psychologist, 28, 1-14.

39. Meeker, M.N. (1969), The structure of Intellect: its interpretation and uses, columbas, Ohio: charles E. Merril.

40. Park, Douglas et.al. (1994), The Influence of Separation Orientation on Life Satisfaction in the Elderly, International Journal of Aging and Human – Development, Vol. 39, No. 2, p. 117-07, 1994.

41. Piaget, J. (1947), The Psychology of Intelligence, London: Routledge and Kegal Paul.

42. Pintner, R. and Upshall, C.C. (1928), Some results of social Intelligence Tests, School and Society, 27, 369-370.

43. Spearman, C. (1923), The Nature of "Intelligence" and the Principles of Cognition, London: McMillan.

44. Spearman, C. (1927), The Abilities of Man, New York: Mac Millan.

45. Stern, W. (1914), The Psychological Methods of Testing Intelligence, (Translated by G.M. Whipple) Educational Psychology Monographs.

46. Thorndike, E.L. (1927), The Measurement of Intelligence, New York://Teachers College, Columbia University.

47. Vernon, P.F. (1948), Indices of Item consistency and validity, British Journal of Psychology 1, 152-166.

48. Young and Margaret. H, The Effect of Parental Supportive Behaviour on Life Satisfaction of Adolescent Offspring, Journal of Marriage and the Family, Vol. 57, No. 3, p. 813-22, Aug. 1995.

APPENDIX – I

SOCIAL INTELLIGENCE SCALE (SIS)

INSTRUCTIONS

In this booklet there are some statements regarding the way in which we behave, feel and act. We want your first response. Please try to make your best possible answer honestly and sincerely. Read and understand each question properly and then put your mark on any cell against every statement on the answer-sheet by making the sign of cross (X) please do not omit any question. Your answer will be kept strictly confidential. We need your full cooperation.

INSTRUCTIONS

Please read the following statements carefully and among the three responses "given for each of them, pick up the one which seems to you to be the most likely way in which you would respond. You are to choose only one response from a, b and c and mark a cross (X) on the appropriate cell on the answer-sheet.

Sr. No.	Statement	*a*	*b*	*c*
1.	Your servant has taken days leave.	You are the first to volunteer help.	You will help if nobody else does.	You find some excuse and avoid helping.
2.	When you hear about a crime.	You sympathise solely with the indifferent Victims.	You remain indifferent.	You do both, sympathise with the victims and emphathise with the criminals.

Sr. No.	Statement	*a*	*b*	*c*
3.	You have been given an award for academic excellence.	How did you manage it?	I deserved it?	Well, nobody else could have got it.
4.	You are forced to rewrite some of your notes because somebody stole them.	I will kill the person.	I wonder why somebody had to do this.	I will never forgive him/ her.
5.	You are requested to switch off the music system as your neighbour is having a severe headache.	You immediately comply.	You ignore the request.	You grumble and aruge.
6.	You come across an accident where a car collided with an elephant. The former was damaged and the latter died. What strikes you first?	The damaged car received.	The dead elephant.	Both.
7.	You are asked to join a rough treck.	I am determined to give it a try.	I wonder if I can stand the strain.	Oh! I won't risk it.
8.	Some one who is dependent on you spends your hard earned money on gambling.	You repirmand severaly.	You take it over.	You decide to throw him out.
9.	If you are asked to come for a picnic you do not really want to go	You will go.	You refuse point blank.	You will try your best avoid going if it were

Sr. No.	Statement	*a*	*b*	*c*
	but your friends would like you to go.			possible.
10.	You hear that some anti-social elements have been given capital punishment.	You are happy.	You are relieved.	You are against capital punishment.
11.	You are invited for a grand party.	I hope I know people there.	I guess I'll make friends.	I wish I did not have to go.
12.	You are asked to make a speech at public function.	Gosh! I am nervous.	I will give them a talk to remember.	I wonder if a substitute can be found.
13.	You come out of a restaurant and find a beggar out side.	You give him some money.	You ignore him.	You feel guilty.
14.	If you had to share you room with a distant cousin for a week.	You hesitate.	You refuse.	You agree immediately.
15.	At a group meeting you find it impossible to flut forward a very pertinent point.	You get disgusted.	You want to scream.	You decide to make it late if possible.
16.	Your friend fails to understand the solution to simple technical problem which you have	You tell your friend that he/she is stupid.	You continue to try.	You dismiss the subject.

Sr. No.	Statement	*a*	*b*	*c*
	explained many times over.			
17.	You are required to stay home to look after someone in your family and hence to cancel an outing.	You wouldn't do it.	You cancel your outing.	You look for an altern-ative solution.
18.	When you see a child being hit by his parent in public.	You sympathise with the child.	You set upset.	You look for an alter-native solution.
19.	You are faced with a stiff problem.	I can't solve it.	I sure some thing will come up.	There can be no possible solution for this.
20.	Your friend arrives 45 minutes late for an appointment.	You are wild at him/her.	You refuse listen to excuses.	You ask for an expla-nation.
21.	You are asked to walk a long way to the market to get something for a party at home.	You refuse.	You agree to go.	You try, persuading other's to go.
22.	If you see a blind man waiting try to cross a road and looking for help.	You want to see if someone else will help.	You imme-diately offer assistance.	You decide to ignore this situaiton.
23.	You have failed your examina-tions.	This is terrible.	I will always fail.	I'm sure I will do better next time.
24.	Caged birds are being sold all over the country.	You consider them decora-tive.	You appre-ciate their beauty.	You think that they ought to be feed.
25.	If you are asked to	You will	You will	You will

Sr. No.	Statement	*a*	*b*	*c*
	step down from some high post for a good cause.	resign.	fight and try to retain the post.	refuse it immediately.
26.	You are asked to baby sit a child for the evening.	You try to quickly put the child to sleep.	You try to form a rapport with the child.	You refuse to baby sit.
27.	You go for a movie with some family friends and find it very boring.	You wait till the end.	You walk out.	You tell your friend that they have had taste.
28.	If you had to sacrifice a holiday for a friend's need.	You would go on your holiday.	You would help your friend out.	You tell your friends that they have bad taste.
29.	You see a man screaming in pain on the roadside.	You help him.	You ignore him.	You can't help him but think about the incident for many days.
30.	You have been accused of a crime you never committed.	I will never be able to prove my self. I will prove my point.	I will prove my self.	There is no way I can get out of this.
31.	If you went home tired and found that you had to entertain some friends for the evening.	You display signs of reluctance.	You keep up a smile and ensure their comfort.	You will try your best to give them a hint.
32.	Suppose you are a team captain and some discussion arose.	You would refuse to accept the views of other members.	You consider yourself supreme.	You believe in over all participation.

Sr. No.	Statement	*a*	*b*	*c*
33.	If you finally find a dress you have been waiting for, for ages and discover that the size is not proper.	You wait for more places to arrive.	You buy it up any way and consider altering it.	You drop the idea completely.
34.	How would you react to the extreme poverty prevalent in slums?	Dirty slums sicken you.	You consider it their bad luck.	You feel responsible in some way.
35.	You are to play the lead role in play.	I can't act at all.	I am not presentable enough.	I will try and do my best.
36.	You are asked to attend a religious function at an old aunt's house.	You are unwilling because you dislike conventional people.	You accept jut to please your aunt.	You can't hear to sit through long ceremonies.

PART - II

INSTRUCTIONS

From each of the following quotations, select the word that most accurately describes the mental state of the person making the statement. Cross out (X) the correct answer on the answer-sheet.

Sr. No.	Statement	a	b	c
37.	The army will defend us. Will it?Won't it?	Despair	Indecision	Confidence
38.	And to think we had looked forward to this party for days.	Disappo-intment	Regret	Disgust
39.	We hate the way you admire her.What about us?	Despair	Jealousy	Posses-siveness

PART-III

INSTRUCTIONS

In this part, *there are some statements regarding the way you behave and act. Each statement has a forced choice response of either 'yes' or 'No', try and decide whether 'Yes' or 'No' represents your usual way of behaving and acting. If yes, cross out (X) the cell below 'Yes' and if no, then cross out (X) the cell below 'No'.

40. If you were the host in a party and had to entertain a mixed crowd in which there were some people you disliked intensely would you gently avoid them and give the other more attention.
41. Your friend brings you a gift for some occasion and it so happens that you don't like it much, would you feelings obviously.

42. If you had to give someone a piece of bad news and after having searched for almost a day, you finally find him / her in a disturbed mood would you give the news?
43. On arrival for dinner at a friend's place you discover that none of the dishes prepared appeals to your appetite. Would you resist showing traces of disappointment?
44. In your various successful enterprises do you think that your opponents experiences strong sense of defeat.
45. Do you go through experiences where you find that in some controversial matter after a while your opponents willingly acknowledge your point of views.
46. If you are asked to intervene in an argument between two persons without supporting any of them, do you expect to be. successful.

PART- IV

INSTRUCTIONS

Given below is a list of incomplete jokes. Against them, there are three choices with which to complete the joke. You are to select and cross out (X) the choice you consider to be the most humorous.

Sr. No.	Statement	*a*	*b*	*c*
47.	Doctor to patients: 'Are you married by any chance?' Patients :	My wife chooses her own doctor.	No the reason I look this way is that I am sick.	That was ten years back.
48.	Two friends were discussing the reasons for their remaining single after all these years. 'Why only a few days', said the first, 'I met a girl and fell in love with her at first sight'. 'Well', then said the second, 'Why didn't you marry her'?	I took a second look.	She was my boss's wife.	Her boy friends punched me.
49.	It was their first fight after marraige and the sordid subject was money. 'Before we were married', She cried, "You told me you were well off'	'So What' he yelled.	'I was', he snarled but I don't know it'.	How right I was he retored.
50.	Why does he suffer from eyestrain?	Lack of spectacles	He lives opposite the YWCA	He sleeps very little
51.	'You're a liar', challenged muscles,' Really', grumbled the small man, 'Say	Forget it	Bye-bye, I have to hurry	Consider it bursted.

Sr. No.	Statement	*a*	*b*	*c*
	that again and I'll burst your law' 'Consider it said', taunted muscles.		home	
52.	'Don't I look good tails?'	No.	We all do don't we.	Why not? Your ancestor did.
53.	Elderly passenger who objects to cigarette smoking. 'If you were my husband, I'd give you poison'. Replied the smoker:	Well if you were my wife I'd take it.	You'd still go to jail.	With or without desert.
54.	Patient to new doctor in the Mental Asylum, 'We all like your more than the old doctor';. 'Why?', queried the surprised doctor.	We feel you are more like one of us.	Well, the old doctor was longer. Slightly mad.	Your hair is longer.

APPENDIX – II

LIFE SATISFACTION SCALE

Sr. No.	Statement time	Always	Often	Some-	Seldom	Never
1.	I set realistic goal for myself	☐	☐	☐	☐	☐
2.	I, on the whole, enjoy my life	☐	☐	☐	☐	☐
3.	I enjoy whatever I do.	☐	☐	☐	☐	☐
4.	I enjoy the way I live	☐	☐	☐	☐	☐
5.	I believe life is for living	☐	☐	☐	☐	☐
6.	I am satisfied with the subject I study	☐	☐	☐	☐	☐
7.	I feel that I am a successful person	☐	☐	☐	☐	☐
8.	I obtain pleasure from domestic affairs	☐	☐	☐	☐	☐
9.	I feel proud that I am successful in my Examination	☐	☐	☐	☐	☐
10.	I love to get myself involved in leisure activities	☐	☐	☐	☐	☐
11.	I feel happy when 1 achieve my goals	☐	☐	☐	☐	☐
12.	I am very much optimistic about my future	☐	☐	☐	☐	☐
13.	I feel my studies are less demanding	☐	☐	☐	☐	☐

Sr. No.	Statement time	Always	Often	Some-	Seldom	Never
14.	I think that I am self-made man	☐	☐	☐	☐	☐
15.	I set priorities by planning the day	☐	☐	☐	☐	☐
16.	I enjoy taking part in social activities	☐	☐	☐	☐	☐
17.	I devote some time to community activities	☐	☐	☐	☐	☐
18.	Money making is not the only motive of my life	☐	☐	☐	☐	☐
19.	Want to make use of my skills to improve the quality of life	☐	☐	☐	☐	☐
20.	I want to raise my standard of living	☐	☐	☐	☐	☐
21.	I take life as it comes	☐	☐	☐	☐	☐
22.	I think I am capable of fulfilling demands of my life	☐	☐	☐	☐	☐
23.	I feel, I have a healthy sense of self	☐	☐	☐	☐	☐
24.	I hold optimistic attitude towards life	☐	☐	☐	☐	☐
25.	I maintain self-respect in different roles	☐	☐	☐	☐	☐
26.	I understand my strength and weaknesses	☐	☐	☐	☐	☐
27.	I believe in self-help and self-sufficiency	☐	☐	☐	☐	☐
28.	I have a lot of control over my life	☐	☐	☐	☐	☐
29.	I never leave a job unfinished	☐	☐	☐	☐	☐

Sr. No.	Statement time	Always	Often	Some-	Seldom	Never
30.	I am interested in sports activities	☐	☐	☐	☐	☐
31.	I can solve my problems effectively	☐	☐	☐	☐	☐
32.	I derive satisfaction from whatever I do	☐	☐	☐	☐	☐
33.	I believe I am a healthy person	☐	☐	☐	☐	☐
34.	I can face unanticipated hardships	☐	☐	☐	☐	☐
35.	I feel, I am a courageous person	☐	☐	☐	☐	☐

CHAPTER 4

Climate and Job Satisfaction of Teachers

INTRODUCTION

Teachers are the backbone of the educational process and play a vital role in building the nation. Teachers act as a pivot around which all the educational programmes rotate and they are crucial in the implementation process also. It is also a fact that the quality of teachers influences the level of achievement of students. Teachers have an impact on all the desired outcomes envisaged in an individual by the society. Thus the role of teachers does not limit itself to impart the knowledge alone, but in broadening the national outlook, enhancing sense of efficacy and competency among the future citizens and preparing individuals for the right type of profession.

CONCEPT OF A PROFESSION

A profession has certain level of skill and knowledge before put to practice. Entry to the profession is thus restricted to those who have already acquired the requisite skills and knowledge. All members of a profession are expected to have a minimum level of competence and share a general belief in what counts good practice.

Professionals have good specific sense of purpose and responsibility and they are bound by codes of ethics that outline how they operate in their professional life. Professionals are generally respected because they have skills that are valuable to the society.

TEACHING AS A PROFESSION

Teaching qualifies the fundamentals of a profession and it posses the qualities of sincere devotion for the betterment of human (Wise 1994) Human interaction gives personal touch in the educational process and that takes place in school environment plays an important role in shaping students in the classroom. "The destiny of India is being shaped in the class room" and - teachers influence the behaviour of students as per Kothari Commission Report on Education 1964-66. Hence, school is a place where web of interaction takes place together among varied people including teacher's students and organisational people creates interactive environment leads to an organisational climate.

Job satisfaction is important to the employee, the worker and the community. The community profits on the score of an individual and well being of the society in general the understanding of the dynamics of job satisfaction therefore requires serious consideration of all concerned. Teaching is one of the most common professions in the society. Job satisfaction among teachers is one of the problems that the administration faces. When the teacher engages in a plan to achieve higher school effectiveness the performance and effectiveness of the teacher and school also improves. For improving job satisfaction among teachers, environment of the institution should be such in which teacher obtain social need satisfaction and enjoy a sense of accomplishment in their job.

THE CONCEPT OF JOB SATISFACTION

Job satisfaction is concerned with the feelings one has towards the job. The satisfaction one gets from out of tasks assigned to him in his job. People especially those above the lower rung of an organisation feel adequately rewarded only when the jobs are challenging and help to exploit their latent talents to the maximum.

Job satisfaction as a "reintegration of effect produced by

individual perception of fulfillment of his needs in relation to his work and the situations surrounding it. In the other hand job satisfaction refers to a general attitude towards work by an individual worker"(Syadain 1995)

DEFINITION OF JOB SATISFACTION

Job satisfaction may be viewed as the pleasurable emotional state resulting from the perceptions of one's job as fulfilling or allowing the fulfillment of one's needs, Edwin A Locke,(1976). According to P.C.Smith (1990) job satisfaction is the persistent feeling towards different aspects of the job situation. E.A. Locke (1969) admits the job satisfaction and job dissatisfaction are seen as function of perceived relationship between the one wants from job and how he perceived it as offering or entailing. Job satisfaction may be global or specific. Some times job satisfaction is referred to as overall feeling of satisfaction (i.e. Global satisfaction). At some other point of times job satisfaction refers to person's feeling towards specific dimensions of the work.

DETERMINANTS OF JOB SATISFACTION

Many factors influence job satisfaction of employees. Review of research reveals the following important determinants of job satisfaction.

(*i*) Supervision

The first and foremost important determinants of job satisfaction are supervision and the style of leadership.

(*ii*) Job Content

Another influential factor of job satisfaction is the job content. Job content refers to the factors such as recognition, responsibility, advancement, achievement etc. in the jobs employee perform.

(*iii*) Specialisation

The relationship between job specialisation and job satisfaction is complex and that leads to greater efficiency in general, but at the same time it lowers the job satisfaction to some people with increasing but after a particular point it starts falling. That is to say after a certain point of specialisation, it leads to dissatisfaction.

(*iv*) Educational level

Keeping the occupational level as constant there we found a negative correlation between the level of education of employees and their satisfaction. A Possible explanation could be that people with educated level have a tendency to set higher expectation from their jobs. Dissatisfaction will be more when an educated person is employed in lower grades.

(*v*) Age

The relationship between age and job satisfaction is both complex and fascinating. Research reveals that old workers are satisfied workers. Job satisfaction usually tends to be high when people enter the work force.

(*vi*) Race and Sex

Sex and race also affects job satisfaction. It has been found that job satisfaction among blacks and other minority groups has been consistently lower than that of whites in America. When males and females were equally affected by such determinants of job satisfaction as wages, prestige and supervisory positions.

CONSEQUENCES OF JOB DISSATISFACTION

Job dissatisfaction can act as a double-edged sword as it reduced absenteeism and labour turn over.

Absenteeism : There exist a relationship between the job satisfaction and frequency of absence of employees weather unexcused absence due to minor aliments. Absenteeism is inversely related to the level of job satisfaction.

Turnover : Research has clearly established that the satisfied worker is less likely than his dissatisfied counterpart to quit the job overtime.

Negative publicity : Another frequently notable consequence of job dissatisfaction is badmouthing the organisation. That is disgruntled employee verbalises his discontent.

THE CONCEPT OF ORGANISATIONAL CLIMATE

In 1950's and 1960's a new line of enquiry captured the attention of the researchers in the field of natural and social sciences. This line of enquiry introduced the concept of environment and organisational climate in to the field of educational research. Studies of 'environments' of organisations became quick popular with the social scientists, particularly with those who are interested in the studies of organisations, their characteristics and effectiveness. After 1970 a new emphasis was laid on the study of human environment. A movement was started to make an all out effort to upgrade the quality of human life.

This created a strong concern for improving the social environment of the human milieu. Hence studies of organisational environment have quite often focused on organisational climate also. In fact scientists have used different methods and dimensions for characterising organisational environments. Thus a distinction that is drawn between the organisational environment and organisational climate is that of 'part' and the 'whole' organisational climate constitutes a specific dimension of the total environment, which may be defined as the environment of an organisation.

DEFINITIONS OF ORGANISATIONAL CLIMATE

It has been classified on the basis of the existing literature that organisational climate is an aspect of organisation's total environment, a characteristics that give a unique quality to the environment. Hence quite often the term 'environment' has been used in place of 'climate'. Physiological environment is considered more often an identical form for 'organisational climate'. Thus number of terms such as atmosphere, climate, physiological environment, ethos, social interaction, inter personal relationships, social emotional climate etc., have been used in literature interchangeably. Benjamin Bloom(1978) regards organisational climate as " a network of forces and factors which surround, engulf and play on the individual."

The environment is a shaping and reinforcing force which acts on the individuals". Miskel(1987) defines climate with special reference to inter personal relations of people in the organisation. He calls this "interpersonal climate" and describes it as the behaviour, attitude and perceptions of the individuals within the building as they interact with each other. Hellreigel and slocum (1984) pointed out that an effective climate is a simple and static environment may prove to be dysfunctional in a dynamic and complex environment. At the same time it should be noted that the climates of different organisational subsystems are seldom radically different. Therefore, instead of taking a fragmented view of climate in a particular sub-system the total system may be more meaningful to study and analyse.

The school is a people developing or changing socio, psychological organisation. The interaction of organisational behaviour within the school gives rise to the climate or personality of the school. Better teaching and learning depends on the climate of schools. Organisational climate is a global construct and creates a common phenomenon in reading various climates of organisation viz. learning environment academic climate, social climate, learning climate etc.,

School organisational climate is always measure in terms of healthy interpersonal dynamics. All human organisations have certain essential features. Firstly they have an objective of a good result to be achieved. Secondly there is structure, the way that people are placed in working relationship with each other. Research shows that school climate can affect many areas and people within schools. For example a positive climate has been associated with fewer behavioural and emotional problems for students. (Kuperminc et al., 2001)

School climate is multi-dimensional and influenced by many factors including students, parents, teachers, management (School personnel) and the community. Additionally school climate can siginificantly impact the educational environment as Freibeg(1998) notes "School climate can be a positive influence on health of learning environment or a significant barrier to learning.

FACTORS AFFECTING ORGANISATIONAL CLIMATE

In every organisation there exist certain elements that exert profound influence on the existing climate. In some organisations certain factors like structures and process play major role, where as in others the level of Technology may be the major influential factor in climate. Lawrence James and Allen Jones (1974) have tried to identify the factors influencing climate and they grouped these factors under 5 heads.

- Organisational content
- Organisational structure
- Process
- Physical environment
- System values and norms

TYPOLOGY OF CLIMATE

Halpin and croft identified that there are six organisational climates

The Open Climate

The open climate teachers enjoy extremely have high spirits and they work well together. They are not overloaded and they have job satisfaction. The principal works hard to set an example to the teachers. He criticizes the actions of the teachers whenever necessary. He considers the social needs of the teachers and helps them. He is in full control of the situation and he clearly provides leadership among teachers

The Autonomous Climate

The teachers enjoy almost complete freedom in the autonomous climate. They are satisfied with their job and work well together. The principal has set up procedures and regulations to facilitate the teacher's task. The teachers are allowed to do things analytically and creatively.

The Controlled Climate

Every teacher works hard under the controlled climate with emphasis on the task. It is task oriented and not employee centered. Teachers are not allowed to do work as they like and the heads controls them. The principal allows little flexibility.

The Familiar Climate

Here the relationship between the teacher and the principal is friendly in manner. Social need satisfaction is extremely high. The principal exerts little control in directing their activities. The principal helps teachers freely and exercises leadership in an indirect manner and tries to keep production satisfactory. The principal's behaviour is job oriented but does not hinder the social needs satisfaction on the part of the teachers.

The Paternal Climate

Under the paternal climate the teachers do not work well together. They are split into fractions. The headmaster's attempt is ineffective to control the teachers and there is only a very little hope to satisfy their social needs. The faculty has to work in the way the principal wants but at the same time the principal as the paternal guardian of the school faculty does not ignore the individual interest and hence his behaviour is perceived as highly considerate (Sharma 1973, p. 264)

Closed Climate

The teachers are dissatisfied with respect to the task achievement or social needs in schools where the closed climate prevails. It is not a genuine climate and it is characterised by a high degree of apathy on the part of all members of organisation. The organisation is not moving. This climate lacks authenticity of behaviour. The principal constrains the emergence of leadership acts from the group. The group members secure neither social needs satisfaction nor job satisfaction stemming from task-accomplishment (Sharma 1973,p.266)

Additionally specific research on school climate in high-risk urban environments indicated that a positive supportive and culturally conscious school climate could significantly shape the degree of academic success experienced by urban students (Haynes & Comer 1993)

The job satisfaction of teachers is important for any educational institutions and it is not new to educational thinking

STATEMENT OF THE PROBLEM

The problem under investigation is Organisational Climate and Job Satisfaction of Higher Secondary School Teachers.

DEFINITION OF TECHNICAL TERMS USED IN THE STUDY:

Organisational climate

In the present study the organisational climate refers to administrative and behavioural aspects of heads of schools

Job satisfaction

Job satisfaction refers to teachers happiness over facilities, security, working condition and liking for the job.

NEED AND SIGNIFICANCE OF THE STUDY

Many researches were conducted to find out the relationship between organisational climate and job satisfaction among college teachers. The research findings on this topic are concentrated mostly on discovering rather than creating a climate although investigators have envisaged the eventful possibility of selecting climate for maximum benefit. Hence this is certainly an area, which needs to be investigated. At the same time, the establishment of an appropriate climate also becomes one of the functions of administrations. The results of the study could bring out the prevailing condition of organisational climate and job satisfaction among higher secondary teachers of Madurai and suggestions could be made for a better organisational set up, consequently a better work morale.

OBJECTIVES OF STUDY

- To study the organisational climate of schools under different types of management
- To study the level of job satisfaction of higher secondary school teachers.
- To study the level of job satisfaction with respect to gender.
- To find out the significant difference between the job satisfaction of higher secondary teachers with respect to their length of experience
- To find out the significant difference between the job satisfaction of higher secondary teachers with respect to the type of school.
- To find out the significant difference between the job satisfaction of higher secondary school teachers with respect to their locality of the school.
- To find out the significant difference between the job satisfaction of higher secondary teachers with respect to their monthly income.
- To find out the correlation between the job satisfaction of higher secondary school with respect to their monthly income.

- To study the level of job satisfaction of higher secondary school teachers under different types of management
- To find out the interrelationship between organisational climate and job satisfaction of higher secondary school teachers

REVIEW OF LITERATURE

INTRODUCTION

This chapter aims in presenting background materials for the development of the present Investigation and also provided the investigator with rich and varied information in the fundamentals of the present problem. A summary of the writings of the recognised authors and the previous research provides evidence that the investigator can move from what is already known to what is still unknown. Review makes the investigator to be interested in knowing the achievements of researchers and helps to understand the significance of the discoveries. Since the effective research is based upon the past knowledge this step is also helpful to eliminate the duplication of the work. It has given the investigator a sound knowledge of all aspects of the problem chosen as a whole, helps to sharpen and define understanding of the existing knowledge in the problem area and also suggested the possible techniques and procedures to be assumed and applied in the current study.

RELATED STUDIES ON ORGANISATIONAL CLIMATE

A large proportion of studies surveyed the existing organisational climate of schools, colleges and universities.

Baylay (1957), Pace, Stern (1970) and others view environment as a powerful determinant of behaviour. Sharma (1969) Sharma,Buch and Rai(1971) Mubayi and Sharma(1971) found that schools differ in terms of their climates(environment). Sharma (1971) found that student's academic performance has significant relationship with school climate. Sharma and Santhanam (1971 and 1972) studied relationship of school climate with classroom teacher behaviour. Sharma and Quraishi (1972) explored into relationship between school climate and teachers morale. Sharma (1973) and Sharma and Parham (1973) studied the relationship between, school climate and initiating the structure behaviour and consideration behaviour of school heads respectively. Sharma (1972) studied school climate in relation with leadership behaviour of the headmaster. Sharma (1975) also studied the relationship of school climate with school effectiveness and teacher satisfaction along with other variables. Sharma (1974) found headmaster's effectiveness as significant predictor of school climate. Sharma (1973) conducted replication study along the lines of its originators and found new dimensions of climate and developed model profiles for Indian schools which have been discussed in this technical Manual. The book "Diagnosing the school climate" by Sharma (1978) gives, details about the development of the school organisational climate questionnaire. Studies referred above have indicated that school climate is related with student performance, teachers satisfaction school and headmaster effectiveness, leadership behaviour of the headmaster and many such other variables. All results have indicated that school environment warrants our immediate attention.

The dimensions of mostly touched upon over intellectual (anality of teaching, research, academic freedom etc., social moral trust, cohesiveness, communication, support, interpersonal relations) and administrative communication, disciplinary policy and structure. Differences were observed between the climate perceptions of faculty and administrators (Anderson 1983) the anti-creativity climate was reported in most of the institutions (Jex 1983,Gibb1968, Ellison et al., 1968, Taylor 1982) the capacity for innovation was facilitated by openness of climate and by teacher morale as well (Pillai, 1979).

The above picture of overall organisational climates of Educational Institutions was not quite clear on the other end of the climate and formed a normal distribution. The largest number came into the intermediate range high on some attitudes and low on others.

A number of studies linked the climate of institutions to the size of the institutions in forms of faculty and students. The size of an institution was found to have a mixed effect on climate, positive for some aspects and negative on others. (Duttlinger 1979, Bhatnagar 1979, China – Tangual, 1980) Negative association between these two was pointed by Rickout 1975 and shelt 1979. But Kumar1979, Metha 1979 and Birch 1982 found them all to be independent of each other.

These studies on educational administration reported its functions and pressure on it, which found a strong relationship, exist between macro social work activities and climate. May Carolyn Stdwey 1984 use activities index (AI) and (OCI) organisational climate index in evaluation and comparing climate in school organisation. The activity index discriminated between groups as expected.

Teachers' perception of school climate may be influenced by additional factors besides the principals leadership behaviours reported by scott and John Erren Jr on 1998.

RELATED STUDIES ON ORGANISATIONAL CLIMATE AND FACULTY MORALE

A substantial part of the studies under this category explored relationship of teacher morale with organisational climate. Halpin and Croft initiated this trend. They found faculty morale to be one of the important dimensions of school climate. Faculty morale was found closely tied to organisational climate (Sharma and Quaraishi, 1972; Murphy 1975; Aderunumu and Chinatangual, 1980)

Studies in 1979 by Pillai,Collica and Mehore found faculty morale to be positively associated with organisational climate(Openness,achievement,leadership behaviour) Institutions with open climate were found to be higher on ;the ladder of morale as compared to other groups.

RELATED STUDIES ON ORGANIZATIONAL CLIMATE AND STUDENT PERFORMANCE

Studies suggested that climates high in control were not conductive to the establishment of morale climate but led to behavioural problems of students. Aspects of social control like production emphasis disengagement hindrance etc affected all participants in an organisation (Plimpton 1979;Raburn 1979)

Students and teachers differed in their attitudes to climate conditions and positive attitudes were tied to better climate (Rao 1971and Friedmann 1979)

Studies indicated that a given climate condition may result in specific attitudes and behavioral responses by teachers and students and that one may affect the other.

STUDIES RELATED ON JOB SATISFACTION

Foreign studies related to Job satisfaction

Marlow (1996) : Studied the attitude of teachers through survey method and the study found that 44 percent of the teachers occasionally considered leaving the profession. Reason cited included student discipline, students' lack of motivation and poor attitudes, emotional factors such as lack of fulfillment boredom with the daily routine stress and frustration, lack of respect from the community, parents, administrators, and/ or students, difficult working condition, and low salaries. Also 49 percent of the population surveyed identified the professional prestige to be as they had expected it or better.

Lam peter (1995) : Studied 350 teacher trainees of Singapore's teacher training institution in their relationship among quality of work life carrier commitment, job satisfaction and withdrawal cognition. Carrier commitment perceptions of the social status of teaching strongly related to commitment to and satisfaction with teaching.

Clarke Robert (1995) : Found out the teachers job satisfaction instrument by brainstorming session with 81 teachers in Pennsylvania and the results were converted in to numerical scores and the findings revealed that pay did not appear to be a satisfier or dissatisfier, that interaction with students was the most satisfying factor and that majority of the subjects should approve of their children following in their factor and teachers were not happy with the state mandated innovations of outcome based education(OBE) and inclusion(NAV)

Kim I (1994) : Investigated predictors of teacher job satisfaction as these predictors through the sample of 2,054 practicing class room teachers. Through their findings the teachers job satisfaction are associated with both intrinsic and extrinsic rewards. That is, the factors salary and opportunities for advancement are generally perceived as extrinsic sources of satisfaction. Job satisfaction such as profession challenge, professional autonomy working conditions interaction with colleagues and interaction with students are generally classified as intrinsic satisfiers. Intrinsic satisfiers refer to factors that make certain activities rewarding in themselves. This study has potential of maximising the achievement of organisational and individual goals through improvement of teacher job satisfaction.

Saad IA (1996) : Studied the job satisfaction in transitional society within some of the Arabian schools and found that the satisfaction of teachers relies with work itself and with social needs too. Also finds that female teachers and teachers with higher educational levels were more likely to be satisfied with their jobs.

Heller H studied the relationship between teacher job satisfaction and principal leadership style.

Here about 45% of the 339 teachers were queried and found dissatisfied. The teachers were least satisfied with teachings financial aspects and most satisfied with co-workers. Job satisfaction was not significantly related to principal leadership style

A survey was conducted by **Hoppock(1935)** on teachers' job satisfaction. The sample of this study was five hundred teachers from North Eastern United States. The job satisfaction was estimated through four attitude scales. By combining these scales a measure of job satisfaction was obtained. Among the sample the most satisfied hundred and the least satisfied hundred was compared and the satisfied were differentiated from the dissatisfied teachers. The satisfied showed fewer indications of maladjustments and enjoyed better human relationships with their superiors. They were more religious and had selected their vocations on their own. They had seven and half years of experience in teaching. The main causes of dissatisfaction were monotony and fatigue.

Anjaneyulu(1968) conducted a study of job satisfaction among secondary school teachers and its impact on the education of pupils with special reference to the state of Andhra Pradesh. This study sought to find out the reasons for dissatisfaction among teachers working under different conditions. A sample of 1000 teachers was taken up using stratified random sampling technique in the Andra Pradesh State. The main findings were that factors like frequent transfers, low standard of teachers caused dissatisfaction among teachers. Indiscipline among pupils, lack of parental co-operation, lack of bright prospects in the job, lack of job security, rigid and orthodox service conditions and too much domination by the management were found to be the chief factors of dissatisfaction.

The job satisfaction of teachers in secondary school depends on the economic and social status and the poor such conditions causing dissatisfaction among teachers in secondary school was reported by **Anjaneyulu 1973.** Rigid rules orthodox service conditions and lack of parental cooperation are the causes of dissatisfaction among teachers working in government institutions.

Sing H L (1974) and **Goyal J.C (1980)** and **Thakkar P.A (1977)** suggested that there was a significant relationship between teachers attitudes and job satisfaction.

Kulsum N (1995) : Correlated a relationship between the dependent and independent variables. Teachers working in corporation schools were highly satisfied than those who were working in other types of schools. Amarsigh(1985)) correlated job satisfaction among different professionals for teachers engineers, advocates and doctors.

RELATED STUDIES ON ORGANISATIONAL CLIMATE AND JOB SATISFACTION

Most of the studies on organisational climate are based on organisational climate descriptive questionnaire. The studies included here reveal that the majority of the Indian schools have a closed climate followed by open and autonomous climates (Baraiya 1985,Swatandra Devi 1985 and Prakasham, 1986) Most of these studies related to organisational climate with set of other variable like teacher morale, job satisfaction performance of the students etc. Class room climate found to play a crucial role in student achievement (Uma Devi 1983;Lalithakumari 1984;singles 1984;and santhappan 1984) Disengagement among teachers was found to be related negatively to school effectiveness while feeling of esprit and feeling of intimacy were found related to school effectiveness (Srivastava 1985,Sriratna 1983). The promotions of a favourable organisational climate for creativity helped to increase productivity, satisfaction and mental health of workers (Ganesan 1987)

Organisational climates viz esprit, trust, consideration and total leadership behaviour are correlated with job satisfaction (Balvender and Kaur 1986) Student activism had a relationship of heads, teachers and improper methods of teaching (Rama 1978, Bassano, Louis V 1997) indicated that climate membership was significantly related to job satisfaction and performance. Pparaji and Timoty I 1988 suggested that teacher were dissatisfied with their jobs and perceived the school system as being unhealthy it suggest that administrators could enhance job satisfaction in their school by improving organisational climate.

Greaves 1991 reported that there is a direct positive correlation between school scoring on the openness index and job satisfaction. Alltrunian and Anita Rose 1992 decided that teachers working within the inter-disciplinary middle school perceived a greater degree of job satisfaction and perceived their school climate. The teachers perceived inter-disciplinary schools as having more open climate with high thrust, esprit engagement and satisfaction than did departmentalised schools.

Dimkpa P (1992) : Studied the impact of organisational climate and job satisfaction on black and white managerial job satisfaction. One hindered and twenty-four managers were assessed on their satisfaction level. Results indicated that black managerial job satisfaction and organisational climate significantly differs from each other and significantly influence one another. Results also suggest that retail organisations may not ready themselves for the multi-racial workforce of the future.

MillerB (1990) : Studied the job satisfaction among the Indian vocational home economics teachers.

Job satisfaction measured by the bray field index of job satisfaction and was found to be low. As per the result as the participation increase the job satisfaction decreased. Analysis of variance indicated a significant difference in job satisfaction between teachers who participated in eight or more activities and those who did not.

Craig FM (1992) has done a survey of organisational climate on the institutional research memo to all the faculty members and administrators at three campuses of the mid plains community college area. The survey instrument utilised likert scale to examine seven areas of institutional functioning and work environments. Study findings were compared to 1989 national norms for faculty and administrator attitudes. Study highlights included the following: (1) of the seven areas examined in the survey, there was least satisfaction among all groups in the area of rewards (relating to salary, benefits and personal growth), 64.8 %of the faculty and 52.9% of administrators rated work conditions as satisfactory or very satisfactory as compared with 63.5% and 74% for the national norms, respectively.

CONCLUSION

Based on the above review, the suitable methodology and procedure for the present investigation are given in detailed in the following chapter.

RESEARCH DESIGN AND METHOD

This chapter explains about the hypothesis relating to job satisfaction and organisational climate of higher secondary school teachers. The teachers of higher secondary schools have been classified on the basis of their respective managements viz Aided, Government and private.

Influence of sociological factors like gender length of experience locale salary on job satisfaction of higher secondary school teachers were also considered.

The present investigation is a survey type of research. The main objective of the present investigation is to find out whether a significant relationship exists between the organisational climate and job satisfaction of high school teachers and to find out the influence of background variables such as gender, type of management, experience, salary etc

The following hypothesis were formulated based on the objectives framed and cited in the first chapter.

HYPOTHESIS

There will be a significant difference in the organisational climate of schools under different types of management.

There will be a significant difference in the organisational climate of aided and government higher secondary teachers.

There will be a significant difference in the organisational climate of aided and private higher secondary school teachers.

There will be a significant difference in the organisational climate of government and private higher secondary teachers.

The over all job satisfaction of higher secondary school teachers will be high.

The gender difference has a hindrance on the level of job satisfaction of higher secondary school teachers with respect to their length of experience.

There will be a significant difference in the level of job satisfaction of higher secondary school teachers with respect to their length of experience.

There will be a significant difference in the level of job satisfaction of higher secondary school teachers under different types of management.

There will be a significant difference in the level of job satisfaction of higher secondary teachers in aided and government schools.

There will be a significant difference in the level of job satisfaction of higher secondary teachers in aided and private schools.

There will be a significant difference in the level of job satisfaction of higher secondary teachers in private and government schools.

There will be a significant positive correlation between organisational climate and job satisfaction of higher secondary school teachers.

RESEARCH TOOLS USED

Tool 1: School Organisational Climate Description Questionnaire (SOCDQ) developed by Sharma M (1978)

Tool 2: Teachers Job Satisfaction Scale (TJSS) developed by Mudgil Y (1998)

ORGANISATIONAL CLIMATE DESCRIPTIVE QUESTIONNAIRE

Description

The organisational climate descriptive questionnaire was meant to collect information from high school teachers. It consists of 63 items of which first 32 items were meant for assessing teacher behaviours and remaining 31 items were to rate the administrative behaviour of the heads of the schools. The distribution of the number of items to assess teachers behaviour is as follows.

DISTRIBUTION OF ITEMS UNDER DIFFERENT SUBTESTS

Sub tests		
Perceived behavioural aspects of teachers		items
1.	Disengagement	1,8,21,32,36,44,52,55,57
2.	Alienation	18,30,39,50
3.	Espirit	3,11,17,24,33,38,45,53,58
4.	Intimacy	5,12,25,34,40,46,54,60
5.	Psychophysical Hindrance	9,23,26,41,47,62
6.	Controls	15,20,27,42,48,63
7.	Production Emphasis	6,14,28,35,43,48,64
8.	Humanized Thrust	2,4,7,10,13,16,19, 22,29,31,37,51,56,59

JOB SATISFACTION SCALE

DESCRIPTION

Job satisfaction tool was administered to study the job satisfaction of higher secondary school teachers. It considered 60 items.

ADMINISTRATION

The test was administered personally to higher secondary school teachers who were required to put a tick mark in the appropriate column against the statements indicating the extent of job satisfaction on a five point scale as 1) Strongly agree 2) Agree 3) Undecided 4) Disagree 5) Strongly Disagree

SCORING

Evolving a tentative scheme of weight age quantitatively treats the response to the job satisfaction test.

In each dimension there are questions with positive and negative attitudes. The score for the response on the 5-point scale and the questions with positive attitudes were scored as follows.

1. Strongly agree - 5
2. Agree - 4
3. Undecided - 3
4. Disagree - 2
5. Strongly Disagree - 1

The score for the response for the response on the 5-point scale questions with negative attitudes were scored in a reverse order as mentioned above. The maximum no of items with positive attitude is 32 and negative attitude is 28.

SAMPLE

For the present study various higher secondary schools located at Madurai district was selected. Twelve Schools were randomly chosen for investigation and questionnaires were administered to the all the postgraduate assistants. Among them, 100 from aided school, 100 from Government school and 100 from private schools. Out of 300 150 respondents were males and 150 were females.

Table 4.1. Distribution of Sample

Sl.No.	Type of School	Frequency	Percentage
1.	Government	62	22.71
2.	Aided	108	39.56
3.	Private	103	37.73

Table 4.2.Distribution of Sample with Respect to Gender

Sl No.	Type of School	No of Males	No of Females	Total
1.	Government	25	37	62
2.	Aided	56	52	108
3.	Private	37	66	103
	Total	118	155	273

Table 4.3. Distributions of Sample with Respect to Locality

Sl.No.	Type of School	Locality		
		Rural	Urban	Total
1.	Government	31	31	62
2.	Aided	70	39	109
3.	Matriculation	15	87	102
	Total	116	157	273

MAIN STUDY

The main study deals with the procedure followed in administering the tests and in collecting data. The samples were randomly chosen from the higher secondary school. The samples of the higher secondary school teachers thus selected wee tested for variables of the present study using organisational climate descriptive questionnaire and job satisfaction test, which have been workable in the pilot study.

The following statistical measures were used in the present study to analyse and interpret the data.

Formula for finding standard deviation (S.D)

I = class interval

N = Total number of scores

F = frequency

D = $x^{-} x$

CONCLUSION

This chapter is outlined with the design of the present study and the type and nature of sample. It describes the hypothesis to be tested, the tools employed and the method of administration and scoring. The data collected is analysed and interpreted in the next chapter.

ANALYSIS AND INTERPRETATION OF DATA

In this chapter the classified datas are presented in tables and statically analysed. A brief interpretation follows each table. Data was processed in terms of mean and standard deviation.

MEANING OF ANALYSIS

After the data was collected it was classified according to the various categories tabulated and analysed. In short, analysis means studying the tabulated material in order to determine facts or meanings. Under ideal conditions of precision and simplicity, analysis present very few problems as the statement of hypothesis and the elaboration of the experimental design will automatically provide for the analysis of the data. The problem raised by the analysis of data is directly related to the complexity of the hypothesis.

TESTING THE HYPOTHESIS

Hypothesis: 1

The over all organisational climate of higher secondary school teachers will be Average

Table 4.4. Showing the frequency and percentage of organisational climate

Sl.No.	Over all Organisational climate	Frequency	Percentage	Cumulative frequency
1.	Low	71	26.01	26.01
2.	Average	129	47.25	73.26
3.	High	73	26.01	100

INTERPRETATION

From the above table it is inferred that the mean of the organisational climate of the scores lying in the average scores. Hence the empirical hypothesis is accepted.

Hypothesis- 2

Over all Job satisfaction of higher secondary school teachers are high.

Table 4.5. Showing the frequency and percentage of job satisfaction

Sl.No	Job Satisfaction	Frequency	Percentage	Cumulative percentage
1.	Low	73	26.74	26.74
2.	Average	129	47.25	73.99
3.	High	71	26.74	100
	Total	273	100	

INTERPRETATION

From the above table it is inferred that the mean score of the job satisfaction is falling in the average category. Hence the empirical hypothesis is rejected.

In order to find out the existence of any significant difference between the number of stay of teachers with regarded to organisational climate the F-ratio was calculated and has been presented in table

Hypothesis- 3

There is no significant difference between the government, aided and private higher secondary schools with regard to their organisational climate.

Inference

From the above table it is inferred that the calculated F value is greater than the table value and hence there is a significant difference between the Government, aided and private higher secondary schools with regard to their organisational climate at 0.01 level. So further critical ratio will be calculated.

Table 4.6. One Way ANOVA showing difference in the mean scores of the higher secondary schools (Government, Aided and Private) with respect to the organisational climate

Source of variation	D.F	Sum of Square	Mean of Square	F ratio	Level of Significance
Between groups	2	12549.15	6274.57		
Within groups	270	96963.37	359.12	17.47	0.01
Total	272	109512.28			

Hypothesis- 3a

There will be no significant difference in the organisational climate of Government, Aided and private higher secondary schools

Table 4.7. Showing the significance of difference in the mean scores of Government and Aided higher secondary schools with respect to organisational climates

Type of Management	N	Mean	S.D	SEMD	C.R	L.S
Government	62	166.14	20.06	2.54	0.78	NS
Aided	108	163.68	19.64	1.89		

INTERPRETATION

From above table it is inferred that there is no significant difference in the organisational climate of Government and Aided schools. Hence the null hypothesis is accepted.

The findings are represented graphically in Fig 4.03

INTERPRETATION

From above table it is inferred that there is a significant difference in the organizational climate of Aided and private schools. Hence the empirical hypothesis is accepted.

INTERPRETATION

From above table it is inferred that there is a significant

difference in the organisational climate of Government and private schools. Hence the empirical hypothesis is accepted.

Table 4.8. Showing the significance of difference in the mean scores of Aided and private higher secondary schools with respect to organisational climate

Type of Management	N	Mean	S.D	SEMD	C.R	L.S
Aided	108	163.68	19.64	1.89	5.05	0.01
Private	103	150.72	17.46	1.72		

Table 4.9. Showing the significance of difference in the mean scores of Government and private higher secondary schools with respect to organisational climate

Type of Management	N	Mean	S.D	SEMD	C.R	L.S
Government	62	166.14	20.06	2.548	5.19	0.01
Private	103	150.72	17.46	1.72		

In order to find out the existence of any significant difference between the number of stay of teachers with regarded to organisational climate the F-ratio was calculated and has been presented in table

Hypothesis- 4

There is no significant difference between the government, aided and private higher secondary school teachers with regard to the job satisfaction

Table 4.10. One Way ANOVA showing difference in the mean scores of the higher secondary school teachers (Government, Aided and Private) with respect to their job satisfaction

Source of variation	D.F	Sum of Square	Mean of Square	F ratio	Level of Significance
Between groups	2	5190.28	2595.14	3.54	0.01
Within groups	270	197746.99	732.39		
Total	272	202937.28			

Inference

From the above table it is inferred that the calculated F value is greater than the table value and hence there is a significant difference between the Government, aided and private higher secondary school teachers with respect to their job satisfaction at 0.01 level. So further critical ratio will be calculated.

Hypothesis- 4a

There will be no significant difference in the job satisfaction of Government and Aided higher secondary schools

Table 4.11. Showing the significance of difference in the mean scores of higher secondary school teachers of Government and Aided schools with respect to the job satisfaction

Type of Management	N	Mean	S.D	SEMD	C.R	L.S
Government	62	256.06	26.04	3.30	2.67	0.05
Aided	108	244.68	27.17	2.61		

INTERPRETATION

From above table it is inferred that there is a significant difference in the job satisfaction of Government and Aided schools. Hence the null hypothesis is rejected.

Table 4.12. Showing the significance of difference in the mean scores of higher secondary school teachers of Aided and private schools with respect to the job satisfaction

Type of Management	N	Mean	S.D	SEMD	C.R	L.S
Aided	108	244.68	27.17	2.61	1.42	NS
Private	103	250.01	27.54	2.71		

INTERPRETATION

From above table it is inferred that there is no significant difference in the job satisfaction of Aided and private schools. Hence the null hypothesis is accepted.

Table 4.13. Showing the significance of difference in the mean scores of higher secondary school teachers of government and private schools with respect to job satisfaction

Type of Management	N	Mean	S.D	SEMD	C.R	L.S
Government	62	256.06	26.04	3.30	1.39	NS
Private	103	250.01	27.54	2.71		

INTERPRETATION

From the above table it is inferred that there is no significant difference in the organisational climate of Government and private schools. Hence the null hypothesis is accepted.

The findings are graphically represented in figure

Hypothesis-5

There will be no significant difference in the organisational climate of higher secondary school teachers with respect to the gender

Table 4.14. Showing the significance of difference in the mean of organisational climate test scores of male and female higher secondary school teachers

Gender	N	Mean	S.D	SEMD	C.R	L.S
Male	118	156.71	17.94	1.65	1.91	NS
Female	155	161.36	21.38	1.71		

INTERPRETATION

From above table it is found that there is no significant difference in the organisational climate of higher secondary school teachers with respect to their gender. Hence the null hypothesis is accepted.

Hypothesis-6

There will be no significant difference in the Job satisfaction of higher secondary school teachers with respect to the gender

Table 4.15. Showing the significance of difference in the mean of Job satisfaction test scores of male and female higher secondary school teachers

Gender	N	Mean	S.D	SEMD	C.R	L.S
Male	118	243.38	27.47	2.52	3.17	0.01
Female	155	253.77	26.40	2.12		

INTERPRETATION

From above table it is found that there is a significant difference in the organisational climate of higher secondary school teachers with respect to their gender. Hence the null hypothesis is rejected.

The findings are graphically represented in figure

Hypothesis- 7

There will be no significant difference in the organisational climate of higher secondary school teachers with respect to the locale

Table 4.16. Showing the significance of difference in the mean of organisational climate test scores of higher secondary school teachers with respect to the locale

Locale	N	Mean	S.D	SEMD	C.R	L.S
Urban	167	157.0.9	20.67	1.60	2.35	0.05
Rural	106	162.91	18.60	1.80		

INTERPRETATION

From above table it is inferred that there is a significant difference in the organisational climate of higher secondary school teachers with respect to the locale. Hence the null hypothesis is rejected.

Hypothesis- 8

There will be no significant difference in the Job satisfaction of higher secondary school teachers with respect to the locale.

Table 4.17. Showing the significance of difference in the mean of Job satisfaction test scores of higher secondary school teachers with respect to the locale

Locale	N	Mean	S.D	SEMD	C.R	L.S
Urban	167	249.08	26.35	2.04	0.15	NS
Rural	106	249.59	28.88	2.80		

INTERPRETATION

From above table it is inferred that there is no significant difference in the job satisfaction of higher secondary school teachers with respect to the locale. Hence the null hypothesis is accepted.

In order to find out the existence of any significant difference between the number of stay of teachers with regarded to organisational climate the F-ratio was calculated and has been presented in table

Hypothesis: 9

There is no significant difference between the organisational climate of higher secondary school teachers with regard to their age.

Table 4.18. One Way ANOVA showing difference in the mean scores of organisational climate of the higher secondary school teachers with respect to their age.

Source of variation	D.F	Sum of Square	Mean of Square	F ratio	Level of Significance
Between groups	2	392.98	196.49	0.48	NS
Within groups	270	109119.54	404.14		
Total	272	109512.53			

Inference

From the above table it is inferred that the calculated F value is not greater than the table value and hence there is no significant difference between the organisational climate of higher secondary school teachers with regard to their age.

Hence the null hypothesis is accepted and further analysis has been undertaken to see group difference in the following table.

In order to find out the existence of any significant difference between the number of stay of teachers with regarded to job satisfaction the F-ratio was calculated and has been presented in table

Hypothesis-10

There is no significant difference between the job satisfaction of higher secondary school teachers with regard to their age.

Table 4.19. One Way ANOVA showing difference in the mean scores of job satisfaction of the higher secondary school teachers with respect to their age.

Source of variation	D.F	Sum of Square	Mean of Square	F ratio	Level of Significance
Between groups	2	392.98	196.49		
Within groups	270	109119.54	404.14	0.48	NS
Total	272	109512.53			

Inference

From the above table it is inferred that the calculated F value is not greater than the table value and hence there is no significant difference between the job satisfaction of higher secondary school teachers with regard to their age. Hence the null hypothesis is accepted.

In order to find out the existence of any significant difference between the number of stay of teachers with regarded to organisational climate the F-ratio was calculated and has been presented in table

Hypothesis-11

There is no significant difference between the organisational climate of higher secondary school teachers with regard to the number of years of stay in the present school.

Table 4.20. One Way ANOVA showing difference in the mean scores of organisational climate of the higher secondary school teachers with respect to the number of years stay in the present school

Source of variation	D.F	Sum of Square	Mean of Square	F ratio	Level of Significance
Between groups	2	211.68	105.84		
Within groups	270	109300.84	404.81	.26	NS
Total	272	109512.53			

Inference

From the above table it is inferred that the calculated F value is not greater than the table value and hence there is no significant difference between the organizational climate of higher secondary school teachers with regard to the no of years of stay in the present school. Hence the null hypothesis is accepted.

In order to find out the existence of any significant difference between the number of stay of teachers with regarded to organisational climate the F-ratio was calculated and has been presented in table

Hypothesis-12

There is no significant difference between the job satisfactions of higher secondary school teachers with regard to the number of years of stay in the present school.

Table 4.21. One Way ANOVA showing difference in the mean scores of job satisfaction of the higher secondary school teachers with respect to the number of years stay in the present school number

Source of variation	D.F	Sum of Square	Mean of Square	F ratio	Level of Significance
Between groups	2	5413.19	2706.59		
Within groups	270	197524.08	731.57	3.6	0.01
Total	272	202937.28			

Inference

From the above table it is inferred that the calculated F value is greater than the table value and hence there is a significant difference between the job satisfaction of higher secondary school teachers with regard to the number of years stay in the present school at 0.01 level. Hence the null hypothesis is rejected.

Hypothesis-13

There will be no significant difference in the Job satisfaction of higher secondary school teachers with related to the number of years of stay in the present school.

Table 4.22. Showing the significance of difference in the mean of Job satisfaction test scores of higher secondary school teachers stayed in the present school up to 5 and 5 – 10 years

Locale	N	Mean	S.D	SEMD	C.R	L.S
Less than 5 years	72	255.51	26.93	3.17	1.51	NS
5 to 10 years	114	249.52	25.94	2.43		

INTERPRETATION

From above table it is inferred that there is no significant difference in the Job satisfaction of higher secondary school teachers stayed in the present school up to 5 and 5 to 10 years. Hence the null hypothesis is accepted.

Table 4.23. Showing the significance of difference in the mean job satisfaction test scores of higher secondary school teachers stayed in the present school of less than 5 years and above 10 years

Locale	N	Mean	S.D	SEMD	C.R	L.S
Less than 5 years	72	255.51	26.93	3.17	2.64	0.01
Above 10 years	87	243.80	28.52	3.05		

INTERPRETATION

From above table it is inferred that there is a significant difference in the job satisfaction of higher secondary school teachers stayed in the present school up to 5 and above 10 years. Hence the null hypothesis is rejected.

Table 4.24. Showing the significance of difference in the mean of Job satisfaction test scores of higher secondary school teachers stayed in the present school up to 5-10 years and above 10years

Locale	N	Mean	S.D	SEMD	C.R	L.S
5 to 10 years	114	249.52	25.94	2.43	1.48	NS
Above 10 years	87	243.80	28.52	3.05		

INTERPRETATION

From above table it is inferred that there is no significant difference in the job satisfaction of higher secondary school teachers stayed in the present school up to having 5 to 10 years and above 10. Hence the null hypothesis is accepted.

ANOVA org climate vs. monthly salary

In order to find out the existence of any significant difference between Salary of the month of higher secondary school teachers with regarded to organisational climate, the F-ratio was calculated and it has been presented in table

Results of ANOVA for organisational climate with respect to the monthly salary of higher secondary school teachers.

Hypothesis-14

There is no significant difference between the salary of the month of higher secondary school teachers with regard to the organisational climate.

Table 4.25. One Way ANOVA showing difference in the mean scores of the salary of the month of higher secondary school teachers with regard to the organisational climate

Source of variation	D.F	Sum of Square	Mean of Square	F ratio	Level of Significance
Between groups	2	12030.45	6015.22	16.66	0.01
Within groups	270	97482.07	361.04		
Total	272	109512.53			

Inference

From the above table it is inferred that the calculated F value is greater than the table value and hence there is a significant difference between the salary of the month of higher secondary school teachers with regard to the organisational climate at 0.01 level. Hence the null hypothesis is rejected.

Hypothesis-15

There will be no significant difference in the organisational climate of higher secondary school teachers with related to their monthly salary.

Table 4.26. Showing the significance of difference in the mean of organisational climate test scores of higher secondary school teachers having the salary range of up to 7,500 and 7,500 to 15,000 per month

Locale	N	Mean	S.D	SEMD	C.R	L.S
Up to 7,500	81	149.14	17.87	1.98	5.36	0.01
7,500 to 15,000	131	163.60	19.78	1.72		

INTERPRETATION

From above table it is inferred that there is a significant difference in the organisational climate of higher secondary school teachers having the salary range of up to 7,500 and 7,500 to 15,000 per month. Hence the null hypothesis is rejected.

Table 4.27. Showing the significance of difference in the mean of organisational climate test scores of higher secondary school teachers having the salary range of 7,500 to 15,000 and above 15,000 per month

Locale	N	Mean	S.D	SEMD	C.R	L.S
7,500 to 15,000	131	163.60	19.78	2.09	2.04	0.05
Above 15,000	61	163.82	18.74	1.95		

INTERPRETATION

From above table it is inferred that there is a significant

difference in the organisational climate of higher secondary school teachers having the salary range of 7,500 to 15,000 and above 15,000 per month. Hence the null hypothesis is rejected.

Table 4.28. Showing the significance of difference in the mean of organisational climate test scores of higher secondary school teachers having the salary range of up to 7,500 and above 15,000 per month

Locale	N	Mean	S.D	SEMD	C.R	L.S
Up to 7,500	81	149.14	17.87	1.98	4.75	0.01
Above 15,000	61	163.82	18.74	2.39		

INTERPRETATION

From above table it is inferred that there is a significant difference in the organizational climate of higher secondary school teachers having the salary range of up to 7,500 and above 15,000 per month. Hence the null hypothesis is rejected.

ANOVA job satisfaction vs. monthly salary

In order to find out the existence of any significant difference between Salary of the month of higher secondary school teachers with regarded to their job satisfaction the F-ratio was calculated and it has been presented in table

Results of ANOVA for monthly salary of higher secondary school teachers with respect to their job satisfaction.

Hypothesis-16

There is no significant difference between the salary of the month of higher secondary school teachers with regard to their job satisfaction.

Inference

From the above table it is inferred that the calculated F value is greater than the table value and hence there is a significant difference between the salary of the month of higher secondary school teachers with regard to the job satisfaction. Hence the null hypothesis is rejected.

Table 4.29. One Way ANOVA showing difference in the mean scores of the salary of the month of higher secondary school teachers with regard to the job satisfaction

Source of variation	D.F	Sum of Square	Mean of Square	F ratio	Level of Significance
Between groups	2	60.68	30.34	0.04	NS
Within groups	270	202876.59	751.39		
Total	272	202937.28			

ANOVA organisational climate vs. Length of total experience.

In order to find out the existence of any significant difference between the length of total experience with regarded to the organisational climate of higher secondary school teachers, the F-ratio was calculated and it has been presented in table.

Hypothesis-17

There is no significant difference between the organisational climate with respect to the length of experience of higher secondary school teachers.

Table 4.30. One Way ANOVA showing difference in the mean scores of the salary of the month of higher secondary school teachers with regard to the organizational climate

Source of variation	D.F.	Sum of Square	Mean of Square	F ratio	Level of Significance
Between groups	2	3601.70	1800.85	4.59	0.01
Within groups	270	105910.83	392.26		
Total	272	109512.53			

Inference

From the above table it is inferred that the calculated F value is greater than the table value and hence there is a significant difference between the salary of the month of higher secondary school teachers with regard to their organisational climate. Hence the null hypothesis is rejected.

Hypothesis-18

There will be no significant difference in the organisational climate of higher secondary school teachers with respect to their length of experience.

Table 4.31. Showing the significance of difference in the mean of organisational climate test scores of higher secondary school teachers with respect to their length of experience of less than 5 and 6 – 15 years

Locale	N	Mean	S.D	SEMD	C.R	L.S
Less than 5 years	72	159.40	18.72	2.20	1.01	NS
6 to 15 years	138	156.47	20.63	1.75		

INTERPRETATION

From above table it is inferred that there is no significant difference in the organisational climate of higher secondary school teachers with respect to their length of experience of less than 5 and 6 – 15 years.

Hence the null hypothesis is accepted.

Table 4.32. Showing the significance of difference in the mean of organizational climate test scores of higher secondary school teachers with respect to their length of experience of less than 5 and above 15 years

Locale	N	Mean	S.D	SEMD	C.R	L.S
Less than 5 years	72	159.40	18.72	2.20	1.90	NS
Above 15 years	63	165.60	19.11	2.40		

INTERPRETATION

From above table it is inferred that there is no significant difference in the organisational climate of higher secondary school teachers with respect to their length of experience of less than 5 and above 15 years. Hence the null hypothesis is accepted.

Table 4.33. Showing the significance of difference in the mean of organisational climate test scores of higher secondary school teachers with respect to their length of experience between 6 to 15 years and above 15 years

Locale	N	Mean	S.D	SEMD	C.R	L.S
6-15 years	138	156.47	20.63	1.75	2.97	0.01
Above 15 years	63	165.60	19.11	2.40		

INTERPRETATION

From above table it is inferred that there is a significant difference in the organisational climate of higher secondary school teachers with respect to their length of experience between 6 to 15 years and above 15 years at 0.01 level. Hence the null hypothesis is rejected.

ANOVA organisational climate vs. Length of total experience.

In order to find out the existence of any significant difference between the length of total experience with regarded to the job satisfaction of higher secondary school teachers, the F-ratio was calculated and it has been presented in table.

Hypothesis-19

There is no significant difference between the job satisfaction with respect to the length of experience of higher secondary school teachers.

Table 4.34. One Way ANOVA showing difference in the mean scores of the salary of the month of higher secondary school teachers with regard to the job satisfaction

Source of variation	D.F.	Sum of Square	Mean of Square	F ratio	Level of Significance
Between groups	2	6778.73	3389.36	4.66	0.01
Within groups	270	196158.55	726.51		
Total	272	202937.28			

Inference

From the above table it is inferred that the calculated F value is greater than the table value and hence there is a significant difference between the salary of the month of higher secondary school teachers with regard to their job satisfaction. Hence the null hypothesis is rejected.

Hypothesis-20

There will be no significant difference in the job satisfaction of higher secondary school teachers with respect to their length of experience.

Table 4.35. Showing the significance of difference in the mean of Job satisfaction test scores of higher secondary school teachers with respect to their length of experience of less than 5 and 6 – 15 years

Locale	N	Mean	S.D	SEMD	C.R	L.S
Less than 5 years	72	255.63	28.67	3.37	2.83	0.01
6 to 15 years	138	244.47	26.34	2.24		

INTERPRETATION

From above table it is inferred that there is a significant difference in the job satisfaction of higher secondary school teachers with respect to their length of experience of less than 5 and 6 – 15 years.

Hence the null hypothesis is rejected.

Table 4.36. Showing the significance of difference in the mean of job satisfaction test scores of higher secondary school teachers with respect to their length of experience of less than 5 and above 15 years.

Locale	N	Mean	S.D	SEMD	C.R	L.S
Less than 5 years	72	255.63	28.67	3.37	0.65	NS
Above 15 years	63	252.55	26.24	3.30		

INTERPRETATION

From above table it is inferred that there is no significant difference in the job satisfaction of higher secondary school teachers with respect to their length of experience of less than 5 and above 15 years. Hence the null hypothesis is accepted.

Table 4.37. Showing the significance of difference in the mean of job satisfaction test scores of higher secondary school teachers with respect to their length of experience between 6 to 15 years and above 15 years

Locale	N	Mean	S.D	SEMD	C.R	L.S
6-15 years	138	244.47	26.34	2.24	2.02	0.05
Above 15 years	63	252.55	26.24	3.30		

INTERPRETATION

From above table it is inferred that there is a significant difference in the job satisfaction of higher secondary school teachers with respect to their length of experience between 6 to 15 years and above 15 years at 0.01 level. Hence the null hypothesis is rejected.

Chi-square test

Hypothesis-21

There is a significant relationship between the overall organisational climates with respect to the different type of schools

Table 4.38. Showing chi square test between the overall organisational climate with respect to the type of school Chi square test

Variable		Organisational climate				Chi square	L.S
		Low	Average	High	Total		
Type of School	Government	10	31	21	62	24.26	0.01
	Aided	22	46	40	108		
	Private	39	52	12	103		

Interpretation

From the above table it is clearly understood that the calculated chi-square value is more than table value and therefore there is a positive relationship between the organisational climate and the different type of schools.

Hence the empirical hypothesis is accepted.

Hypothesis-22

There is a significant relationship between the overall organizational climates with respect to the locality of schools.

Table 4.39. Showing chi square test between the overall organisational climate with respect to the locality of school

Variable		Organisational climate				Chi square	L.S
		Low	Average	High	Total		
Locality of Schools	Rural	52	79	36	167	8.67	0.01
	Urban	19	50	37	106		

Interpretation

From the above table it is clearly understood that the calculated chi-square value is more than table value and therefore there is a positive relationship between the organisational climate and the locality of schools.

Hence the empirical hypothesis is accepted.

Hypothesis-23

There is a significant relationship between the overall organisational climates with respect to the gender of higher secondary school teachers

Table 4.40. Showing chi square test between the overall organisational climate with respect to the gender of higher secondary school teachers Chi square test

Variable		Organisational climate				Chi square	L.S
		Low	Average	High	Total		
Gender	Male	36	57	25	118	4.06	NS
	Female	35	72	48	155		

Interpretation

From the above table it is clearly understood that the calculated chi-square value is less than table value and therefore there is no relationship between the organisational climate and the gender of the higher secondary school teachers. Hence the empirical hypothesis is rejected.

Hypothesis-24

There is a significant relationship between the overall organisational climates with respect to the age group of higher secondary school teachers.

Table 4.41. Showing chi square test between the overall organisational climate with respect to the age group of higher secondary school teachers Chi square test

Variable		Organizational climate				Chi square	L.S
		Low	Average	High	Total		
Age (in Years)	Below 35	21	43	17	81	2.74	NS
	35-45	29	51	30	110		
	45 and above	21	35	26	82		

Interpretation

From the above table it is clearly understood that the calculated chi-square value is less than table value and therefore there is no relationship between the organisational climate and the age group of the higher secondary school teachers. Hence the empirical hypothesis is rejected.

Hypothesis-25

There is a significant relationship between the overall organisational climate with respect to the Number of years stay in the present school of the higher secondary school teachers.

Interpretation

From the above table it is clearly understood that the calculated chi-square value is less than table value and therefore there is no relationship between the organisational climate and Number of years stay in the present school of the higher secondary school teachers. Hence the empirical hypothesis is rejected.

Table 4.42. Showing chi square test between the overall organisational climate with respect to Number of years stay in the present school of the higher secondary school teachers

Variable		Organisational climate				Chi square	L.S
		Low	Average	High	Total		
No of years stay in the present school	Up to 5	17	40	15	72	4.32	NS
	5 to 10	34	47	33	114		
	10 and above	20	42	25	87		

Hypothesis -26

There is a significant relationship between the overall organisational climate with respect to the Salary of the month of the higher secondary school teachers.

Table 4.43. Showing chi square test between the overall organisational climate with respect to the salary of the month of the higher secondary school teachers Chi square test

Variable		Organisational climate				Chi square	L.S
		Low	Average	High	Total		
Salary of the month (In Rs.)	Up to 7,500	34	39	8	81	25.78	0.01
	7500-15,000	24	66	41	131		
	15,000 & above	13	24	24	61		

Interpretation

From the above table it is clearly understood that the calculated chi-square value is more than table value and therefore there is a positive relationship between the organisational climate and salary of the month of the higher secondary school teachers. Hence the empirical hypothesis is accepted.

Hypothesis-27

There is a significant relationship between the overall organisational climate with respect to the total years of experience of the higher secondary school teachers.

Table 4.44. Showing chi square test between the overall organisational climate with respect to the total years of experience of the higher secondary school teachers Chi square test

Variable		Organisational climate				Chi square	L.S
		Low	Average	High	Total		
Total Years of experience	Up to 5	17	39	16	72	9.49	0.05
	6 to 15	44	61	33	138		
	15 and above	10	29	24	63		

Interpretation

From the above table it is clearly understood that the calculated chi-square value is more than table value and therefore there is a positive relationship between the organisational climate and the total years of experience of the higher secondary school teachers. Hence the empirical hypothesis is accepted.

Hypothesis-28

There is a significant relationship between the job satisfactions of higher secondary school teachers with respect to the type of schools.

Table 4.45. Showing chi square test between the job satisfaction of higher secondary school teachers with respect to the type of schools Chi square test

Variable		Job Satisfaction				Chi square	L.S
		Low	Average	High	Total		
Type of school	Government	13	29	20	62	4.04	NS
	Aided	30	56	44	108		
	Matriculation	30	44	29	103		

Interpretation

From the above table it is clearly understood that the calculated chi-square value is less than table value and therefore there is a no relationship between the job satisfaction of higher secondary school teachers with respect to the type of schools. Hence the empirical hypothesis is rejected

Hypothesis-29

There is a significant relationship between the job satisfactions of higher secondary school teachers with respect to the locality of schools

Table 4.46. Showing chi square test between the l job satisfaction of higher secondary school teachers with respect to the locality of school Chi square test

Variable		Organisational climate				Chi square	L.S
		Low	Average	High	Total		
Locality of Schools	Rural	45	80	42	167	9.43	0.01
	Urban	28	49	29	106		

Interpretation

From the above table it is clearly understood that the calculated chi-square value is more than the table value and therefore there is a positive relationship between the job satisfaction of higher secondary school teachers with respect to the locality of schools.Hence the empirical hypothesis is accepted.

Table 4.47. Showing chi square test between the job satisfaction of the higher secondary school teachers with respect to the gender of higher secondary school teachers Chi square test

Variable		Organisational climate				Chi square	L.S
		Low	Average	High	Total		
Gender	Male	44	52	22	118	13.42	0.05
	Female	29	77	49	155		

Hypothesis-30

There is a significant relationship between the job satisfaction of higher secondary school teachers with respect to the gender.

Interpretation

From the above table it is clearly understood that the calculated chi-square value is more than table value and therefore there is a positive relationship between the job satisfaction and the gender of the higher secondary school teachers. Hence the empirical hypothesis is accepted.

Hypothesis-31

There is a significant relationship between the job satisfaction with respect to the age group of higher secondary school teachers.

Table 4.48. Showing chi square test between the job satisfaction with respect to the age group of higher secondary school teachers Chi square test

Variable		Organisational climate				Chi square	L.S
		Low	Average	High	Total		
Age (in Years)	Below 35	26	28	27	81	9.74	NS
	35-45	30	59	21	110		
	45 and above	17	42	23	82		

Interpretation

From the above table it is clearly understood that the calculated chi-square value is less than table value and therefore there is no relationship between the job satisfaction and the age group of the higher secondary school teachers. Hence the empirical hypothesis is rejected.

Hypothesis-32

There is a significant relationship between the Job satisfaction with respect to the Number of years stay in the present school of the higher secondary school teachers.

Table 4.49. Showing chi square test between the l Job satisfaction with respect to Number of years stay in the present school of the higher secondary school teachers Chi square test

Variable		Organisational climate				Chi square	L.S
		Low	Average	High	Total		
No of Years stay in the present school	Up to 5	18	28	26	72	6.09	0.01
	5 to 10	29	60	25	114		
	10 and above	26	41	20	87		

Interpretation

From the above table it is clearly understood that the calculated chi-square value is more than the table value and therefore there is a positive relationship between the job satisfaction and Number of years stay in the present school of higher secondary school teachers. Hence the empirical hypothesis is accepted.

Hypothesis-33

There is a significant relationship between the job satisfaction with respect to the Salary of the month of the higher secondary school teachers

Table 4.50. Showing chi square test between the job satisfaction with respect to the salary of the month of the higher secondary school teachers Chi square test

Variable		Organisational climate				Chi square	L.S
		Low	Average	High	Total		
Salary of the month (In Rs)	Up to 7,500	26	32	23	81	5.55	NS
	7500-15,000	35	61	35	131		
	15,000 & above	12	36	13	61		

Interpretation

From the above table it is clearly understood that the calculated chi-square value is less than table value and therefore there is no relationship between the job satisfaction and salary of the month of higher secondary school teachers. Hence the empirical hypothesis is rejected.

Hypothesis-34

There is a significant relationship between the job satisfaction with respect to the total years of experience of higher secondary school teachers

Table 4.51. Showing chi square test between the job satisfaction with respect to the total years of experience of the higher secondary school teachers Chi square test

Variable		Organisational climate				Chi square	L.S
		Low	Average	High	Total		
Total Years of experience	Up to 5	18	27	27	72	15.77	0.01
	6 to 15	46	67	25	138		
	15 and above	9	35	19	63		

Interpretation

From the above table it is clearly understood that the calculated chi-square value is more than table value and therefore there is a positive relationship between the job satisfaction and the total years of experience of higher secondary school teachers. Hence the empirical hypothesis is accepted.

Hypothesis-35

There is a significant relationship between the overall organisational climate with respect to the job satisfaction of the higher secondary school teachers.

Interpretation

From the above table it is clearly understood that the calculated chi-square value is more than table value and therefore there is a positive relationship between the organisational climate and the job satisfaction of the higher secondary school teachers. Hence the empirical hypothesis is accepted. Correlation coefficient .

Table 4.52. Showing chi square test between the overall organisational climate with respect to the job satisfaction of the higher secondary school teachers Chi square test

Variable		Organisational climate				Chi square	L.S
		Low	Average	High	Total		
Job satis-faction	Low	32	28	11	71	24.01	0.01
	Average	34	60	35	129		
	High	7	41	25	73		

SUMMARY, FINDINGS AND CONCLUSION

INTRODUCTION

Research is not only compiling counting and tabulating the consequences of hypothesis rather it is the careful observation, enquiry and application of rigorous logic. Research is a process of testing rather than providing, hence the investigator listed this finding in this chapter.

OBJECTIVES

To study the organisational climate of schools under different types of school management.

To study the significant difference between the organisational climate with regard to the Gender.

To study the significant difference between the organisational climate with regard to the Locale of the School.

To study the significant difference between the organisational climate with regard to the Age of the higher secondary school teachers.

To study the significant difference between the organisational climate with respect to the Number of years stay in the present school.

To study the significant difference between the organisational climate with respect to the monthly salary.

To study the significant difference between the organisational climate with respect to the total experience.

To study the level of job satisfaction of higher secondary school teachers.

To study the level of job satisfaction of higher secondary school teacher with regard to the gender.

To study the level of job satisfaction of higher secondary school teacher with regard to the Locale of the school.

To study the level of job satisfaction of higher secondary school teacher with regard to the Age.

To study the level of job satisfaction of higher secondary school teacher with regard to the Number of years stay in the present school.

To study the level of job satisfaction of higher secondary school teacher with regard to the monthly salary.

To study the level of job satisfaction of higher secondary school teacher with respect to their total experience.

To study the relationship between organisational climate and job satisfaction of higher secondary school teachers.

SAMPLE

The study consists of 275 higher secondary school teachers spread over fifteen schools in Madurai. The sample represents Higher Secondary teachers belonging to different types of schools like government, private and aided. Hence the sample is a stratified random sample.

TOOLS AND MATERIALS USED

To verify the different types of hypothesis framed, the following tools were used.

Organisational climate.

Job satisfaction

MAJOR FINDINGS OF THE STUDY

The over all organisational climates of higher secondary school teachers is moderate.

There is a significant difference in the organisational climate of schools under different types of management.

There is a significant difference in the organisational climate of aided and government higher secondary schools.

There is a significant difference in the Organisational Climate of aided and private higher secondary schools.

There is a significant difference in the organisational climate of Government and private higher secondary schools.

Gender has no bearing on the level of organisational climate of higher secondary school teachers.

There is a significant difference in the organisational climate of schools with respect to the locale.

Age has no bearing on the level of organisational climate of higher secondary school teachers.

There is no significant difference in the organisational climate of schools with respect to the number of years stay of teachers in the present schools.

There is a significant difference in the organisational climate of schools with respect to the salary of teachers.

There is a significant difference in the level of organisational climate of higher secondary school teachers with respect to their length of experience.

There is a significant difference in the level of job satisfaction of higher secondary school teachers under different types of management.

There is a significant difference in the level of job satisfaction of aided and government higher secondary schools.

There is a significant difference in the level of job satisfaction of aided and private higher secondary schools.

There is a significant difference in the level of job satisfaction of Government and private higher secondary schools.

Gender has a bearing on the level of job satisfaction of higher secondary school teachers.

There is no significant difference in the job satisfaction of schools with respect to the locale.

Age has no bearing on the level of job satisfaction of higher secondary school teachers.

There is a significant difference in the level of job satisfaction of higher secondary school teachers with respect to the number of years stay in the present schools.

There is no significant difference in the job satisfaction higher secondary school teachers with respect to the salary.

There is a significant difference in the level of job satisfaction of higher secondary school teachers with respect to their length of experience.

There is a significant positive correlation between organisational climate and job satisfaction of higher Secondary school teachers.

REFERENCE

1. Abdhul Samnd, study of organisational climate of government High Schools of chandigarh and its effect on Job satisfaction of Teachers, 1986 as quoted in Fourth Survey of Research in Education, VII M.B Bush(Ed.) National Council of Educational research and Training, Delhi.
2. Abu Saad, Ismael, Organisational climate and teachers Job satisfaction in the Bedouism elementary schools of Negev in Southern Israel, Dissertation Abstracts International, 50,9,March 1990, 2712 – A.
3. Aderunmu William Olushda, An Analysis of teachers and principal perceptions of the organisational climates of secondary schools, Dissertation, Abstracts, International A, 39, Feb 1979, 4609 Alltouniam, Anita Rose The relationship between middle school organisational school climate and teacher job satisfaction in selected Southern California Schools and Teachers job satisfaction Dissertation Abstracts Interanational 523, 4 Oct 1992, 1994 – A.

4. Amarnath, Comparative study of the organisational climate of government and privately managed Higher Secondary Schools in Jullandar District, PhD Edu Pam. 11, 1980 as quoted in third survey of Research in Educational research and training, Delhi.
5. Bamonte, Locus John. A study of the Religious Atmosphere of Catholic Secondary Schools, Dissertation Abstracts International A 44-10, Apr, 1984, 2033.
6. Bassano Louis V Perception of organisational climate, job satisfaction and job performance, Dissertation Abstracts International, 49 3, Sept 1988, 404.
7. Birch, Louis Vinoth Kumar Perception of organisational climate, job satisfaction and job performance, Dissertation Abstracts International, 49, 3, Sept, 1988, 404.
8. Birch, Louise. Teachers growth and Development, Organisational Climate of Elementary Schools. Dissertation Abstracts International, A, 43, Nov, 1982, 1353.
9. Bloom, Benjamin. Stability and change in human characters, 1968, John Wiley and Son's New York.
10. Breiner, John M cause for Discharge, personal journal, 6, 171-172, 1972 348.
11. Buch M.B (Ed) Fourth Survey of Research in Education, 4th international Council of Educational Research and Training, New Delhi.
12. Chiratangul, Sirichal. A study of organisational climate of secondary schools in Bangkok, Thailand, Dissertation Abstract International, 40 Feb.
13. Chttam Sava Austin The relationship between secondary teacher's satisfaction and their perception of school climate, 51 11, May, 1991, p. 3508.
14. Chopra R.K Organisational climate in relation to teacher's job satisfaction and students achievement, Indian Educational Review, 38, 4, Oct, 1983.
15. Chris, Argivris. Personality and organization, the conflict between the system and individuals. Harper and IQOW Publishers, 1972.

16. Christopher, Van M The organisational climate of an inner city secondary schools, Dissertation Abstract International, 35, 12(1), June, 1975, p. 7547.

17. Darji, D.R. A study of Leadership Behaviour and its correlates in the secondary schools at panchmals District, Second Survey of Research in Education, M.B. Buch (Ed), 1997, p. 466.

18. Ellison, R.L. et al An investigation of organisational climate, Grensboro, N.C. Richardson Foundation, 1968.

19. G.A.Forehand and B.Vonjgilmer (E964), Environmental variations in studies of organisational Behaviour, Psychological bulletin, 62,6 1964, A. 362.

20. Forsyrth, Rutgers. Isolation and Alienation in Educational organization Dissertation Abstracts International, 37, 11, 12, 1978, p. 7996.

21. Gorton, R. A School Administration, Challenge and opportunity for leadership, Lowa, Brown, 1976.

22. HERTZNERG R. in anager, B. and syderman, B. The motivation to work, New York, Wiley. 1959.

23. Katz, D. and Kahn, R. The social psychology of organization, 196, John Willey and Sons New York.

24. Likert, R. The human organization, its management and value, 1967, Mc Graw Hill, New York.

25. Maslow, A.H. Motivation and personality (Ind.Edun.) New York, Harper and Row, 1970.

26. Mothilal Sharma. School Climate and its relationship with principle effectiveness and teacher satisfaction, Journal and psychological Researches, 21.3, Sept, 1975, p. 105-107.

27. Pace C.R. Five college environments, collegian Board Reviews, and 41, 1961, p. 24-28.

28. Stern, G.G. People in Context, 1970, John Wiley and Sons, Inc New Yor.

29. Vroom V.R. Work and motivation, New York Wiley 1964.

30. Wahba: M.A.Bridwell, L.G. Maslow De-considered. A review of research on the lead hierarchy theory

organisational Behaviour and Human performance, 1976, 15, p. 112–140.

31. Walberg, H. Social environment as a mediator of classroom learning, journal of Educational Psychology, 60, 1969, p. 443-448.
32. Wright, Hearbert F et al Towards a psychological Ecology of classroom, Journal of Educational Research, 45, 1951, p. 187 – 200.
33. Wyman, S.A. Relationship of organisational climate of the job satisfaction and satisfactoriness of school counsellor Dissertations Abstracts International, 35, 8, p. 5046.

CHAPTER 5

Intelligence and Teaching Competence of Teacher Trainees

—K. RAJAN

PROBLEM AND ITS PERSPECTIVES

Introduction

Teachers should be the living incarnation of the great trinity of truth, goodness and beauty. They must have a deep sense of reasoning, non-violence and objective outlook towards everything and they must appreciate beauty and orderliness. Teacher must have robust optimism and free from frustration and compassion; his personality will be dead wood without tender feelings for anybody. His vision of life must be based on love sympathy and affection for all in general and for the needy and deprived classes of the society in particular.

According to **Vishwakavi Rabindranath Tagore** "A lamp never lights another lamp unless it continues to burn its own flame. A teacher can never truly teach unless he is still learning himself."

IMPORTANCE OF EDUCATION

Education is an exclusively human activity. Man inherits his cultural heritage from his elders in society, through education. A person without education is really like a blind. In the words of **Rousseau**, "Plants are developed by cultivation and men by education" Education nourishes us like a mother. It directs us to the proper path like the father. It guides us to reach our destination like a teacher.

According to **John Dewey,** "True education comes through the stimulation of child's power by the demands of social stimulation in which he finds himself".

CONCEPT OF INTELLIGENCE

Intelligence is the general mental adaptability for new problems and new situations of life. It is the power within a person to analyze what to do and act accordingly. It also emphasis the ability to learn, that is one's intelligence is educable. It also emphasis on effective use of concept and symbols in dealing with situations. Intelligence is an inherited capacity of an individual. It is the capacity to improve upon native tendency in the light of past experiences. This is manifested through his ability to adopt and to reconstruct the factors of his environment in accordance with his group. Most psychologists accept the idea that learning capacity is an essential aspect of intelligence. There are instances of pupils who face special fields like art and mechanics. Intelligence is the general capacity of an individual to consciously adjust his thinking to new requirements.

Intelligence

Intelligence is the capacity to acquire and apply knowledge. Intelligence is the general ability Intelligence is assumed to be basically a matter of relationships. Many psychologists observe the positive relationships between different types of performance. There are various definitions given by the psychologists as follows.

According to **Colvin** "An individual possess intelligence in so far as he has learned or can learn to adjust himself to an environment".

Freeman states "An individual is intelligent in proportion as he is able to carry on abstract thinking".

Gates observes, "Intelligence is a composite organisation of abilities to learn, to grasp broad and stable facts especially abstract facts with alertness accuracy, to exercise mental control and to display flexibility ingenuity in seeking the solutions to problems".

Rex Knight notes, "Intelligence is the ability to discover the relevant qualities and relations of the objects or ideas that are before us and to evoke relevant idea; in other words it is capacity of relational thinking, directed to the attainment of some end".

Characteristics of Intelligence

According to **Woodworth,** "An intelligent person makes use of his past experience to an immediate problem or seek a goal. He can adopt himself to a novel situation and face to solve a new problem or master a complex situation. He try to understand the cause of the problem before trying a solution for it. Thinks ahead of time, keeps a broader outlook and tries to be different from others.

Types of Intelligence

Intelligence is the aggregate or global capacity of the individual to act purposefully to think rationally and to deal effectively with his environment. Philosophers and psychologists developed various types with regard to nature of intelligence; they classified intelligence into various categories.

CONCRETE INTLLIGENCE

This type of intelligence is applicable when the individual is handling concrete objects or machines. The person uses this intelligence in the operation of tools and instruments. Engineers and mechanics generally have this type of intelligence.

ABSTRACT INTELLIGENCE

This type of intelligence is acquired after an intensive study of book and related literature. It is mostly literary in content. Mostly good teachers, lawyers, doctors and philosophers have this type of knowledge.

SOCIAL INTELLIGENCE

Persons having this type of intelligence have a dynamic personality. They know the art of winning friends and influencing them. They present their views in an attractive manner and generally seek the approval of their friends and associates. Leaders, ministers, members of the diplomatic sources and social workers have it.

It is difficult to say about the distribution of the above three types of intelligence. Some may have more of concrete intelligence though he may not be an engineer. It is also possible that an engineer may have more of abstract intelligence and less of concrete.

Howard Gardner classified the intelligence into nine types based on multiple intelligence theory, they are:

Naturalist Intelligence

Musical Intelligence

Logical Mathematical Intelligence

Existential Intelligence

Interpersonal Intelligence

Bodily-Kinesthetic Intelligence

Linguistic Intelligence

Intra-personal Intelligence

Spatial Intelligence

Measurement of Intelligence

Some of the basic expressions for the measurement of intelligence are mental age, chronological age and intelligence quotient.

Chronological Age

Chronological age is the physical age of a person, counted from the date and time of his birth. It is counted in terms of years, month and date etc.

Mental Age

Mental age is an index of intelligence rank. Mental age means that a given child's performance of a test is like the average performance on the same test of children of a given chronological age.

Intelligence Quotient

Intelligence quotient is synonymous with intelligence. Intelligence quotient (I.Q) means a child's Mental Age (M.A) divided by his Chronological Age (C.A) multiplied by IQ = (MA / CA) 100.

Intelligence and Educational Implication

Mental development is influenced by both heredity and environment. A very little change can be alone to change the influence of heredity. But the parents, the teachers and the school can provide a healthy and motivating intellectual environment for the child. In this regard, the combined efforts of the child, the family and the society can do a great deal of work. The cultural and social experiences, learning opportunities and discipline, which he receives in the learning environment contributes significantly towards his mental development in contrary to the notion that many students who fail in examination do have sufficient intelligence, but are unable to progress because of certain personality inadequacies, family problems and social factors.

TEACHNG COMPETENCE

The teacher has a major role in the educational development **Gandhiji** remarked that "no country can make any progress without good teachers" The quality and standard of education depends on the quality and standard of teachers. Teacher is the torch bearer of the race and guardian of the feature of the mankind.

According to **Humagun Kabir:** "Teachers are literally the architects of a nations destiny " **Mrs. Indira Gandhi** stated, "The nations well being depends upon the teachers well being our teachers are the 'custodians' of future. No society can afford to neglect them".

"Competency" ordinarily is defined as "Adequate for the purpose; suitable, sufficient, or as capable". In a sense it refers to adequate preparation to begin a professional career, and has a direct linkage to verification requirements.

Cooker (1976) defined "competence is seen as the ability to cope with a certain class of problems encountered on the job. A teacher who can deal with problems in certain area is said to be competent in that area a fully competent teacher is one who can cope successfully with any "propositional problem." Competency in teaching stems forms the capacity to reach out differing children and to create a rich and multidimensional environment for them **(Joyce** and **Well 1985).**

To study the effectiveness "competency based teacher training (CBTT) Strategy" for developing following basic teaching competencies among pre service teacher;

1. Cognitive- based teaching competency
2. Performance -based teaching competency
3. Affective - based teaching competency
4. Consequence - based teaching competency
5. Managerial - based teaching competency

Concepts of Teaching Competence

A competent teacher has good command of subject matter and solid core of teaching skills. They have excellent instructional strategies supported by methods of goal setting, instructional planning and classroom management. They know how to motivate, communicate and work effectively with students. The teachers play an important role in molding and shaping the attitudes, habits, and manners and above all, the character and personality of the students. The teacher with competency does the planning, organisation, reading and controlling of teaching. He is free to perform various activities to provide a learning experience to the learners.

Definitions

In the words of **Murthy** and **Lulla,** "Competence based teacher education is that type of professional education of classroom teachers that takes the pre-determined competence of teaching behaviours as the base of teacher education programs".

The Education Commission (1964-66) observed, "Of all the different factors, which influence its quality of education and its contribution to national development, the quality, competence and characters are undoubtedly the most significant".

Competencies to be Developed

Competence in the use of any methodology involves being able to choose intelligently with the knowledge, experience and skill to make chosen methods work effectively. This can only be acquired by experience, which requires confidence, risk taking and reflection on what happens, so the competencies that are to be developed among the teacher trainees are as follows.

1. Competence to understand the sight process of learning, including learning, learning by doing, learning to be, learning to do and learning to become.
2. Competence to devise dynamic methods in the day-to-day situations based on the needs and interests of children.
3. Competence to organise the classroom in such a manner that different kinds of activities may be organised in it so that children may receive required guidance from teacher.
4. Competence to become an example of qualities that he/she wants to develop among his/her students, realising that example is superior to mere instruction and preaching.
5. Competence in regard to language, delivery of speech and other method of communication.

6. Competence in regard to the contents of the subject that he /she is supposed to teach. The teacher should be able to answer questions that belong to the immediate reason or even to some remotely related subject matter, which may occur in subsequent reason.
7. Competence to engage children in a meaningful manner so that children may develop capacity to ask question and may be inspired to find out the answers by themselves.
8. Competence to innovate so as to create proper environment in the classroom to enable children to develop wider horizons of perceptions.
9. Competence to develop among students a scientific temper, which is often confined to cultivation of various attitudes, includes objective observation, experimentation and consideration of every point of view relevant to the enquiry in a logical manner.

The competencies mentioned above suggest that the school teacher in the developing countries may inspire a change in the impulses of the pupils growing personality so as to have a balanced blending of knowledge, power, love and skills that are required for his/her development as a good individual and useful member of the society. The teacher has to develop competence to innovative methods oriented and learner's need based. The teachers may be apprised what they are supposed to teach.

Competency Areas

National Council for Teacher Education **(NCTE)** has identified tén competency areas in teacher preparation:

(*i*) Contextual competencies including development of education in society and teacher's role in it.

(*ii*) Conceptual competencies comprising various concepts of education and learning and psychological, sociological and physiological aspects of education.

(*iii*) Curricula and content competencies relating different stages of education like primary, upper-primary and secondary.

(*iv*) Transitional competencies as regards general subject-wise and stage-wise dimensions.

(*v*) Competencies in other educational activities such as planning and organising morning assembly, etc.

(*vi*) Competencies relating to teaching-learning materials.

(*vii*) Evaluation competencies including preparation, selection, use of tools, justice etc.

(*viii*) Management competencies including organisation of classroom, school and community activities.

(*ix*) Competencies related to working with parents understand the role; discuss the problems; active co-operation; organise parent teacher meetings; explore and utilise educational resources etc. utilise.

(*x*) Competencies related to working with the community and other agencies through understand the importance; contribute for improvement; realise the objectives; develop wholesome relationship; explore and exploit community educational resources activities etc.

A to Z of Teaching Competencies

Teaching is an interactive process involving many aspects of teacher, student, learning process and learning situations. So in order to be a competent teacher one must have competent in the following dispositions.

'A' is for alertness.

'B' is for business like attitude to keep busy in worthwhile tasks.

'C' is for clarity and co-operative teaching learning.

'D' is for devotion and discovery.

'E' is for enthusiasm, expecting children to learn and evaluation.

'F' is for feedback for the guidance of the learner and evaluation.

'G' is for goal setting and achieving.

'H' is for hard work, honest work, humility and humor.

'I' is for involvement of children.

'J' is for judicious attitude and just action.

'K' is for knowledge of the students, subject-matter of oneself.

'L' is for linking learning with daily experiences and life.

'M' is for motivation.

'N' is for need-based learning.

'O' is for objectivity and providing out of classroom learning experiences.

'P' is for practice and praising children when needed.

'Q' is for quiz organizing for monitoring learning progress.

'R' is for relationships and review.

'S' is for stimulation.

'T' is for tolerance and the technology of teaching learning.

'U' is for unbiased attitude and unexpected encounters and situations.

'V' is for a variety of learning experience.

'W' is for warmth and wisdom.

'X' is for x-ray of the learning process.

'Y' is for yearning and eagerness.

'Z' is for zeal.

Essential Qualities of a Competent Teacher

In order to be a competent teacher, he must possess certain special qualities such as:

1. Qualities relating to professional requirements.

2. Qualities relating to character and personality.
3. Qualities relating to human relationship.
4. Qualifications relation to professional educational/ training

SIGNIFICANCE OF THE STUDY

Intelligence is the important aspect of an individual. Through intelligence one can know his abilities and capabilities. Intelligence test is used to categories people into different group. Person having intelligence is capable of doing all things. Teaching is an interactive process, involving four aspects teacher, student, learning process and learning situation. A competent teacher possesses all the necessary qualities to interact with the school and community. Teacher with intelligence will be able to teach students with all capabilities. So the present study has been conducted to verify how intelligence is correlated with the teaching competency of the B.Ed teacher trainees. It is that every teacher trainee should have minimum intelligence to be perfect in his teaching competency. Hence this study has been conducted to verify these interesting aspects.

CONCLUSION

The first chapter is chiefly concerned with the conceptual framework of the problem chosen for the present study. The descriptions on teaching competence and intelligence among the teacher trainees have been presented to highlight the conceptual position with which this study has been planned and conducted.

REVIEW OF RELATED LITERATURE

Introduction

The key to the vast store house of the published literature may open door to source of significant problems and exclamatory hypothesis and provide helpful orientation for definition of the problem, background for selection of procedure and comparative data for interpretation of results. In order to be truly creative and original one must read extensively and critically as stimulus to thinking good (1959).

Review of related literature gives a broad idea to the investigator to carry out his research work in a successful manner. It also helps him get thorough knowledge in his research work. Review tells the researcher what has been done and what needs to be done in a particular topic.

The related literature available on the proposed study is presented in this chapter under the following heads.

1. Studies related to intelligence.
2. Studies related to teaching competence.
3. Studies on intelligence and teaching competence.

FOREIGN STUDIES ON INTELLLIGENCE

Ann (2000) conducted an investigation on, "The influence of preference for novelty and gender on intelligence." The purpose of this research was to further investigate the link between preference for novelty and intelligence. A total sample of 86 children in grade V was selected. The result showed positive effect of cognitive novelty preference on intelligence.

Asthana (2000) made an attempt to assess the differences in some cognitive variables of general intelligence in rural and urban children. The study was conducted on 60 rural and 60 urban primary school children. Alexander along pass Test was used to measure general intelligence. The findings of the study showed that the rural children were less intelligent into comparison to the urban primary schools children.

Hoenig (2002) conducted a study on the relation between memory and intelligence in children with learning disabilities. Memory of the ability to retain information was evaluated using the Test of Memory and Learning, a recently released test that gives a comprehensive measure of global memory functioning. Winchester's intelligence Scale for children used to assess intelligence. The tests to 80 students (aged 6-12 years) with learning disabilities. The correlation between global measure of memory and global measure of intelligence was significant indicating that the memory should be viewed as an important component when evaluating children with learning disabilities.

De. Smedt (2003) conducted a research on pre-academic and early-academic achievement in children with relocardio facial syndrome of borderline or normal intelligence. The study focused on pre-academic and early -academic skills in borderline to normal intelligent children within the last year of kindergarten and first grade of a primary school in Flanders. In the Kindergarten group, meta-linguistic awareness and counting skills were examined. In the group of first graders, children were tested on reading, spelling and mathematics. 13 children participated in this study. There were no differences in intelligence and academic outcomes between boys and girls, and no differences in IQ and academic achievement between children with cardiac defects or severe velopharyngeal insufficiency (IPI) and children without these deficits. With regard to pre-academic achievement in general, a characteristic profile with clearly better results for meta-linguistic awareness in comparison with counting skill was found, but this difference was not statistically significant. However, at an individual level – especially within the domain of counting skills and mathematics, there is wide variability, with some children showing remarkable learning difficulties already at an early age.

Demethiou (2003) conducted research on, "The Missing link in the relations between intelligence and personality". The researcher studied relationship between performance tasks representing five cognitive domains (quantitative, categorical, spatial, causal and prepositional reasoning) and self-attribution of ability in regard to them and also in regard to four general cognitive functions (processing speed, working memory, self-monitoring and self-regulation), and the big five factors of personality (extraversion, agreeableness, conscientiousness, neuroticism and openness to experience) on students in the age group of 12-17 years. Structural equations modelling showed that self-attribution of ability are to some extent, dependent on cognitive performance. Cognitive performance is weakly related only to two of the five factor (openness and conscientiousness) of personality Self-attribution of ability is substantially related to all but the neuroticism factor differs. Apart from openness to experience, the dependence of personality dimensions on the dimensions of cognitive self-representation tends to weaken with age. It is concluded that influence of cognitive abilities on personality can be mediated by self-awareness about them.

Garlick (2003) conducted a research on "integrating brain science research with intelligence research" and he says that the possible causes of differences unintelligence are crucial to children who are to achieve their full potential. Such understanding has been hampered until recently, however, because researchers who study intelligence have neglected recent findings in the brain sciences suggesting that the brain develops in response to environmental stimulation. These findings contradict intelligence research, which suggests that intelligence abilities are inherited. However the findings from intelligence research and the brain sciences can be integrated if it is accepted that there are individual differences in the process by which the brain adapts to the environment, such that some peoples' brains are better at adapting than others. The findings obtained from intelligence research are consistent with this integrated model. Such integration has implications for better understanding of the nature of intelligence.

Kinlaw (2003) conducted a research on "The Development of children's beliefs about intelligence." Research was focused on the development of children's beliefs about intelligence and proposed that this development requires simultaneous processes of concept acquisition and theory building. Research in beliefs about the nature of intelligence has focused on children's definitions of intelligence, beliefs about the component structure of intelligence and the criteria, children use to evaluate ability. Children's beliefs about the stability of intelligence have been examined in terms of constancy, controllability, capacity and the origins of intelligence and mechanisms of change. It was found that intelligence and achievement are positively related.

Meullum (2003) conducted a research on comprehensive test of nonverbal intelligence. It discuss the apprehensive test of nonverbal intelligence, which was designed to provide an estimate of the intelligence of individuals who are not proficient in English, or who are deaf, disadvantaged, language disordered, or motor impaired. The test formats and items were selected on the basis of statistical analysis. The results showed that items contained little gender or no ethnic bias.

Petrill (2003) conducted a research on, "The development intelligence behavioural genetic approaches". The purpose was to outline the behavioural genetic literature on the development of intelligence in childhood, adolescence and adulthood; to describe the implications of these findings for neuroscience and to search for genetic makers and evil factors influencing intelligence. Behavioural genetic research suggests that genetic influences relating to intelligence becomes the greatest across development stages.

Rushton (2003) conducted a research on African white IQ differences from Zimbabwe on the Weshsler's Intelligence Scale for children revised, mainly in the 'g' factor. It was noted that African white differences on the sub tests of the Weschler's Intelligence Scale in Zimbabwe were like the black white, differences in the US being positively associated with the sub tests. 12-14 years old Zimbabweans in Canada in the ten sub-tests were compared against white Americans.

Junhi (2004) conducted a research on "Low intelligence and levels of lead and cadmium in children. The researcher studied the influence levels of lead and Cadmium in the bodies of children on their intelligence. 112 children with low intelligence and 80 children with high intelligence were selected from 3,700 elementary schools (7-12 years) by using an intelligence test peripheral blood and first urine of both the groups were collected in the morning to measure the levels of lead and Cadmium. The results showed that there was significant difference in the level of lead in the blood between the two groups.

INDIAN STUDIES ON INTELLIGENCE

Sinha and Vibha (1998) studied the relationship between level of bed exposure and intelligence and vigilance performance in a sample of 960 school going children of Agra. Biological monitoring of lead through nadir analysis was done to assess the level of lead exposure. The tool used for intelligence and vigilance was Whechster Intelligence Scale for children. It was found that increased level of lead in the hair caused a decrease in intelligence and vigilance test scores.

Archana (1998), made an investigation on intelligence to find out whether there is any relationship between intelligence, gender, religion and socioeconomic status. The study was done on 480 students. The tools were Mohsin Gender Intelligence test and Socio-economic Status scale by Kuppuswamy. The study revealed the following: General does not exercise any significant influence on the intelligence level. Socio-economic status has significant effect on the subjects. Religion and socio-economic status, independently as well as internationally are significant factors in the determination of IQ. She explored the independent as well as interactions effect of religion on intelligence. Two religious groups –Hindus and Muslims with an incidental sample of 480 college students, were administered using Mohsin General Intelligence Test. A three way ANOVA revealed that religion had significant impact on intelligence level, religions interacting with socio- economic status creates significant difference in intelligence scores.

Agarwal (1999) made an attempt to compare the failed and passed students on the basis of their intelligence, family relations, socio-economic status and adjustment. The sample size was 200, who were selected from the higher secondary schools of Uttar Pradesh. The tool used were Jalotai Group Test of General Ability, Bharadwaj, Gupta and Chauhan's Socio-Economic Scale and Sherry and Sinha's Adjustment Inventory for school students. The major findings intelligence, family relations and socio-economic status are permanent factors related to the scholastic achievement of high school students. Intelligence is innate and cannot be increased beyond limit.

Tyagi (1999) made a study to compare the acoustic behaviour of boys and girls as a function of intelligence. A Stratified random sample of 480 boys and 480 girls was administered using the Mental Ability Test (Joshi) and Altruism Scale (Tyagi). The results revealed that girls were more intelligent and altruistic than boys. Altruism correlated with intelligence.

Sharma and **Kumar (1999)** made an attempt to compare the intelligence of the first born child The sample consisted of 120 children and tools used were: For the children of 5-11 years of age, Raven's Colored Progressive Matrices. For the children above 11 years of age, Raven's Advanced Progressive Matrices. The major findings were that there was no significant difference in intelligence of the first –born and the second born child, and no significant difference in intelligence of the first-born and the third born child.

Prabha and **Monika (2000)** examined the role of sex, intelligence and socio-economic status in the achievement of computer education. The sample size was 223. The tools were the Group Test of Intelligence (Ahuja) and Socio-Economic Status Scale by Bharadwawj. The examination marks scored in computer education were used as an index for computer achievement scores. The study showed that intelligence and computer education are positively and significantly correlated.

Gupta (2000) explored the effect of prolonged deprivation on intelligence and attainment of academic achievement of students. The sample consisted of 1453 students of grade 10. The Bengali version of Prolonged Deprivation Scale (PDS) by Misra and Tripathi and Raven's Progressive Matrices were administered to the subjects. Examination marks were taken as academic achievement score. The main findings were: Boys scored higher on the measures of both the intelligence and academic achievement than girls. There is a positive correlation between intelligence and academic achievement. Prolonged deprivation adversely affects the intelligence of boys and girls.

Deshmukh (2000) designed his study to compare high and low self-concept groups of junior college students with intelligence. The sample consisted of 832 students ranging in the age group of 16-20 years, studying in XII standard. The main finding was that high and low self-concept groups of junior college students differ significantly on intelligence.

Varma and **Varma (2000)** examined the relationship between academic achievement and intelligence, parental involvement, subject's motivational resources and assessed father and mother's contribution. Samples of 206 secondary school girls were administered using the tests. Analysis of the results. Control shows the understanding; perceived competence and self-regulation were more powerful than intelligence in academic achievement. Intelligence affect directly and indirectly by influencing motivational variables. Intelligence is not the only factor, which affect academic achievement.

Sangwan (2001) examined the relationship between intelligence and ecological factors in a Sample of 42 slow learn, with an IQ range of 90-110. The Stanford Binet Intelligence Scale was administered to assess the IQ of these children and an Interview Schedule was used to obtain the information on ecological factors like birth order, type of family, school environment, parent's education and occupation. The study revealed that these entire factors except birth order play an unimportant role in children's cognitive development and IQ.

Aswal (2001) made an attempt to examine the relationship between intelligence and achievement in Mathematics across different socio-economic status levels. A Sample of 200 students of grade 11 was administered. Group Test, and the Socio-Economic Status Scale and marks in Mathematics, scored in the high school board examination, were used as indices of Mathematics achievement. The major findings were: there is a significant correlation between intelligence and achievement in Mathematics. The relation between intelligence and achievement is significant across high, average and low socio-economic status. According to this study, intelligence, achievement and socio-economic status are interrelated.

Himain and **Asha (2001**) examined the relationship of Piaget stages of cognitive development and intelligence and creative thinking potential of female primary school students. The tools used were Culture Fair Test of Intelligence of 'g' and Piaget tasks, Verbal and Figural form of Torrance Test of Creative Thinking. The findings were: There is significant difference in the creative thinking at different stages of Piaget's stages of development and IQ is significant for all the subjects.

Lakxmi Thakur (2001) designed her study to see the effect of the different factors of home (conformity, reward, deprivation, permissiveness) that influence intelligence and educational aspirations. The sample for the study was selected randomly. In the total sample 50% students were males and 50% were females. The findings of the study were: intelligence and educational aspirations positively correlated with each other, which indicate a linear incremental relationship between them. Conformity plays positive role intelligence. Reward is positively correlated with intelligence. Deprivation always has an effect on intelligence. Permissiveness has positive but non-significant correlation with intelligence.

Malini (2003) investigated on the main effect and interactive effect of non-verbal intelligence and mastery learning strategy on achievement in mathematics. Non-equivalent parallel group experimental design was used for the study. Two variations of mastery learning strategy were tried on two experimental groups. The sample size was 46 drawn from standard IX Students. The major findings were: The main effect due to non-verbal intelligence is found to be significant. The interaction between non-verbal intelligence on achievement and mastery learning strategy on achievement in mathematics were significant.

Raina (2003) made a study entitled, "Does preference for sons have a differential impact on the intelligence of boys and girls?" The study examined impact of son preference on the intelligence of boys and girls from a developing country. It was hypothesized that preference for sons enhances the intelligence among boys whereas it hampers the intelligence of girls. About 204 boys and 213 girls studying in grade VI to VII in an urban center of the state of Himachal Pradesh was taken as the sample.

FOREIGN STUDIES ON TEACHING COMPETENCE

Gregrersen and **Traves (1968)** used the projective technique for making a study of the child concept of the teachers. They made use of drawing of children, environment, which have special significance for them. Choeng and Devault at university of Wisconsin also made similar study in 1966.

Richard M. Galger and **Tom. D. Freyo (1974)** investigated to two research questions (a) would rewarding items on a questionnaire for evaluating faculty teaching effectiveness substantially affect students ratings (b) Would students ratings of professors teaching quality be totally consistent with their ratings of benefits derived from courses? Results shows that students' ratings were affected very little by a major rewarding of items and that a substantial degree of linear independence existed between students perception of the quality benefited from the instructional process.

Garrett and **George, W. (1978)** Studied the teachers perception of selected factors affecting the success of teaching process. A study sought to determine how various groups of teachers rated selected factors in teaching success. A review of literature of the topic indicated that both teachers and non–teacher was conducted to collect data from teachers of 64 elementary and secondary schools that were part of the test.

Lawrenz, Frances (1987) studied the gender effects for students' perception of the classroom psycho-social environment. This study compared to classroom environments as perceived by fourth grade, seventh grade and high school boys and girls in classes taught by males and females to determine if any perceptual differences existed. The analyses showed no difference for fourth grade students, one for seventh grade students, and three for high school students.

Brosious Janice A. and **Smith R. Lyle (1990)** studied the impact of Teachers Attractiveness and Gender on Students Perception of the Teacher's Ability. A group of seventh grade maths students (N=28) was chosen for the experiment, the students rated photograph of teachers in the area of organisation, classroom management, motivation, communication, sensitivity, imagination, and competence. The results of this analysis revealed a significant main effect of student perceptions due to the attractiveness of the teacher in the area of organisation, classroom significant main effect on student's perceptions due to the gender of the teacher. The students rated the female photographs higher than male photographs in the area of organisation. Finally, there was a significant interaction between the attractiveness of the teacher and gender of teacher in the areas of organisation, sensitivity and imagination. Overall, females rated higher than males and teachers considered attractive were given higher ratings than teachers considered average and unattractive.

Ocepek, Linda Jeanne (1993) tested some "Selected elements of effective teaching: A study of perception of high school teachers in Illinois, Indian and Ohio." This study utilised an export co-relational design. A 42 item Value Rating Scale (VRS) was mailed to a stratified random sample of 384 public high school teachers in Illinois, India and Ohio. The teachers rated 42 indicator behaviours subsumed under the six elements of effective teaching.

Kim Keyng Suk (1999), studied "Teacher's perceptions of competencies needed for working inclusive early childhood education programs". A survey using five-point Likert scales included 7 teacher competency domains, each with a set of competency statements, and 12 teachers roles needed for working in inclusive pre-school program. 23 ECE teachers and 52 ECSE teachers in non-inclusive programs and 39ECE teacher and 25 ECSE teachers inclusive program participated in this study. To determine the early childhood education (ECE) and Early Childhood. Special Education (ECSE) teacher's perceptions of importance teacher competencies, current levels of these competencies and appropriate teacher roles for working in inclusive early childhood programme. They found the ECSE teacher had significantly higher perceptions than the ECE teachers of their self-proficiency of competencies related to child development, curriculum and instruction, assessment procedures, working with other adults, and professionalism.

Kastair, Jamal (1999) carried out a study on "An evaluation of professional teaching competency of the instructors of the institute of Agriculture Sabah, Malaysia." A survey was carried out at the institute involving the instructors, the principal and the first and second year students as respondents. Each instructor and the principal completed questionnaires containing 40 competency items of 7 categories, while each of the first and the second year students completed a questionnaire containing 33 competency items on 5 categories. The respondents were asked to assess the competence level of the instructors based on a five point Likert type scales. Evaluation by the professional teaching competency of the instructors of the Institute of Agriculture

Sabah, Malaysia. They found that instructors' competence level was relatively high with respect to personal characteristics / attribute category, and lower with respect to planning and application of the principles of teaching-learning process.

INDIAN STUDIES ON TEACHING COMPETENCE

Chatter Jee, B.B *et al.* (1965) studied about the predication of teaching competency as a function of sharing a common frame of reference. The major findings were: The range of the scaled teaching competency scores given by the staff judges increased in the post-presentation assessments as compared to the pre-presentation predication, while the post-presentation scaled scores of teaching competency given by the instructors themselves were found to have low range compared to scores distributions obtained from the staff judges.

Saraswathi, L.S (1973) conducted a study about the jobs held by home scientists and the competencies needed on the jobs held as perceived by the employed home scientists and their employers in the District. The Major Findings were; The high competency perception proportion indicated that majority of the items included in the competency tests were perceived by the two sets of respondents (Teachers and research workers and those on miscellaneous jobs) as required as the job with an exception of those of the jobs of the assistant lecturers in colleges and teachers in secondary schools.

Nair, S.R (1974) reported about and impact of certain sociological factors on teaching ability in the classroom of government training college in Tiruchur. The major finding of this work was that private school teachers in general were found to have better teaching ability than the government school Teachers. Sex was not found to be affecting teaching ability. A positive relationship existed between age and teaching ability. Caste and religion were not found to be affecting teaching ability.

Sharma, S.K (1981) analyzed the various relationship of teaching effectiveness in terms of competency. The study was carried out at three different stages. In the final study 220 classrooms teaching learning situations were observed. The major findings were: There were no significant relationship between the ages of Hindi teachers, their attitude, interest and intelligence and their teaching competency. Male and female Hindi teachers did not differ significantly in their teaching competency. There was significant negative correlation between the self-perception of Hindi teachers teaching at higher secondary level and their teaching competency. There was a significant positive correlation between the teaching competency of teachers at higher secondary level and academic achievement of their pupil of grade XI in Hindi. The teaching competencies identified were: giving assignments, loud reading, asking questions, introducing lessons, pacing, managing the classroom, presenting verbal mode, clarification, using the black board, using appropriate reinforcement, achieving closure, probing question, creation interest and improving pupils reading behaviour.

Rajan, S. Sathyagiri (1985) conducted a study about the competency, personality, motivation, perception and profession of college teachers. The major findings were; Teacher competency was related to intelligence, emotional stability, conscientiousness, tender mindedness, trusted nature, and placid nature, self-sufficiency, and placed nature, self-sufficiency and relaxedness factors of Cattell's 16PF questionnaires. It was significantly related to creativity, dynamism, organised demeanors and warmth and acceptance, self-actualisation and professional perception of teachers. The more competent teachers significantly differed from the less competent teachers in all the above variables. Those variables that correlated significantly with teacher competence inter correlated with one another significantly.

Das, B.C (1993) conducted a study about the effectiveness of concept attainment model in terms of teaching competency of pre-service student teachers. It was found that concept attainment model effectively developed the teaching competency of pre-service students teachers.

Naseema, C. (1994) reported about a teaching competence of secondary schools physical science teachers in relation to satisfaction of teaching physical science. The major findings were: It was found that 30.92 percent of physical science teachers differed in perceived teaching competence which can be attributed to work (0.01) rewards (1.73), context of work (0.87), self (0.61), others (0.56); 26.89 percent of physical science teachers differed in observed teaching competence which can be attributed to work (0.86), reward (0.002) context of work (1.5), self (2.32), others (1.91).

Kukreti, B.R. (1994) reported about a correlation study between job motivation and teaching competency. The major findings were: the competent teachers had joined the teaching profession because they regarded teaching as a prestigious job. They believed that the teaching profession provided them reasonable salary, security, opportunity of social service, to establish human relation and enhance their knowledge. Incompetent teachers entered the teaching profession because they thought that their profession would get fame, personal freedom, influencing opportunity and enough leisure with little burden of work.

Thigarajan, A. *et.al.* (1995) conducted a study about the teaching competency and achievement. The major findings were; The teaching competency and achievement of boys had significant relationship. The relationship between teaching competency and achievement of boys and girls differed significantly.

Panda, S.C. (1996), Conducted a study about the effect of competency-based instruction in achieving MLL competencies in grade IV Oriya medium schools. The major findings were: There was remarkable difference in the achievement of both the groups. The competency-based instruction yielded significantly better results than the traditional method of teaching.

Shamala, S.K. (1997) reported about enhancing teaching competency through integration of art education for effective language teaching at the primary stage. The major findings were: Prior the implementation of MLL based curriculum, it was highly essential to orient the primary school teachers to know how to develop local specific competencies based on different activities. There was a positive impact of module to empower primary school teachers in developing competency based local specific curriculum. The main Objective are: To determine the value of high school teachers place on these elements: classroom climate, questioning, set induction, stimulus variation, reinforcement and closure. In this study classroom climate, questioning, set induction, stimulus variation, reinforcement and closure are sported as a set of selected elements for improving instruction.

Thamilmani, P.(2000) conducted a study on teacher competency, teacher personality and teacher attitude on student achievement in science in high schools. The study included a sample of 100 teachers (58 male, 42 female teaching science and 300 students X studying under those teachers). The tools used were: Teacher Competency – Student Rating Scale, Teacher personality and teacher attitude of science teachers are related to the academic achievement of X standard students in science. They revealed male and female teachers differed significantly in their personality traits and attitude towards teaching.

Palaniyandi, R (2001) investigated the competency needs of pre-service teacher trainees. The teacher educators and student teachers from six DIETs constituting 273 pre-service Teacher trainees 106 teacher educators and 462 practicing teachers working in these districts were the samples for the study. To identify the competency needs of pre-service teacher trainees as perceived by the pre-service trainees. They revealed learning process related competencies emerged as a group having the highest number of competencies.

Manjula P. Rao (2002) studied Teacher Competencies and learners' achievement in Tribal areas of Karnataka.

Twenty schools belonging to 3 taluks, 261 students of third standard and 31 teachers teaching the same students constituted the sample of this study. The research tool used in this study are: The achievement test developed based on the competencies specified for class III in Language, Mathematics, EVS-I and EVS-II to assess teachers' competence in subject areas. To study the relationship between teachers' competency and students achievement: in language, Mathematics, EVS-I and II. They found that majority of the teachers do not have the knowledge competencies in EVS-I (66.5%) and EVS-II (89.9%).

Amaladoss Xavirer, S and Amalraj, A. (2002), conducted a correlative study on teaching competency and its dimensions in post-graduate chemistry teachers. The study included data from 89 postgraduate chemistry teachers of higher secondary schools in Kanyakumari District in Tamil Nadu. A Teaching Competency Rating Scale was used to assess the teaching competency of chemistry teachers. They revealed that there exists significant relationship between the low-level of post- graduate chemistry teachers with regard to the teaching competency dimensions: content, organisation, knowledge, clarity, communication, rapport, audio-visual aids and personality.

Jayakanthan, S. (2003) conducted a study of general teaching competency of secondary school teachers in relation to their attitude in teaching. The study included samples of 3000 teacher from 14 schools. The General Teaching Competency Scale of Passi *et al*, and Teacher Attitude Scale of Ahulwalia were used to carry out the study found that Government and aided school teachers differed significantly in general teaching competency. Male and female teachers differed significantly in teaching competency.

Krishna Prasad, B. and Mthiah, P.N.(2003). carried out a study on teacher effectiveness and temperament variables of secondary school teacher. The study was carried out to a sample of 300 teachers of various secondary schools in Thirunelveli District in Tamil Nadu. MTA-test of Personality for measuring the variables of Temperament, Checklist on Teacher Effectiveness developed and validated by the investigators, and a Personal Information Schedule were used. They found that there exist significant differences among high, average and low effective teachers in five variables (inferiority, self sufficiency, sociability, stability, objectivity) of temperament.

Laxmidhar Bhara (2004) made an attempt to find out the performance of B.Ed trainees. of IASEs and CTEs. Six fifty student-teachers (259 male and 391 female) drew purposively from tow CTEs and one IASE of Orissa in two consecutive sessions 1995-96 and 1996-97. The Major findings were: that women student teachers excel their male counter parts in their aggregate (theory and practical) performance.**Jeba A., (2005)** studied the teaching competency and mental health of student teachers in DIETs. The size of the sample was 300 student-teachers in a DIET undergoing B.Ed.. Elementary Teachers Training course. Tools used in this study are: Mental Health status scale constructed by M. Abraham and K.C.B. Praszanna. Teaching Competency Scale the study was conducted to find out gender and group (Arts, science) difference in teaching competency and mental health status, the relationship between teaching competency and mental health status of student teachers in DIET. A major finding was that there is no significant difference between man and women student teacher.

CONCLUSION

In this chapter, the related literature with regard to the variables, intelligence and teaching competence have been reviewed so as to get proper theoretical orientation of the problem and the design of the study is followed in the next chapter.

METHODOLOGY

Introduction

This chapter gives an over all view of the design of the study, research tools used in the study, nature and selection of the sample and a brief description of the procedure adopted for collection of data.

NEED AND SIGNIFICANCE OF THE STUDY

Teachers play a vital role in the development of future citizens. Teaching is an interactive process, involving four aspects teacher, student, learning process and learning situation. A competent teacher possesses all the necessary qualities to interact with the school and community. Intelligence is the important aspect of an individual, through intelligence one can know his abilities and capabilities. Intelligence test is used to categorise people into different group. Intelligence helps a person to understand the concept and to interpret on it. So, the present study has been conducted to evaluate the level of intelligence and its influence on the teaching competence of the B.Ed teacher trainees.

STATEMENT OF THE PROBLEM

The problem for the present study is titled as, "Intelligence and Teaching competence among the B.Ed teacher trainees".

OPERATIONAL DEFINITION OF KEY TERMS

Intelligence

In this study, intelligence was assessed by the Standard Progressive Matrices, developed and standardised by Raven. The score obtained by the subject in the test indicate the level of intelligence.

Teaching Competence

Teaching competence of the teacher trainees indicates the score obtained by the subjects on the basis of the assessment made by their subject teachers, to know the level of teaching competence of the teacher trainees, the investigator adapted the Teaching Competence Rating Scale (TCRS) developed and standardised byS. Mani (2005).

B.Ed Teacher Trainees

In this investigation the teacher trainees refer to the trainees with minimum qualification of graduation who pursue pre serviced teacher education in course of study to acquire a general B.Ed degree during the academic year 2006-2007 in College of Education.

OBJECTIVES OF THE STUDY

The following objectives are set in the present study;

1. To assess the level of intelligence of B. Ed. teacher trainees.
2. To find out the level of teaching competence of B.Ed teacher trainees.
3. To find out whether there is significant difference between overall scores on intelligence of B. Ed teacher trainees with respect to:

   Gender
   Educational Qualification
   Optional Subject
   Types of Management of Colleges
   Medium of Instruction
   Location of the College
   Parental Occupation
   Parental Qualification

4. To find out whether there is any significant difference between the overall score on teaching competence of B. Ed teacher trainees with respect to:

   Gender
   Educational Qualification
   Optional Subject
   Types of Management of Colleges
   Medium of Instruction

Location of the Colleges
Parental Occupation
Parental Educational Qualification:

5. To find out whether there is significant association between intelligence and teaching competence of B. Ed teacher trainees.
6. To find out the relation between intelligence and teaching competence of B.Ed., teacher trainees.

HYPOTHESIS

1. The B.Ed., teacher trainees have above average level of intelligence.
2. The B.Ed., teacher trainees are competent in teaching.
3. There is no significant difference between the overall scores on intelligence of the B. Ed teacher trainees with respect to;

    Gender
    Educational Qualification
    Optional Subject
    Types of Management of Colleges
    Medium of Instruction
    Location of the Colleges
    Parental Occupation
    Parental Educational Qualification.

4. There is no significant difference between the overall scores on teaching competency of B. Ed teacher trainees with respect to:

    Gender
    Educational Qualification
    Optional Subject
    Types of Management of Colleges
    Medium of Instruction
    Location of the Colleges
    Parental Occupation
    Parental Educational Qualification:

5. There is no significant association between intelligence and teaching competence of B. Ed teacher trainees.
6. There is no significant relation between intelligence and teaching competence of B.Ed., teacher trainees.

METHOD OF STUDY

In the present study survey method is employed. This method is used to describe and interpret, what exist at present. It is concerned with the condition of relationships that exist, practices that prevails, beliefs, points of view or attitudes that are held, processes that are going on and effects that are being felt.

VARIABLES OF THE STUDY

Research Variables

1. Intelligence
2. Teaching competence

Personal Variables

1. Gender
2. Educational Qualification
3. Optional subject
4. Parental Occupation
5. Parental Educational Qualification

Institution Related Variables

1. Types of the management of collage
2. Medium of Instruction
3. Location of the Colleges

TOOLS USED IN THE STUDY

1. Personal Data Sheet developed by the Investigator. (Appendix I).
2. Standard Progressive matrices developed and standardised by Raven. (Appendix II).

3. Teaching Competence Rating Scale (TCQS) developed and standardised by S. Mani (appendix III).

PERSONAL DATA SHEET

The personal data sheet was prepared to collect information on personal and institutional related details, such as gender, educational qualification, and medium of instruction, types of management, locality, parental annual income, parental educational qualification and parental occupation.

INTELLIGENCE

Description

Raven's Progressive Matrices Test was used to measures the intelligence of the B.Ed teacher trainees, as the purpose of the study is to find out the relationship between intelligence and teaching competence. Intelligence questionnaires consist of 60 questions, which were divided into 5 sets (A, B, C, D and E) of 12 each. In each set, the first problem is as nearly as possible self-evident. The problems, which follow, become progressively more difficult. The order of the tests provides the standard training in the method of working. The five sets provide five opportunities for grasping the method and five progressive assessments of a person's capacity for intellectual activity.

Administration

The investigator with the help of respective school teachers did the administration of the test. The investigator met the students and explained the instructions to them on how to answer the test. The students were asked to answer all the questions without fail and they were given only 30 minutes to answer.

Scoring Procedure

Each item carried one mark. Adding the total marks obtained by the B.Ed. teacher trainees in 5 sets of test was done. By taking the total marks obtained by the students further calculations were done and they were clarified into intelligence average, above average superior.

TEACHING COMPENTENCY - DESCRIPTION

To find the level of teaching competency among the teacher trainees Teaching Competency Rating Scale was used. The tool consists of 3 dimensions and 8 components in classroom teaching.

The Dimensions and the Components are:

A. Planning Preparation and Organisation.
   1. Planning
   2. Preparation
   3. Organisation

B. Knowledge of the Subject –Matter
   1. Mastery in Subject

C. Presentation and Classroom Management
   1. Motivation
   2. Communication
   3. Interaction
   4. Evaluation and Closure

The items are rated in 5 point scale as follows

Options	Scores
Very poor	1
Poor	2
Average	3
Good	4
Very good	5

Administration

The Teaching Competence Rating Scale (TCRS) meant to assess teaching competence of teacher trainees were given to the respective optional subject teachers (supervisors/teacher educators). They were requested to rate the teaching competence of their students only after the completion of the intensive teaching practice. The supervisors/teacher educators were asked to encircle only one numerical value for each component of all the three dimensions with the help of the indicators given in the tool. Time limit was not prescribed to finish the rating.

Scoring

The maximum score for all the three dimensions would be 40 and minimum 8. On the basis of the overall score, the teacher-trainees were classified into less competent, competent and more competent by using the m ±1s procedure.

PILOT STUDY

A Pilot study was carried out to test the suitability of the time required to administer to test, and to establish the validity and reliability of the tool. The test was administered to a group of 50 B. Ed. teacher trainees in the month of September 2006.

ESTABLISHING RELIABILITY AND VALIDITY OF THE TOOLS

Reliability of Intelligence Test

In the present study reliability of this tool Standard Progressive Matrices has been established by odd even method on 50 B. Ed. teacher trainees selected for the pilot study. The reliability of this tool has been found as 0.64

Validity of Intelligence Test

The validity is computed as the square root of reliability and this works out to be 0.8.

Reliability of Teaching Competence Rating Scale

Test-retest technique was used to establish the reliability of the tool and it was found to be -------0.87

Validity of Teaching Competence Rating Scale

The validity is computed as the square root of reliability and this works out to be 0.93.

MAIN STUDY

The validated tools were used for the main study to collect the necessary data. The study was carried out in the month of November 2006 in six B.Ed colleges in and around Chennai, which are affiliated to University of Madras in the state of Tamil Nadu.

SAMPLE OF THE STUDY

The present study is mainly concerned with 220 B. Ed. teacher trainees of six B.Ed colleges in and around Chennai, which are affiliated to University of Madras, in the state of Tamil Nadu.

COLLECTION OF DATA

Necessary permission was obtained from the head of the institutions to administrate the tools. Data are collected from six B.Ed colleges, and five students form each department are selected for the study. In addition to this the optional teachers co-operation was also sought to assess the teaching competency of the B.Ed teacher trainees.

DELIMITATION

1. The sample for the present study has been restricted to 220 B. Ed. teacher trainees as stratified random sample selecting only 5 samples from each optional subject.
2. The study was restricted to in and around Chennai City only.
3. The age of the sample was restricted to 20-25 years only.
4. The teaching competence assessment was done only by the teacher educator and not by the investigator.

STATISTICAL TECHNIQUES USED

Descriptive and inferential statistical techniques are used in the interpretation of the data to draw out a meaningful picture of results from the obtained data. In the present study the following statistical techniques are used

- Percentile
- Differential (Mean, Standard deviation, t-test and ANOVA)
- Correlation (correlation co-efficient and Chi-square)

CONCLUSION

This chapter outlines the design of the present study. The procedure followed and the nature of the sample. It describes the hypothesis to be tested, the tools used and the methods of administration and scoring. Adopting the methods and procedures discussed earlier in this chapter, tests were administered and information was gathered. The obtained datas were then analyzed using appropriate statistical techniques described above and its results are presented in the next chapter.

Categorywise distribution of the sample

Variables	Category	Total (220)	Percentage
Gender	Male Female	104 116	47.27 52.73
Educational Qualification	U.G. P.G.	94 122	43.52 56.48
Optional subjects	Language Arts Science	59 47 114	26.82 21.36 51.82
Types of management of colleges	Government Aided Self-financed	81 60 79	36.82 27.27 35.91
Medium of Instruction	Tamil English	81 139	36.82 63.18
Location	Urban Rural	141 79	64.09 35.91
Father's Occupation	Employe Unemployed Self-employed	110 41 69	50 18.64 31.36
Mother's Occupation	Employed Unemployed Self-employed	42 140 38	19.09 63.64 17.27
Father's Education	Illiterate School level College level	18 128 74	8.18 58.18 33.64
Mother's Education	Illiterate School level College level	49 141 30	22.27 64.09 13.64

ANALYSIS AND INTERPRETATION OF THE DATA

INTRODUCTION

This chapter presents the results obtained from the analysis of data collected from six different educational colleges based on two variables viz., intelligence and teaching competence. The data has been subjected to various descriptive and inferential statistics correlation among the different variables was computed.

Hypothesis-1

The B.Ed., teacher trainees have above average level of intelligence.

Table 5.1. The level of intelligence of B.Ed., teacher trainees

Groups	Number of Students (N = 220)	Percentage %
Average	63	28.6
Above average	139	63.2
Superior	18	8.2

It is observed from the above table (5.1) that the intelligence of B.Ed teacher trainees is above average. Hence, hypothesis is accepted.

Hypothesis-2

The B.Ed., teacher trainees are competent in teaching.

It is observed from table (5.2) that B.Ed teacher trainees are competent in teaching. Hence the hypothesis is accepted.

Table 5.2. The level of teaching competence of B.Ed., teacher trainees

Classication	Score	Number of Students (N = 220)	Percentage %
Low Competent	Below 90	57	25.9
Competent	90 to 160	86	39.1
More Competent	Above 160	77	35.0

Hypothesis-3a

There is no significant difference between the overall scores of Intelligence of B.Ed teacher trainees with respect to gender.

Table 5.3. Significant difference between the mean scores of Intelligence of B.Ed teacher traineeswith respect to gender

Variables	Gender				t - value	L S
	Male		Female			
	Mean	SD	Mean	SD		
Overallintelligence Score	45.87	7.41	46.95	6.35	1.17	NS

As the calculated value (1.17) is less than the table value (1.96), it is concluded that there is no significant difference between mean scores of intelligence of B.Ed teacher trainees Hence, the hypothesis is accepted.

Hypothesis-3b

There is no significant difference between the overall scores of Intelligence of B.Ed teacher trainees with respect to their Education qualification.

As the calculated value of the above table (1.34) is less than the table value (1.96), it is concluded that there is no significant difference between the Intelligence mean scores of B.Ed teacher trainees with respect to their educational qualification. Hence the hypothesis is accepted.

Hypothesis-3c

There is no significant difference between the overall scores of Intelligence of B.Ed teacher trainees with respect to the Medium of Instruction.

Table 5.4. Significant difference between the mean scores of Intelligence of B. Ed teacher trainees with respect to their Education Qualification

Variables	Educationl Qualification				t-value	L S
	UG		PG			
	Mean	SD	Mean	SD		
Intelligence Score	47.12	6.69	45.84	7.08	1.34	Ns

Table 5.5. Significant difference between the mean scores of Intelligence of B.Ed teacher trainees with respect to the Medium of Instruction

Variables	Medium of Instruction				t - value	L S
	English		Tamil			
	Mean	SD	Mean	SD		
Intelligence Score	Mean	SD	Mean	SD	1.38	NS
	45.95	6.29	47.27	7.74		

Since the calculated value (1.38) is less than the table value (1.96), it is concluded that there is no significant difference between the intelligence mean scores of B.Ed teacher trainees with respect to the medium of instruction. Hence, the hypothesis is accepted.

Hypothesis-3d

There is no significant difference between the overall mean scores of Intelligence of B.Ed teacher trainees with respect to the location of colleges.

As the calculated value (1.12) of the above table is less than the table value (1.96), no significant difference between the intelligence mean scores of B.Ed teacher trainees with respect to the location of the colleges. Hence, the hypothesis is accepted.

Table 5.6 Significant difference between the mean scores of Intelligence of B.Ed teacher trainees with respect to the location of colleges.

Variables	Location				t - value	L S
	Urban		Rural			
	Mean	SD	Mean	SD		
Intelligence Score	Mean 46.05	SD 7.92	Mean 47.13	SD 4.38	1.12	NS

Hypothesis-3e

There is no significant difference between the overall mean scores of Intelligence of B.Ed teacher trainees with respect to their Optional subject.

Table 5.7. Significant difference between the mean scores of optional Subject on Intelligence

Sources	df	Sum of squares	Mean sum of squares	F-ratio	LS
Between group	2	106.617	53.39	1.129	NS
Within the group	217	10243.491	47.21		
Total	219	10350.109			

From the above table, it is noticed that the calculated table value (1.13) is less than the table value (1.96). So it is concluded that there is no significant difference between the mean scores of Intelligence of B.Ed teacher trainees with respect to their optional subject. Hence, the hypothesis is accepted.

Hypothesis-3f

There is no significant difference between the overall mean scores of Intelligence of B.Ed teacher trainees with respect to the types of management of college.

Therefore, further analysis of multiple comparisons of the significant difference of the mean scores of Intelligence among the types of management of colleges have been computed, the details of which are presented in table 5.9.

Table 5.8. Significant difference between the mean scores of Types of management of colleges

Sources	df	Sum of squares	Mean sum of squares	F-ratio	LS
Between group	2	342.950	171.475	3.718	0.05
Within the group	217	10007.158	46.116		
Total	219	10350.109			

As the calculated value (3.72) is grater than the table value (1.96) at 0.05 level in the table 5.8, it is concluded that there is significant difference in the mean scores of Intelligence of B.Ed teacher trainees with respect to the types of management of colleges.

Table 5.9. Multiple comparison of significant difference between the mean scores on Intelligence of B.Ed teacher trainees with respect to the management of colleges

Groups	Mean	SD	SE of Mean	t-value	LS
Government vs Aided	47.27	7.74	0.86	2.15	0.05
	44.40	7.93	1.02		
Government vs Self-financed	47.27	7.74	0.86	0.15	NS
	47.12	4.28	60.49		
Aided vs Self-financed	44.40	7.93	1.02	2.58	0.05
	47.12	4.28	0.49		

From the above table, in the first comparison as the calculated table value (2.15) is greater than table value (1.96). Significant difference is found on the mean scores of intelligence of B.Ed. teacher trainees with respect to the types of management of college.

In the second comparison, no significant difference is found between the mean scores of intelligence among the B.Ed teacher trainees with respect to the types of management of college.

In the third comparison, as the calculated table value (2.58) is greater than table value (1.96), significant difference is found between the mean scores on intelligence of B. Ed. teacher trainees with respect to the types of management of colleges. Hence, the hypothesis is partially accepted.

Hypothesis-3g

There is no significant difference between the overall mean scores of intelligence of B.Ed teacher trainees with respect to their parental occupation.

Table 5.10. Significant difference between the mean scores of Fathers' occupation on intelligence of B.Ed teacher trainees

Sources	df	Sum of squares	Mean sum of squares	F-ratio	LS
Between group	2	173.283	86.641	1.848	NS
Within the group	217	10176.826	46.987		
Total	219	10350.109			

Table 5.11. Significant difference between the mean scores of Mothers' occupation on intelligence of B.Ed teacher trainees

Sources	df	Sum of squares	Mean sum of squares	F-ratio	LS
Between group	2	39.722	19.861	0.418	NS
Within the group	217	10310.388	47.513		
Total	219	10350.109			

As the calculated values are less than (1.848, 0.418) table value (1.96), no significant difference is found between the means scores on intelligence of B.Ed teacher trainees with respect to their parental(Father & Mother) occupation, Hence, the hypothesis in accepted.

Hypothesis-3h

There is no significant difference between the overall mean scores of Intelligence of B.Ed teacher trainees with respect to parental educational qualification.

Table 5.12. Significant difference between the mean scores of Intelligence of B.Ed teacher trainees with respect to their Fathers' Educational Qualification

Sources	df	Sum of squares	Mean sum of squares	F-ratio	LS
Between group	2	12.617	6.308	0.532	NS
Within the group	217	2571.069	11.848		
Total	219	2583.686			

Table 5.13. Significant difference between the mean scores of Intelligence of B.Ed teacher trainees with respect to Mothers' Educational Qualification

Sources	df	Sum of squares	Mean sum of squares	F-ratio	LS
Between group	2	61.175	30.587	0.645	NS
Within the group	217	10288.934	47.414		
Total	219	10350.109			

As the calculated table values (0.532, 0.645) is less than table value (1.96) it is concluded that there is no significant difference between the means scores of intelligence of B.Ed teacher trainees with respect to their Parental education qualification. Hence, the hypothesis in accepted.

Hypothesis-4a

There is no significant difference between the overall mean scores of teaching competence of B.Ed teacher trainees with respect to gender.

Table 5.14. Showing the significant difference between the mean scores of Teaching competence of B.Ed teacher trainees with respect to gender

Variables	Gender				t-value	LS
	Male		Female			
	Mean	SD	Mean	SD		
Teaching Competency	Mean 29.25	SD 3.96	Mean 29.58	SD 2.89	0.71	NS

From the above table (5.14) no significant difference is found between the mean scores on the teaching competence of B.Ed teacher trainees. Hence, the hypothesis is accepted.

Hypothesis-4b

There is no significant difference between the overall mean scores of teaching competence of B.Ed teacher trainees with respect to their education qualification.

Table 5.15. Significant difference between the mean scores of teaching competence of B.Ed teacher trainees with respect to their education qualification

Variables	Educational Qualification				t - value	LS
	UG		PG			
	Mean	SD	Mean	SD		
Teaching Competency	29.54	3.36	29.33	3.55	0.45	NS

As the calculated table value (0.45) is less than the table value (1.96), no significant difference is found between the mean scores of teaching competence of B.Ed teacher trainees with respect to their educational qualification. Hence the hypothesis is accepted.

Hypothesis-4c

There is no significant difference between the overall man scores of teaching competence of B.Ed teacher trainees with respect to their Medium of Instruction.

Table 5.16. Significant difference between the mean scores of teaching competence of B.Ed teacher trainees with respect to their Medium of instruction

Variables	Medium of Instruction				t - value	LS
	English		Tamil			
	Mean	SD	Mean	SD		
Teaching Competency	29.04	3.79	30.07	2.61	2.17	0.05

In the above table the calculated value (2.17) is greater than the table value (1.96) at 0.05 level, significant difference is found between the mean scores on teaching competence of B.Ed teacher trainees with respect to the medium of instruction. Hence, the hypothesis is rejected.

Hypothesis-4d

There is no significant difference between the overall mean scores of teaching competence of B.Ed teacher trainees with respect to the location of college.

Table 5.17. Significant difference between the mean scores of teaching competence with respect to the location of colleges

Variables	Location				t - value	LS
	Urban		Rural			
	Mean	SD	Mean	SD		
Teaching Competency	29.26	3.66	29.71	2.99	0.92	NS

In the above table, the calculated value (0.92) is less than the table value (1.96), no significant difference is found between teaching competences of B.Ed teacher trainees with respect to the location of colleges. Hence, the hypothesis is accepted.

Hypothesis-4e

There is no significant difference between the overall mean scores of teaching competence of B.Ed teacher trainees with respect to their optional subject.

Table 5.18. Significant difference between the mean scores of optional subject on teaching competence.

Sources	df	Sum of squares	Mean sum of squares	F-ratio	LS
Between group	2	44.498	22.249	1.90	NS
Within the group	217	2539.188	11.701		
Total	219	2583.686			

From the above table (5.18), the calculated table value

(1.90) is less than table value (1.96), no significant difference is found between the mean scores of teaching competence of teacher trainees with respect to their optional subject. Hence, the hypothesis is accepted.

Hypothesis-4f

There is no significant difference between the overall mean scores of teaching competence of B.Ed teacher trainees with respect to the types of management of colleges.

Table 5.19. Significant difference between the mean scores of teaching competence of B.Ed teacher trainees the types of management of college

Sources	df	Sum of squares	Mean sum of squares	F-ratio	LS
Between group	2	135.493	67.746		
Within the group	217	2448.193	11.282	6.005	0.01
Total	219	2583.686			

In the above table (5.19) as the calculated value (6.005) is greater than the table value (2.58) at 0.01 level, significant different is observed between the mean scores of teaching competence of B.Ed teacher trainees with respect to the types of management of colleges

Therefore further analysis of multiple comparison of the significant difference of the mean scores of teaching competence among the three types of management of colleges have been computed, the details of which are presented in table (5.20).

From the above table, in the first comparison the calculated table value (3.16) is greater than table value (2.56), which shows the significant difference is found at 0.01 level, between the men scores of teaching competence of B.Ed. teacher trainees. It is also noted that the teacher trainees of government colleges got higher mean value (30.07) than the teacher trainees of aided colleges.

Table 5.20. Multiple comparison of significant difference between the mean scores of teaching competence of B.Ed teacher trainees with respect to the types of management of colleges

Groups	Mean	SD	SE of Mean	t-value	LS
Government VsAided	30.07 28.17	2.61 4.52	0.290 0.583	3.16	0.01
Government Vs Self-financed	30.07 29.71	2.61 2.99	0.290 0.337	0.82	NS
Aided Vs Self-financed	28.17 29.71	4.52 2.99	0.583 0.337	2.42	0.05

In the second comparison, no significant difference is observed between the mean scores of B. Ed teacher trainees teaching competence with respect the types of management of college.

In the third comparison, the calculated table value (2.42) is greater than table value (1.96) at 0.05 level, which indicates the significant difference between the mean scores of teaching competence of B.Ed teacher trainees with respect to Aided and Self-finance colleges.

Therefore, the hypothesis is partially accepted.

Hypothesis-4g

There is no significant difference between the overall mean scores of teaching competence of B.Ed teacher trainees with respect to their parental occupation.

From the above tables (5.21, 5.22) it is observed that the calculated table (0.362, 0.589) value is less than the table value no significant difference are observed between the means scores of teaching competence of B. Ed teacher trainees with respect to their parental occupation, Hence, the hypothesis is accepted.

Table 5.21. Significant difference between the teaching competences mean scores of B.Ed teacher traineesof with respect to their fathers' occupation

Sources	df	Sum of squares	Mean sum of squares	F-ratio	LS
Between group	2	8.595	4.297		
Within the group	217	2575.091	11.867	0.362	NS
Total	219	2583.686			

Table 5.22. Significant difference between the teaching competences mean scores of B.Ed teacher trainees with respect to their Mothers' occupation

Sources	df	Sum of squares	Mean sum of squares	F-ratio	LS
Between group	2	13.969	6.985		
Within the group	217	2528.716	11.842	0.589	NS
Total	219	2583.687			

Hypothesis-4h

There is no significant difference between the overall mean scores of teaching competence of B.Ed teacher trainees with respect to their parents educational qualification

Table 5.5. Significant difference between the teaching competences mean scores of B.Ed teacher trainees with respect to their Fathers' educational qualification

Sources	df	Sum of squares	Mean sum of squares	F-ratio	LS
Between group	2	9.574	4.787		
Within the group	217	1274.808	5.875	0.815	NS
Total	219	1284.382			

From table (5.23) it is noticed that the calculated value (0.815) is less than the table value (1.96), no significant difference is found between the mean scores of teaching competence of B.Ed teacher trainees with respect to their fathers' educational qualification.

Table 5.24. Significant difference between the teaching competences mean scores of B.Ed teacher trainees with respect to their Mothers' educational qualification

Sources	df	Sum of squares	Mean sum of squares	F-ratio	LS
Between group	2	90.238	45.119	3.926	0.05
Within the group	217	2493.448	11.490		
Total	219	2583.686			

From table (5.24) it is noticed that the calculated value (3.926) is greater than the table value (1.96) at 0.05 level, significant difference is found between mean scores of teaching competence of B.Ed teacher trainees with respect to their mothers' educational qualification.

Hence, further analysis of multiple comparisons of the significant difference of the scores of teaching competence among the parental education qualification have been computed, the details of which are presented below.

Table 5.25. Multiple comparison of significant difference between the mean scores of teaching competence of B.Ed teacher trainees with respect to parental education qualification

Source of variation	Mean	SD	SE of Mean	t-value	LS
Illiterate Vs School level	29.59 29.04	3.47 3.37	0.496 0.284	0.98	NS
Illiterate Vs College level	29.59 30.92	3.47 3.36	0.496 0.614	1.69	NS
School level Vs College level	29.04 30.92	3.37 3.36	0.284 0.614	2.79	0.01

From the above table, in the first and second comparison, there no significant difference is found between the mean scores of teaching competence of B.Ed teacher trainees with respect to their parental educational qualification.

But in the third comparison, the calculated value (2.79) is grater than table value (2.56) at 0.01 level, significant difference is observed between the mean scores of teaching competence of B.Ed teacher trainees with respect to their mothers' educational qualification Hence, the hypothesis is partially accepted.

Hypothesis-5

There is no significant association between intelligence and teaching competence of B.Ed teacher trainees.

Table 5.26. Significant association between Intelligence and teaching competence of B.Ed teacher trainees

Intelligence	Teaching Competence			Total
	Less competent	Competent	More competent	
Average	25 (16.3)	25 (24.6)	13 (22.1)	63 (28.6)
Above average	32 (36)	51 (54.3)	56 (48.7)	139 (63.2)
Superior	0 (4.7)	10 (7)	8 (6.3)	18 (8.2)
Total (%)	57 (25.9)	86 (39.1)	77 (35)	220 (100)

Chi-square value 16.466 df-4 LS - 0.01

From the above table, the Chi-square value (16.466) is greater than the table value (13.28) for df 4 it is concluded that there exist significant association between intelligence and teaching competence of B. Ed. teacher trainees. Hence, the hypothesis is rejected.

Hypothesis-6

There is no significant relation between intelligence and teaching competence of B. Ed teacher trainee.

In the above table as the correlation co-efficient value (0.2878) is greater than the table value (0.273). it is concluded that there exist significance positive correlation between intelligence and teaching competence of B. Ed. teacher trainees. Hence, the hypothesis is rejected.

Table 5.27. Significant relation between the overall scores of and Intelligence and teaching competence of B. Ed. teacher trainees

Variables	Intelligence	LS
Teaching Competency	0.2878	0.01

df =219

MAJOR FINDINGS

- The B.Ed., teacher trainees have above average level of intelligence.
- The B.Ed., teacher trainees are competent in teaching.
- No significant difference is found between male and female B.Ed., teacher trainees in intelligence.
- No significant difference is found in intelligence between the U.G. and P.G. qualified B.Ed., teacher trainees.
- No significant difference is found in intelligence between the English and Tamil medium B.Ed., teacher trainees.
- No significant difference is found in intelligence between the Urban and Rural B.Ed., college teacher trainees.
- No significant difference is found in intelligence of different optional subject B.Ed., teacher trainees.
- Significant difference is found in intelligence among the B.Ed., teacher trainees studying in different types of management of colleges (Government vs aided, Aided vs Self-Finance).
- Parents' Occupation do not influence the intelligence of B.Ed., teacher trainees.
- Parental Educational Qualification do not influence the intelligence of B.Ed., teacher trainees.

- Gender does not influence the teaching competence of B.Ed., teacher trainees.
- Educational qualifications of B.Ed., teacher trainees do not have bearing on the teaching competence.
- Medium of instructions in B.Ed., colleges influences the teaching competence of B.Ed., teacher trainees.
- No significant difference is found between urban and rural colleges B.Ed., teacher trainees teaching competence.
- No significant difference is found between the different optional subjects B.Ed., teacher trainees teaching competence.
- Significant difference is found in teaching
- competence of B.Ed., teacher trainees studying in different types of management of colleges (Government vs aided, aided vs self-finance).
- Parental Occupations do not influence the teaching competence of B.Ed., teacher trainees.
- Parental Educational Qualifications (Mothers') significantly influence the teaching competence of B.Ed., teacher trainees (Mothers' school level vs college level education).
- Significant positive correlation is found between intelligence and teaching competence of B.Ed., teacher trainees.
- Significant association is found between intelligence and teaching competence of B.Ed., teacher trainees.

CONCLUSION

This chapter analyses the hypothesis of the study. The finding and conclusions thus obtained from the analysis of this chapter have been summarised and presented along with a brief report of the research study and implications of the study in the following chapter.

SUMMARY AND CONCLUSION

Introduction

The present chapter provides a brief summary of the entire study and it also gives the statistical analysis of data presented in the previous chapter. The implications along with suggestions for replicating the study or for investigation at other closely related problems in other settings and with different samples and tools are also presented.

REVIEW OF THE RELATED LITERATURE

Review of related literature gives a broad idea to the investigator to carry out his research work in a successful manner. It also helps him get thorough knowledge in his research work reviews tells the researcher what has been done and what needs to be done particular topic.

METHODOLOGY

Need and Significance of the Study

Teachers play a vital role in the development of future citizens. Teaching is an interactive process, involving four aspects teacher, student, learning process and learning situation. A competent teacher possesses all the necessary qualities to interact with the school and community. Intelligence is the important aspect of an individual, through intelligence one can know his abilities and capabilities. Intelligence test is used to categorise people into different group. Intelligence helps a person to understand the concept and to interpret on it. So, the present study has been conducted to evaluate the level of intelligence and its influence on the teaching competence of the B.Ed teacher trainees.

Statement of the Problem

The problem for the present study is titled as, "Intelligence and Teaching competence among the B.Ed teacher trainees".

Operational Definitaions of Key Terms

Intelligence

In this study, the intelligence was assessed by the Standard Progressive Matrices, which was developed and standardised by Raven. The score obtained by the subject in the test indicate the level of intelligence.

Teaching Competence

Teaching competence of the teacher trainees indicates the score obtained by the subjects on the basis of the assessment made by their subject teachers, for the purpose the investigator adapted the Teaching Competence Rating Scale developed and standardised by Dr.S. Mani (2005).

B.Ed Teacher trainers

In this investigation the teacher trainees refer to the trainees with minimum qualification of graduation who pursue pre serviced teacher education in course of study to acquire a general B.Ed degree during the academic year 2006-2007.

Objectives Of The Study

The following objectives are set in the present study;

1. To assess the level of intelligence of B. Ed. teacher trainees.
2. To assess the level of teaching competence of B.Ed teacher trainees.
3. To find out whether there is significant difference between overall scores on intelligence of B. Ed teacher trainees with respect to:

    Gender

    Educational Qualification

    Optional Subject

    Types of Management of Colleges

    Medium of Instruction

Location of the College

Parental Occupation

Parental Educational Qualification

4. To find out whether there is any significant difference between

   (*a*) The overall score on teaching competence of B. Ed teacher trainees with respect to:

   Gender

   Educational Qualification

   Optional Subject

   Types of Management of Colleges

   Medium of Instruction

   Location of the Colleges

   Parental Occupation

   Parental Educational Qualification:

5. To find out whether there is significant association between intelligence and teaching competence of B.Ed teacher trainees.

Hypothesis

1. The B.Ed., teacher trainees have above average level of intelligence.
2. The B.Ed., teacher trainees are competent in teaching.
3. There is no significant difference between the overall mean scores on intelligence of the B. Ed teacher trainees with respect to;

   Gender

   Educational Qualification

   Optional Subject

   Types of Management of Colleges

   Medium of Instruction

Location of the Colleges

Parental Occupation

Parental Educational Qualification.

4. There is no significant difference between the overall mean scores on teaching competency of B. Ed teacher trainees with respect to:

   Gender

   Educational Qualification

   Optional Subject

   Types of Management of Colleges

   Medium of Instruction

   Location of the Colleges

   Parental Occupation

   Parental Educational Qualification:

5. To find out the relation between intelligence and teaching competence of B.Ed., teacher trainees.
6. There is no significant association between intelligence and teaching competence of B. Ed teacher trainees.

Method of Study

In the present study survey method is employed. This method is used to describe and interpret, what exist at present. It is concerned with the condition of relationships that exist, practices that prevails, beliefs, points of view or attitudes that are held, processes that are going on and effects that are being felt.

Variables of the Study

Research Variables

1. Intelligence
2. Teaching competence

Personal Variables

1. Gender
2. Educational Qualification
3. Optional subject
4. Parental Occupation
5. Parental Qualification

Institutional Related Variables

1. Types of the management of collage.
2. Medium of Instruction
3. Location of the Colleges

Tools Used in the Study

1) Personal data sheet developed by the investigator.
2) Standard Progressive matrices developed and standardised by Raven.
3) Teaching Competence Rating Scale developed and standardised by S. Mani

Personal Data Sheet

The personal data sheet was prepared to collect information on personal and institutional related details, such as gender, educational qualification, and medium of instruction, types of management, locality, parental annual income, parental educational qualification and parental occupation.

Sample of the Study

The present study is mainly concerned with 220 B. Ed. teacher trainees of six B.Ed colleges in and around Chennai, which are affiliated to University of Madras, Tamil Nadu.

Collection of Data

Necessary permission was obtained from the head of the institutions to administrate the tools. Data are collected from six B.Ed colleges, and five students form each department are selected for the study. In addition to this the optional teachers co-operation was also sought to assess the teaching competency of the B.Ed teacher trainees.

Delimitation

1. The sample for the present study has been restricted to 220 B. Ed. teacher trainees as stratified random sample selecting only 5 samples from each optional subject.
2. The study was restricted to in and around Chennai City only.
3. The age of the sample was restricted to 20-25 years only.
4. The teaching competence assessment was done only by the teacher educator and not by the investigator.

Statistical Techniques Used

Descriptive and inferential statistical techniques are used in the interpretation of the data to draw out a meaningful picture of results from the obtained data. In the present study the following statistical techniques are used

- Percentile
- Differential (Mean, Standard deviation, t-test and ANOVA)
- Correlation (correlation co-efficient and Chi-square)

MAJOR FINDINGS

- The B.Ed., teacher trainees have above average level of intelligence.
- The B.Ed., teacher trainees are competent in teaching.
- No significant difference is found between male and female B.Ed., teacher trainees in intelligence.
- No significant difference is found in intelligence between the U.G. and P.G. qualified B.Ed., teacher trainees.
- No significant difference is found in intelligence between the English and Tamil medium B.Ed., teacher trainees.

- No significant difference is found in intelligence between the Urban and Rural B.Ed., college teacher trainees.
- No significant difference is found in intelligence of different optional subject B.Ed., teacher trainees.
- Significant difference is found in intelligence among the B.Ed., teacher trainees studying in different types of management of colleges (Government vs aided, Aided vs Self-Finance).
- Parents' Occupation do not influence the intelligence of B.Ed., teacher trainees.
- Parental Educational Qualification do not influence the intelligence of B.Ed., teacher trainees.
- Gender does not influence the teaching competence of B.Ed., teacher trainees.
- Educational qualifications of B.Ed., teacher trainees do not have bearing on the teaching competence.
- Medium of instructions in B.Ed., colleges influences the teaching competence of B.Ed., teacher trainees.
- No significant difference is found between urban and rural colleges B.Ed., teacher trainees teaching competence.
- No significant difference is found between the different optional subjects B.Ed., teacher trainees teaching competence.
- Significant difference is found in teaching competence of B.Ed., teacher trainees studying in different types of management of colleges (Government vs aided, aided vs self-finance).
- Parental Occupations do not influence the teaching competence of B.Ed., teacher trainees.
- Parental Educational Qualifications (Mothers') significantly influence the teaching competence of B.Ed., teacher trainees (Mothers' school level vs college level education).

- Significant positive correlation is found between intelligence and teaching competence of B.Ed., teacher trainees.
- Significant association is found between intelligence and teaching competence of B.Ed., teacher trainees.
- The B.Ed., teacher trainees have above average level of intelligence.
- The B.Ed., teacher trainees are competent in teaching.
- No significant difference is found between male and female B.Ed., teacher trainees in intelligence.
- No significant difference is found in intelligence between the U.G. and P.G. qualified B.Ed., teacher trainees.
- No significant difference is found in intelligence between the English and Tamil medium B.Ed., teacher trainees.
- No significant difference is found in intelligence between the Urban and Rural B.Ed., college teacher trainees.
- No significant difference is found in intelligence of different optional subject B.Ed., teacher trainees.
- Significant difference is found in intelligence among the B.Ed., teacher trainees studying in different types of management of colleges (Government vs aided, Aided vs Self-Finance).
- Parents' Occupation does not influence the intelligence of B.Ed., teacher trainees.
- Parental Educational Qualification does not influence the intelligence of B.Ed., teacher trainees.
- Gender does not influence the teaching competence of B.Ed., teacher trainees.
- Educational qualifications of B.Ed., teacher trainees do not have bearing on the teaching competence.
- Medium of instructions in B.Ed., colleges influences the teaching competence of B.Ed., teacher trainees.

- No significant difference is found between urban and rural colleges B.Ed., teacher trainees teaching competence.
- No significant difference is found between the different optional subjects B.Ed., teacher trainees teaching competence.
- Significant difference is found in teaching competence of B.Ed., teacher trainees studying in different types of management of colleges (Government vs aided, aided vs self-finance).
- Parental Occupations do not influence the teaching competence of B.Ed., teacher trainees.
- Parental Educational Qualifications (Mothers') significantly influence the teaching competence of B.Ed., teacher trainees (Mothers' school level vs college level education).
- Significant positive correlation is found between intelligence and teaching competence of B.Ed., teacher trainees.
- Significant association is found between intelligence and teaching competence of B.Ed., teacher trainees.

EDUCATIONAL IMPLICATION

1. Necessary facilities and opportunities need to be provided to teacher trainees to acquire and develop the essential competences that are required in teaching profession.
2. Selection of teacher trainees should be made on certain criteria like testing their oral expressions and presence of mind, testing the depth knowledge of the subject and interpersonal relationships.
3. Entry behaviour of teacher trainees needs to assess and necessary supportive programme need to be organised to develop competences required for the teaching profession.

SUGGESTION FOR FURTHER STUDY

1. The study also may be extended to school teachers and college teachers.
2. This study can also be done to the DIET teacher trainees.
3. This inquiry can also be carried out to teacher trainees and teachers in other districts of Tamil Nadu.
4. A comparative study of gender difference among the teachers with respect to teaching competence and intelligence can also be done.
5. A study on the teaching competence and psychological factors of the different subject teachers can be taken up.

CONCLUSION

The quality of the teacher is determined by many factors and intelligence is the most vital factor among them. The present study indicates the close relationship between intelligence and teaching competence. Further it is also ensured in this present study that there is positive correlation between intelligence and teaching competence. The significant aspect, the types of management of college greatly influences not only the intelligence of the teacher trainees but also their teaching competence. However quality in education is possible only by preparing competent teacher.

REFERENCE

1. Arachana (1998). "Intelligence as a function of Religion Gender and socioeconomic status". *Indian Psychological Review*. 3: 153-157.
2. Asheval. G.G (2001). "Intelligence as a correlate of achievement in mathematics across Different levels of socio-economic status". *Indian Psychological Abstracts and Reviews* X(1): 186.
3. Asthana. M. (2000). "General intelligence visual motor perception and memory in rural and urban children. *Indian Education Review*. 54 (1&2): 94-99.

4. Das, B.C. (1993). "Effectiveness of concept attainment model in terms of teaching competency of pre-service student teachers [perspectives in Education. *Indian Educational Abstracts* (Issue-4) 9(1): 34-35.
5. Das, R.C. *et al* (1976). A study of effectiveness of micro teaching of teachers dept of teachers education. NCERT. New Delhi (Abridged Report).
6. Kukreti (1994). Job motivation and teacher competency. A correlation and study. Experiments in education. Indian Educational Abstract Issue-2. 22(1): 10-14.
7. Laxmi Thakur (2001). "Effect of Home environment on intelligence and educational aspirations". *Journal of Education and Psychology*. 59(4): 8-15.
8. Maline, P.M. (2003). "Effect of Intelligence and Mastery learning strategy of instruction of IX standard Pupils". *Experiment in Education*. XXXI(8): 149-153.
9. Panda, S.C. (1996). Effect of competency based instruction in achieving MLL competencies in Grade IV. National council of educational research. *Educational Abstract Issue*-6.
10. Prabha, I. and Gupta, Monika(2000). "Effect of sex, Intelligence and socioeconomic status on the achievement of students in Computer Education". *India Psychological Abstracts and Reviews*. III(2).
11. Renuga. N (2003). A study on intelligence and creativity among XI standard Arts and Science Students in chennai city M. Ed Thesis, Madras University.
12. Sadhya Giri Rajan (1985). Competency and personality. Motivation and profession perception of college teachers. Fourth serve of research in education 1983-1988. Volume-11.
13. Shamala, S.K. (1998). Enhancing teaching competency through integration of arts education for effective language teaching at the primary stage. National council of educational research and training. *Indian educational Abstract Issue*-5.
14. Sharma. A and Kumar, H (1999). Birth order and intelligence", *Indian Psychological Review*. 52(6): 85-93.
15. Singhal (1996). Teacher's self-efficacy and competency for improving quality of primary school. National council of

educational research and training. *Indian Educational Abstracts* Issue-6.

16. Sinha, S.P and Bvibha (1998). "Intelligence and Vigilance Performance as related to lead Exposure among children", *Indian Psychological Abstracts and Reviews.* VIII(1): 183.
17. Srivastsa.R.k (1999). A correlation study of intelligence and academic achievement of High School pupils. *The Progress of education.* XXI(10): 218.
18. Thamilmani. P. (1990). Teacher competency and teacher personality in relation to Achievement of High School. Students in science V *Survey of Educational Research* 11: 19-26.